CERTIFICATION CIRCLE™

MOUS

Microsoft Access

Lisa Friedrichsen

EXPERT

APPROVED COURSEWARE

COURSE
TECHNOLOGY
THOMSON LEARNING™

Australia • Canada • Mexico • Singapore • Spain • United Kingdom • United States

MOUS Microsoft Access 2002

CERTIFICATION CIRCLE™ EXPERT
Lisa Friedrichsen

Managing Editor:
Nicole Jones Pinard

Product Managers:
Debbie Masi
Julia Healy

Editorial Assistant:
Christina Kling Garrett

Production Editor:
Debbie Masi

Contributing Author:
Carol Cram

Developmental Editors:
Holly Lancaster, Kim Crowley

Composition House:
GEX Publishing Services

QA Manuscript Reviewers:
Nicole Ashton, John Freitas,
Jeff Schwartz, Alex White

Book Designers:
Joseph Lee, black fish design

COPYRIGHT © 2002 Course Technology, a division of Thomson Learning. Thomson Learning is a trademark used herein under license.

ISBN 0-619-05718-1

Printed in Canada

1 2 3 4 5 6 7 8 9 WC 06 05 04 03 02

For more information, contact Course Technology, 25 Thomson Place, Boston, Massachusetts, 02210.

Or you can visit us on the World Wide Web at www.course.com

For permission to use material from this text or product, contact us by

Tel (800) 730-2214
Fax (800) 730-2215

www.thomsonrights.com

Thank You, Advisory Board!

This book is a result of the hard work and dedication by authors, editors, and more than 30 instructors focused on Microsoft Office and MOUS certification. These instructors formed our Certification Circle Advisory Board. We looked to them to flesh out our original vision and turn it into a sound pedagogical method of instruction. In short, we asked them to partner with us to create *the* book for preparing for a MOUS Exam. And, now we wish to thank them for their contributions and expertise.

ADVISORY BOARD MEMBERS:

Linda Amergo	Old Westbury
Shellie Besharse	Mississippi County Community College
Margaret Britt	Copiah Lincoln Community College
Becky Burt	Copiah Lincoln Community College
Judy Cameron	Spokane Community College
Elizabeth T. De Arazoza	Miami-Dade Community College
Susan Dozier	Tidewater Community College
Dawna Dewire	Babson College
Pat Evans	J. Sargent Reynolds
Susan Fry	Boise State University
Joyce Gordon	Babson College
Steve Gordon	Babson College
Pat Harley	Howard Community College
Rosanna Hartley	Western Piedmont Community College
Eva Hefner	St. Petersburg Junior College
Becky Jones	Richland College
Mali Jones	Johnson and Wales University
Angie McCutcheon	Washington State Community College
Barbara Miller	Indiana University
Carol Milliken	Kellogg Community College
Maureen Paparella	Monmouth University
Mike Puopolo	Bunker Hill Community College
Kathy Proietti	Northern Essex Community College
Pamela M. Randall	Unicity Network
Theresa Savarese	San Diego City College
Barbara Sherman	Buffalo State
Kathryn Surles	Salem Community College
Beth Thomas	Hagerstown Community College
Barbara Webber	Northern Essex Community College
Jean Welsh	Lansing Community College
Lynn Wermers	North Shore Community College
Sherry Young	Kingwood College

Preface

Welcome to the *CERTIFICATION CIRCLE SERIES*. Each book in this series is designed with one thing in mind: preparing you to pass a Microsoft Office User Specialist (MOUS) exam. This strict focus allows you to target the skills you need to be successful. You will not need to study anything extra—it's like getting a peek at the exam before you take it! Read on to learn more about how the book is organized and how you will get the most out of it.

Table of Contents
This book is organized around the MOUS exam objectives. Each Skill on the exam is taught on two facing pages with text on the left and figures on the right. This also makes for a terrific reference; if you want to brush up on a few skills, it's easy to find the ones you're looking for.

Getting Started Chapter
Each book begins with a Getting Started Chapter. This Chapter contains skills that are *not* covered on the exam but the authors felt were vital to understanding the software. The content in this chapter varies from application to application.

Skill Overview
Each skill starts with a paragraph explaining the concept and how you would use it. These are clearly written and concise.

File Open Icon
We provide a realistic project file for every skill. And, it's in the form you need it in order to work through the steps; there's no wasted time building the file before you can work with it.

Skill Steps
The Steps required to perform the skill appear on the left page with what you type in green text.

Tips
We provide tips specific to the skill or how the skill is tested on the exam.

Skill Set 8
Integrating with Other Applications

Import Data to Access
Import Data from an Excel Workbook

You can import data into an Access database from several file formats, including an Excel workbook or another Access, FoxPro, dBase, or Paradox database. It is not uncommon for a user to enter a list of data into Excel and later decide to convert that data into an Access database, because the user wants to use Access's extensive form or report capabilities or wants multiple people to be able to use the data at the same time. (An Access database is inherently **multi-user**; many people can enter and update data at the same time.) Since the data in an Excel workbook is structured similarly to data in an Access table datasheet, you can easily import data from an Excel workbook into an Access database by using the **Import Spreadsheet Wizard**.

Activity Steps
ClassesO1.mdb

1. Click **File** on the menu bar, point to **Get External Data**, then click **Import**

2. Navigate to the drive and folder where your Project Files are stored, click the **Files of type list arrow**, click **Microsoft Excel**, click **Instructors**, then click **Import** to start the Import Spreadsheet Wizard
   See Figure 8-1.

3. Select the **First Row Contains Column Headings check box**, then click **Next**

4. Click **Next** to indicate that you want to create a new table, then click **Next** to not specify field changes

5. Click the **Choose my own primary key option button** to set InstructorID as the primary key field, then click **Next**

6. Type **Instructors** in the Import to Table box, click **Finish**, then click **OK**

7. Double-click **Instructors** to open it in Datasheet View
   See Figure 8-2. Imported data works the same way as any other table of data in a database.

8. Close the Instructors table

tip

Step 4
You can also import Excel workbook data into an existing table if the field names used in the Excel workbook match the field names in the Access table.

Additional Projects

For those who want more practice applying the skills they've learned, there is a project for each skill set located at the back of each book. The projects ask you to combine the skills you've learned to create a meaningful document – just what you do in real life.

Project for Skill Set 1

Working with Cells and Cell Data

Sales Projection for Alaska Adventures

You work for Alaska Adventures, a small company based in Juneau, Alaska, that offers sea kayaking, mountain biking, and hiking tours. You've received a workbook containing a sales projection for the sea kayaking tours that the company hopes to sell in the busy summer months of June, July, and August. In this project, you will complete and format this worksheet. The workbook also contains a second worksheet that includes a list of the guests who purchased sea kayaking tours on a single day during the previous summer. You'll use the AutoFilter features on this list to determine the number of customers who came from countries other than the United States and Canada.

Activity Steps

open EC_Project1.xls

1. Clear the contents and formats of cell **A3**, drag cell **A4** up to cell **A3**, then delete cell **D14** and shift the cells left

2. Merge cell **A3** across cells **A3** to **E3**, then check the spelling in the worksheet and correct any errors

3. Enter **Total** in cell **E5**, use the **Go To** command to navigate to cell **C13**, then change the value in cell **C13** to **1200**

4. Use the **SUM** function in cell **E12** to add the values in cells **B12** through **D12**, then copy the formula to cells **E13** through **E15**

5. Select cells **B12** through **B16**, then use the **AutoSum** button to calculate the totals required for cells **B16** through **E16**

6. In cell **B18**, enter the formula required to subtract the value in cell **B16** from the value in cell **B9**, then copy the formula to cells **C18** through **E18**

7. Use **Find and Replace** to locate all instances of **1500** and replace them with **500**

8. Format cells **B7** through **E7**, **B9** through **E9**, **B12** through **E12**, **B16** through **E16**, and **B18** through **E18** with the **Currency** style, format cells **B8** through **E8** and cells **B13** through **E15** with the **Comma** style, then compare the completed worksheet to Figure EP 1-1

9. Switch to the **Customers worksheet**, then use AutoFilter to show only the **International** customers in the Category column
The filtered list appears as shown in Figure EP 1-2

close EC_Project1.xls

tip

Step 8
To save time, press and hold the [CTRL] key, select each group of cells, and then click the Currency Style button.

2   Certification Circle

Skill 1
Import Data to Access

Figure 8-1: Import Spreadsheet Wizard dialog box

Figure 8-2: Imported Instructors table in Datasheet View

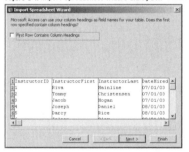

Seven records were imported

Figures

There are at least two figures per skill which serve as a reference as you are working through the steps. Callouts focus your attention to what's important.

extra!

Using delimited text files
You can import data from a **delimited text file**, a file of unformatted data where each field value is delimited (separated) by a common character, such as a comma or a tab. Each record is further delimited by a common character, such as a paragraph mark. A delimited text file usually has a **txt** (for text) file extension. You can use delimited text files to convert data from a proprietary software system (such as an accounting, inventory, or scheduling software system) into a format that other programs can import. For example, most accounting software programs won't export data directly into an Access database, but they can export data to a delimited text file, which can then be imported by Access.

Extra Boxes

This will *not* be on the exam–it's extra–hence the name. But, there are some very cool things you can do with Office xp so we had to put this stuff somewhere!

Target Your Skills

At the end of each unit, there are two Target Your Skills exercises. These require you to create a document from scratch, based on the figure, using the skills you've learned in the chapter. And, the solution is provided–there's no wasted time trying to figure out if you've done it right.

Additional Resources

There are many resources available with this book—both free and for a nominal fee. Please see your sales representative for more information. The resources available with this book are:

INSTRUCTOR'S MANUAL

Available as an electronic file, the Instructor's Manual is quality-assurance tested and includes unit overviews, lecture topics, solutions to all lessons and projects, and extra Target Your Skills. The Instructor's Manual is available on the Instructor's Resource Kit CD-ROM, or you can download if from www.course.com.

FACULTY ONLINE COMPANION

You can browse this textbook's password protected site to obtain the Instructor's Manual, Solution Files, Project Files, and any updates to the text. Contact your Customer Service Representative for the site address and password.

PROJECT FILES

Project Files contain all of the data that students will use to complete the lessons and projects. A Readme file includes instructions for using the files. Adopters of this text are granted the right to install the Project Files on any stand-alone computer or network. The Project Files are available on the Instructor's Resource Kit CD-ROM, the Review Pack, and can also be downloaded from www.course.com.

SOLUTION FILES

Solution Files contain every file students are asked to create or modify in the lessons and projects. A Help file on the Instructor's Resource Kit includes information for using the Solution Files.

FIGURE FILES

Figure Files contain all the figures from the book in bitmap format. Use the figure files to create transparency masters or in a PowerPoint presentation.

SAM, SKILLS ASSESSMENT MANAGER FOR MICROSOFT OFFICE XP SAM^{xp}

SAM is the most powerful Office XP assessment and reporting tool that will help you gain a true understanding of your students' proficiency in Microsoft Word, Excel, Access, and PowerPoint 2002.

TOM, TRAINING ONLINE MANAGER FOR MICROSOFT OFFICE XP TOM

TOM is Course Technology's MOUS-approved training tool for Microsoft Office XP. Available via the World Wide Web and CD-ROM, TOM allows students to actively learn Office XP concepts and skills by delivering realistic practice through both guided and self-directed simulated instruction.

Certification Circle Series, SAM, and TOM: the true training and assessment solution for Office XP.

Preparing for the MOUS Exam

Studying for and passing the Microsoft Office User Specialist (MOUS) exams requires very specific test preparation materials. As a student and reviewer of MOUS exam materials, I am proud to be a part of a team of creators that produced a new series specifically designed with the MOUS exam test taker in mind.

The Certification Circle Series ™ provides a fully integrated test preparation solution for MOUS Office^{XP} with the powerful combination of its Core and Expert textbooks, testing software with Skills Assessment Manager (SAM^{XP}) and Training Online Manager (TOM^{XP}). This combination coupled with the Exam Reference Pocket Guide for quick test taking tips and Office^{XP} materials will provide the skills and confidence a student will need to pass the MOUS exams.

How does the Certification Circle Series provide the best test preparation materials? Here's how:

▶ Core and Expert texts are based entirely on MOUS exam objectives.

▶ Table of Contents in each book maps directly to MOUS exam objectives in a one to one correlation.

▶ "Target Your Skills" exercises in the end of unit material presents problem solving questions in similar fashion to the MOUS 2002 exams.

▶ Skills Assessment Manager (SAM^{XP}) provides a simulated testing environment in which students can target their strengths and weakness before taking the MOUS exams.

If you are an experienced Access user, you'll probably want to go directly to the Target Your Skills exercise at the end of the Skill Set and Test your mastery of the objectives in that Skill Set. If you are unsure about how to accomplish any part of the exercise, you can always go back to the individual lessons that you need to review, and practice the steps required for each MOUS objective.

If you are relatively new to Access, you'll probably want to complete the lessons in the book in a sequential manner, using Target Your Skills exercise at the end of each Skill Set to confirm that you've learned the skills necessary to pass each objective on the MOUS test.

The Target Your Skills exercises simulate the same types of activities that you will be requested to perform on the test. Therefore, your ability to complete them in a timely fashion will be a direct indicator of your preparedness for the MOUS exam.

Judy Cameron, Spokane Community College
and the Certification Circle Series Team

SAM, Skills Assessment Manager for Microsoft Office XP

SAM XP–the pioneer of IT assessment.

How can you gauge your students' knowledge of Office XP? SAM XP makes teaching and testing Office XP skills easier. SAM XP is a unique Microsoft Office XP assessment and reporting tool that helps you gain a true understanding of your students' ability to use Microsoft Word, Excel, Access, and PowerPoint 2002, and coming soon Outlook 2002, Windows 2000 and Windows XP.

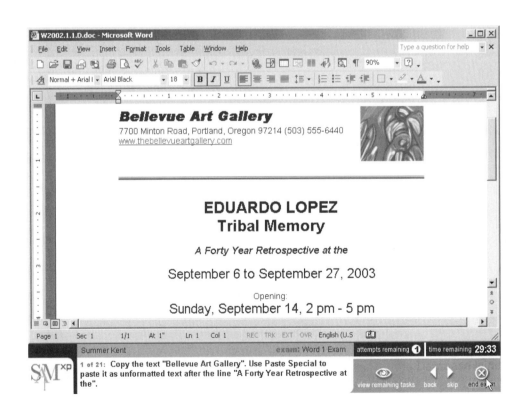

TOM, Training Online Manager for Microsoft Office XP

TOM—efficient, individualized learning when, where, and how you need it.

TOM is Course Technology's MOUS-approved training tool for Microsoft Office XP that works in conjunction with SAM XP assessment and your Illustrated Office XP book. Available via the World Wide Web or a stand-along CD-ROM, TOM allows students to actively learn Office XP concepts and skills by delivering realistic practice through both guided and self-directed simulated instruction.

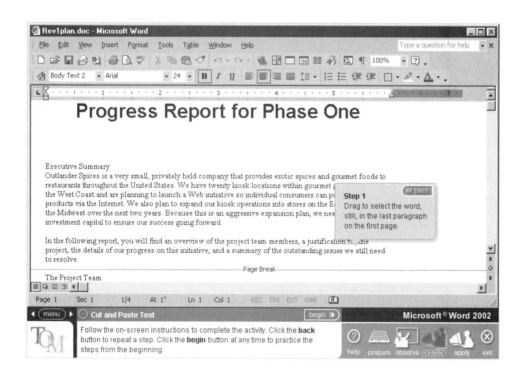

Certification Circle: Exam Reference Pocket Guide

The Microsoft Office ^{XP} Exam Reference Pocket Guide is a reference tool designed to prepare you for the Microsoft Office User Specialist (MOUS) exams. The book assumes that you are already familiar with the concepts that are the basis for the skills covered in this book. The book can therefore be used as a study companion to brush up on skills before taking the exam or as a desk reference when using Microsoft Office programs.

There are six chapters in this book. The first chapter in the book, *Exam Tips*, provides some background information on the MOUS Certification program, the general process for taking an exam, and some helpful hints in preparing and successfully passing the exams.

The remaining five chapters each cover a different Office program: Word, Excel, Access, PowerPoint, and Outlook. Each program-specific chapter begins by covering program basics in a brief *Getting Started* section. This section covers the basic skills that are not specifically covered in the MOUS exams, but that are essential to being able to work in the program. The *Getting Started* section is followed by the complete set of skills tested by the Microsoft MOUS Certification exams, starting with the Core or Comprehensive exam, and then followed by the Expert exam where applicable. These sections are labeled and ordered to exactly match the Skill Sets and Skill Activities tested in the MOUS Certification Exam. Clear, bulleted steps are provided for each skill.

Because there are often different ways to complete a task, the book provides multiple methods where appropriate for each skill or activity, including Menu, Button, Keyboard, Mouse, and Task Pane methods. The MOUS exams allow you to perform the skills using any one of these methods, so you can choose the method with which you are most comfortable to complete the task. It is the perfect companion to any of the Certification Circle Series textbooks or as a stand-alone reference book.

Contents

MOUS Microsoft Access 2002

CERTIFICATION CIRCLE™ EXPERT

MOUS Microsoft Access 2002

CERTIFICATION CIRCLE™ *EXPERT*

MOUS Microsoft Access 2002

CERTIFICATION CIRCLE™ *EXPERT*

MOUS Microsoft Access 2002

CERTIFICATION CIRCLE™ *EXPERT*

MOUS Microsoft Access 2002

CERTIFICATION CIRCLE™ *EXPERT*

Skill List

1. What you need to know before you start
2. Start Access and open a database
3. Identify the parts of the Database window
4. Understand database terminology
5. Understand the benefits of using a relational database
6. Manage toolbars and understand views
7. Use the Help system
8. Close a database and exit Access

This book will help you prepare for the Access 2002 Microsoft Office User Specialist (MOUS) exams and learn more about Access 2002. An Access database provides an efficient way to enter and maintain data, as well as fast and flexible ways to report and analyze information. Also, by relating several lists of data, an Access database can minimize data redundancy, which decreases the possibility of errors in your database. To enjoy the benefits of an Access database, you must be comfortable with the terminology specific to Access databases and be able to navigate through Access.

This Skill Set will introduce you to database terminology and will outline the benefits of using an Access database. It will provide information that you'll use throughout the book to open and close databases and to manage various Access screen elements, such as toolbars, menu bars, and windows. It will also introduce you to the Access Help system so that you can find and troubleshoot problems.

Before you get started, you need to store a copy of the Project Files on your computer to complete the exercises (or **Activities**) in this book. If you store the Project Files on floppy disks, use one floppy disk for each chapter (or **Skill Set**) to avoid running out of room. Within each activity, you are not usually instructed to specifically open, close, or save your files, so to get the correct results, use the specific file(s) listed at the beginning of the activity to the right of the floppy disk icon. If you want to practice an activity more than once, use a new, unmodified copy of the file each time.

Getting Started

Getting Started with Access 2002

Start Access and Open a Database

The Windows desktop is often customized to show icons that you can use to start commonly used programs quickly. But whether or not your computer has a desktop icon for Access, you can start the program by clicking the Start button on the taskbar, then clicking Microsoft Access on the Programs menu. Once you've started Access, you can open an existing database or create a new one. You can also open an existing database from either the My Computer or Windows Explorer windows by double-clicking the database file, which will automatically open both Access and the database.

Activity Steps

Step 1
If you don't see
Microsoft Access
on the Programs
menu, point to the
Microsoft Office
group icon to see
if the Microsoft
Access icon
appears there.

1. Click the **Start button** 🗗 Start on the taskbar, point to **Programs**, then click **Microsoft Access**
   See Figure GS-1. The **task pane** displays links that allow you to open an existing file or start a new database.

2. Click the **More files link**, click the **Look in list arrow**, then navigate to the drive and folder where your Project Files are stored
   See Figure GS-2. Access database files have an **mdb** file extension. A file **extension** consists of one to three characters attached to the end of a filename, and it tells the computer what type of information is stored in that file. Typically, file extensions are three characters and are always separated from the filename by a period. Depending on your Windows settings, you might not see the file extensions for the files on your computer.

3. Click **Employees01**, then click **Open**
   See Figure GS-3. The Employees01 Database window appears. Since you can only work on a single database in an Access window, once you open or start a new database, the task pane closes.

Figure GS-1: Task pane

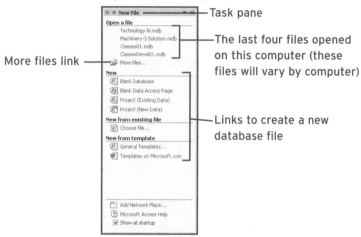

Task pane

The last four files opened on this computer (these files will vary by computer)

More files link

Links to create a new database file

Figure GS-2: Open dialog box

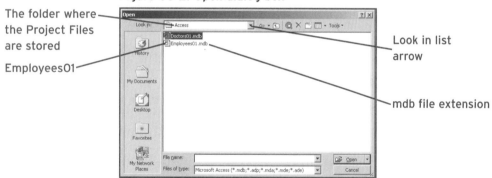

The folder where the Project Files are stored

Employees01

Look in list arrow

mdb file extension

Figure GS-3: Employees01 Database window

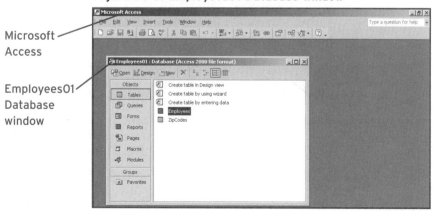

Microsoft Access

Employees01 Database window

Identify the Parts of the Database Window

Access contains the same screen elements as other Microsoft Office programs: a title bar, a menu bar, one or more toolbars, and Minimize, Maximize/Restore, and Close buttons. Access also contains other elements that are specific to managing a database. One such element is the Database window, the first window you see after you open a database. The **Database window** displays the name of the current database in its title bar. Icons that represent existing database objects (as well as shortcuts to create new objects) appear in the body of the Database window. On the left side of the Database window is the **Objects bar**, which you use to access the seven types of database **objects**, the major parts of the database file. The **Database window toolbar** contains buttons to help create a new database object or modify an existing one. Table GS-1 describes some of the elements of the Database window.

Activity Steps

EmployeesO1.mdb

1. Click **File** on the menu bar, then point to **Edit**, **View**, **Insert**, **Tools**, **Window**, and **Help** on the menu bar to view menu options

2. Press **Esc** twice

3. Point to the **New button** on the Database toolbar, then point to the other buttons on the Database toolbar to view their ScreenTips
   A **ScreenTip** is descriptive information that automatically appears in a small box by the pointer when you point to a toolbar button.

Step 6
The first and most important Access object is the table because it contains all the data.

4. Point to the **Open button**  on the Database window toolbar, then point to the other buttons on the Database window toolbar to view their ScreenTips

5. Click the **Queries button** Queries on the Objects bar
   See Figure GS-4. The Database window displays the new object shortcut links as well as any existing objects of that type.

6. On the Objects bar, click the **Forms button** Forms, click the **Reports button** Reports, click the **Pages button** Pages, click the **Macros button** Macros, click the **Modules button** Modules, then click the **Tables button** Tables

7. Click the **Maximize button** on the Database window
   The Maximize button is a toggle that resizes a window.

8. Click the **Restore Window button** on the Database window

Figure GS-4: Elements of the Access window and Database window

Access title bar
Menu bar
ScreenTip
Objects bar
Queries button is selected
Existing query objects

Access Minimize, Restore/Maximize, and Close buttons
Database toolbar
Database Minimize, Maximize/Restore, and Close buttons
New object shortcuts

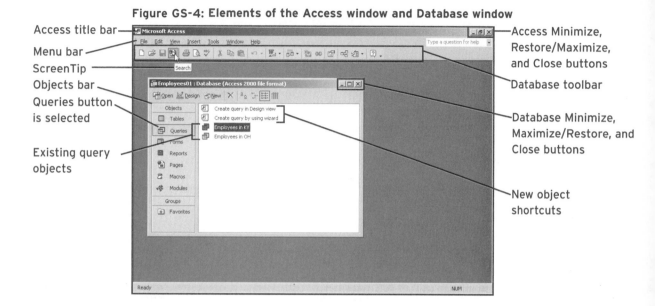

TABLE GS-1: Access window and Database window elements

element	description
Access title bar	Contains the name of the active program: Microsoft Access.
Access Minimize, Maximize, Restore Down, and Close buttons	Minimizes, resizes, or closes the entire Microsoft Access program and an opened database. When the Access window is maximized, the Restore Down button appears and can be used to restore the window to a smaller size.
Menu bar	Contains menus with options that are appropriate for the current view.
Database toolbar	Contains buttons for commonly performed tasks that affect the entire database (such as New, Open, or Relationships) or are common to all database objects (such as Print, Copy, or Spelling).
Database Minimize, Maximize, Restore Window, and Close buttons	Minimizes, resizes, or closes the current database. The Database Close button will close the current database, but Access will still be open.
Database title bar	Contains the filename of the active database.
Database window toolbar	Contains buttons to open, modify, create, or delete the selected database object. The view buttons (Large Icons, Small Icons, List, and Details) on the Database window toolbar are used to display the icons in different sizes and arrangements.
Database window	Allows you to work with the individual objects stored within the database.
Objects bar	Contains one button for each database object type.
Status bar	Displays messages regarding the current database operation.

Getting Started

Getting Started with Access 2002

Understand Database Terminology
Understand Fields, Records, and Tables

At the most basic level, a database is a list of structured data. The "structure" is a column and row grid in which each piece of data is stored. Data organized in this type of structure is very easy to find, update, and analyze. In database terminology, a column of the structure is called a **field** and represents one category or type of information. For example, a database storing information about employees might contain the three fields FirstName, LastName, and HireDate. Each item of data that you enter into each field, such as Mark in the FirstName field or 1/1/2003 in the HireDate field, is called a **value**. All the fields for one employee compose a **record**. Therefore, you'd have as many records in your database as you have employees. The records for a single subject, such as all employee records, are collectively called a **table**. When you open a table, the data that it stores is displayed in a spreadsheet-like grid called a **datasheet**.

Step 5
Be sure to click the Close button for the Employees table rather than the Close button for the Access window, or you'll close the entire Employees01 database and Access.

Activity Steps

 Employees01.mdb

1. Click the **Tables button** 🔲 Tables on the Objects bar (if it's not already selected), click **Employees** (if it's not already selected), then click the **Open button** 📇 Open on the Database window toolbar
   See Figure GS-5. Field names are displayed on the first row of the datasheet.

2. Press **Enter** or **Tab** several times to move through the fields of the first record

3. Press **[Down Arrow]** several times to move through the records of the table

4. Press **[Ctrl][Home]** to return to the first field of the first record

5. Close the Employees table

Figure GS-5: Employees table

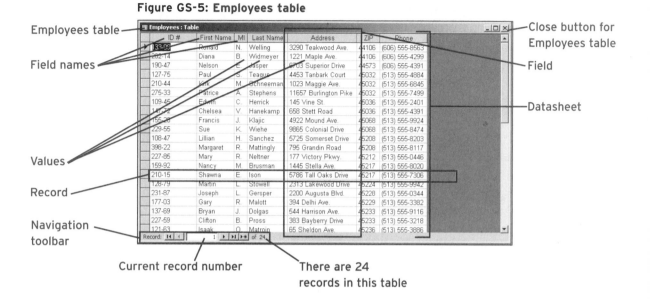

Employees table

Field names

Values

Record

Navigation toolbar

Close button for Employees table

Field

Datasheet

Current record number

There are 24 records in this table

extra!

Using relational databases

In Access, you can create multiple tables of data and link them together. When two tables are linked, or related, your database becomes a **relational database.** The purpose of creating multiple tables of data is to eliminate duplicate data entry. For example, by providing a ZipCodes table in the Employees01 database, you can enter each ZipCode record (each containing a ZIP, City, and State value) only once, but reuse those records if multiple employees live in the same ZIP code.

Getting Started

Getting Started with Access 2002

Understand Database Terminology
Understand Database Objects

Access includes seven types of database objects that represent the major pieces of the database and correspond with the seven buttons on the Objects bar. The most important objects are tables, because tables contain all the data in an Access database. All object types are described in Table GS-2. You can enter data into a database using the table, query, form, or page objects. However, all data that you enter is stored only in the table objects. This means that no matter where you enter or edit data, the data will be updated throughout all objects and views of the data at all times. For example, if you create a report that displays a company name and change the company name later using a form, the report will automatically show the updated company name the next time that you open or print it.

Step 4
A form typically displays the fields of only one record at a time. Often the fields of a form are are displayed in a vertical arrangement (unlike the horizontal arrangement of fields on a datasheet).

Activity Steps

EmployeesO1.mdb

1. Click the **Queries button**  on the Objects bar (if it's not already selected), click **Employees in KY** (if it's not already selected), then click the **Open button** Open on the Database window toolbar
   See Figure GS-6.

2. Double-click **Ronald** in the First Name field of the first record for Ronald Welling, then type **Jack**

3. Close the Employees in KY query
   Entries to a record are automatically saved when you move to another record or when you close the window.

4. Click the **Forms button** Forms on the Objects bar, click **Employee Entry Form** (if it's not already selected), then click the **Open button** Open on the Database window toolbar
   See Figure GS-7. The name "Jack" appears in the first record even though you entered "Jack" into a query object.

5. Double-click **Welling** in the Last Name field of the form, type **Goodspeed** then close the Employee Entry Form

6. Click the **Tables button** Tables on the Objects bar, click **Employees** (if it's not already selected), then click the **Open button** Open on the Database window toolbar
   Jack Goodspeed (formerly Ronald Welling) is listed as the first record in the Employees table.

7. Close the Employees table

Figure GS-6: Employees in KY query

Employees
in KY query

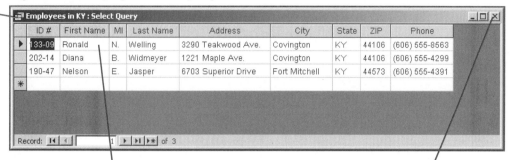

The value "Ronald" in the First
Name field of the first record

Close button for the
Employees in KY query

Figure GS-7: Employee Entry Form

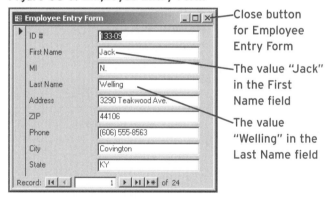

Close button
for Employee
Entry Form

The value "Jack"
in the First
Name field

The value
"Welling" in the
Last Name field

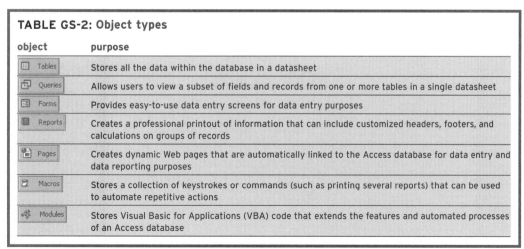

TABLE GS-2: Object types

object	purpose
Tables	Stores all the data within the database in a datasheet
Queries	Allows users to view a subset of fields and records from one or more tables in a single datasheet
Forms	Provides easy-to-use data entry screens for data entry purposes
Reports	Creates a professional printout of information that can include customized headers, footers, and calculations on groups of records
Pages	Creates dynamic Web pages that are automatically linked to the Access database for data entry and data reporting purposes
Macros	Stores a collection of keystrokes or commands (such as printing several reports) that can be used to automate repetitive actions
Modules	Stores Visual Basic for Applications (VBA) code that extends the features and automated processes of an Access database

Getting Started

Getting Started with Access 2002

Understand the Benefits of Using a Relational Database

You've already used databases even if you've never used Access before. Any structured list of information that is stored in electronic or paper format can be considered a database, such as a telephone book, collection of business cards, or address book. Many people choose to create an electronic database in Microsoft Excel, because an Excel spreadsheet provides a tabular grid, making it easy to enter fields and records. However, if you manage your lists in Access, which can link multiple tables of data to create a relational database, you'll enjoy several additional benefits that single-list management systems such as Excel cannot provide. See Table GS-3 for a list of these benefits.

Activity Steps

 Employees01.mdb

1. Click the **Tables button** 🔲 Tables on the Objects bar (if it's not already selected), click **ZipCodes**, then click the **Open button** 📑 Open on the Database window toolbar

2. Click the **expand button** ➕ to the left of the third record for ZIP **45032**
   See Figure GS-8. Three related records that also contain the value 45032 in the ZIP field from the Employees table appear in a **sub-datasheet**, a datasheet within a datasheet. The presence of a sub-datasheet indicates that the tables of your database are related.

3. Double-click **Fairfield** in the City field of the third record, then type **Bridgewater**

4. Close the ZipCodes table

5. Click the **Reports button** 🔲 Reports on the Objects bar, click **Employees Listed by City** (if it's not already selected), then click the **Preview button** 🔍 Preview on the Database window toolbar

6. Maximize the report in the Print Preview window, then click the report to zoom to 100%
   See Figure GS-9. When a relational database is working properly, changes made to a record in one object are automatically updated in all other views of that information.

7. Click the **Restore Window button** 🗗 on the Employees Listed by City report window

8. Close the Employees Listed by City report

Step 6
You use reports to view and print data. You cannot enter data into a report object.

Figure GS-8: ZipCodes table

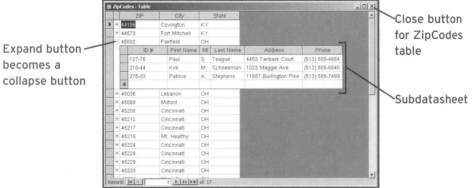

Close button for ZipCodes table

Expand button becomes a collapse button

Subdatasheet

Figure GS-9: Employees Listed by City report

Restore Window button for Employees Listed by City report

"Bridgewater" entry appears as the City value for ZIP 45032

Employees Listed by City

City	First Name	Last Name	State	ZIP
Bridgewater	Paul	Teague	OH	45032
Bridgewater	Kirk	Schneeman	OH	45032
Bridgewater	Patrice	Stephens	OH	45032
Cincinnati	Mary	Neltner	OH	45212
Cincinnati	Margaret	Mattingly	OH	45208
Cincinnati	Nancy	Brusman	OH	45217

TABLE GS-3: Benefits of using Access to manage data

feature	benefit
Relational tables	Storing tables in multiple tables and linking them versus storing information in one large table reduces redundant data, which improves data accuracy.
Querying capabilities	Being able to query the database using **SQL (Structured Query Language)** makes the data available to other programs.
Data entry screens	Creating data entry screens (forms) makes it easier to enter and find data in the database.
Advanced reporting tools	Using the advanced reporting tools of an Access database allows you to quickly summarize and analyze data in many ways. You can save the reports that you build so that you can quickly view data in multiple arrangements without recreating the report.
Web page connectivity	Connecting an Access database to a Web page means that you can provide data entry, editing, and reporting capabilities to users through World Wide Web technologies.
Multi-user file	An Access database is inherently **multi-user**; multiple people can enter and update data in the same database at the same time.

Getting Started
Getting Started with Access 2002

Manage Toolbars and Understand Views

Access displays different toolbars and menu bar options depending on the object you are working with. Furthermore, each object has multiple views, each of which displays a different default toolbar and menu bar. A **view** is a presentation of an object that allows you to perform certain tasks. Most objects have two views. Table GS-4 contains more information on object views. The toolbars that are displayed in each view show the buttons for the commands that are most common to that view. But since it's easy to accidently reposition or remove toolbars, it's also important that you know how to redisplay and move toolbars to the screen location that works best for you.

Activity Steps

 Employees01.mdb

1. Click the **Tables button** [⊞ Tables] on the Objects bar (if it's not already selected), click **Employees**, then click the **Open button** [🗐 Open] on the Database window toolbar

2. Click **View** on the menu bar, point to **Toolbars**, click **Formatting (Datasheet)** (if it's not already checked) to toggle the Formatting (Datasheet) toolbar on, point to the left edge of the Formatting (Datasheet) toolbar so that your pointer changes to ⁺↓⁺, then drag the toolbar to move it just below the Table Datasheet toolbar (if it's not already positioned there)
See Figure GS-10. The Formatting (Datasheet) toolbar contains buttons that apply formatting characteristics such as font size, bold, and text color. After you toggle on a toolbar, it will appear each time you open the view that you displayed it in.

3. Close the Employees table, click **ZipCodes** in the Database window, then click the **Open button** [🗐 Open] on the Database window toolbar

4. Click **View** on the menu bar, point to **Toolbars**, then click **Formatting (Datasheet)** to toggle the Formatting (Datasheet) toolbar off

5. Click the **View button** [🖉] on the Table Datasheet toolbar
See Figure GS-11. The View button icon acts as a toggle to help you quickly switch between the "open" and "design" views of an object. When you are in Table Design View, the View button displays a datasheet icon [⊞], and when you are in Table Datasheet View, the View button displays a designer's tools icons [🖉].

6. Click the **View button** [⊞] on the Table Design toolbar

7. Close the ZipCodes table

Step 2
Two toolbars can also be positioned on the same row, which hides some of the buttons on each toolbar. If this happens, point to the left edge of one of the toolbars so that your pointer changes to ⁺↓⁺, then drag the toolbar to reposition it in the way that works best for you.

Figure GS-10: Table Datasheet toolbar and Formatting (Datasheet) toolbar

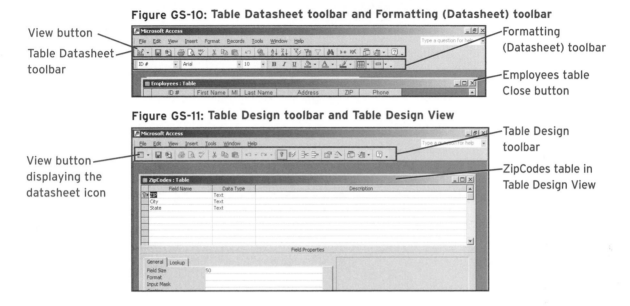

View button

Table Datasheet toolbar

Formatting (Datasheet) toolbar

Employees table Close button

Figure GS-11: Table Design toolbar and Table Design View

View button displaying the datasheet icon

Table Design toolbar

ZipCodes table in Table Design View

TABLE GS-4: Object views

object	view displayed if you click the object, then click the Open button [Open] on the Database Window toolbar	view displayed if you click the object, then click the Design button [Design] on the Database toolbar
Table	**Table Datasheet View** is used to view, enter, edit, and delete data.	**Table Design View** is used to enter, modify, and delete fields from a table.
Query	**Query Datasheet View** is used to view, enter, edit, and delete data.	**Query Design View** is used to define the fields and records displayed by Query Datasheet View.
Form	**Form View** is used to view, enter, edit, and delete data.	**Form Design View** is used to define the layout and formatting characteristics of the form.
Report	Reports do not have an "Open" view. If you double-click a report object in the Database window, you'll open it in Print Preview.	**Report Design View** is used to define the layout and formatting characteristics of a report.
Page	**Page View** is used to view, enter, edit, and delete data; shows you how the Web page will appear when opened in Internet Explorer.	**Page Design View** is used to define the layout and formatting characteristics of a Web page.
Macro	Macros do not have an "Open" view. If you double-click a macro object in the Database window, you'll run the macro.	**Macro Design View** is used to define macro actions.
Module	Modules do not have an "Open" view. If you double-click a module object in the Database window, you'll run the VBA code that the module stores.	Modules contain VBA code. When you design a module, you work in the **Microsoft Visual Basic window.**

Getting Started

Getting Started with Access 2002

Use the Help System

Access provides an extensive **Help system** that you can use to learn more about Access or to troubleshoot problems. You can open the Access Help window through the Help menu, Ask a Question box, toolbar buttons, or by pressing the F1 key. Help menu options are further described in Table GS-5. Once the Help window is open, you can search for information by scanning a table of contents, by searching through an index of keywords, or by typing a question.

Activity Steps

 Employees01.mdb

1. Click the **Ask a Question box** on the menu bar, type **create a table**, then press **Enter**
   See Figure GS-12. Based on your entry, the Help system displays a list of topics for you to choose from.

2. Click the **About creating a table link**, then maximize the Microsoft Access Help window
   The Help page contains information about creating a table.

3. Click the **fields** link on the Help page
   Glossary words appear as blue links on a Help page. Definitions appear in green text.

4. Click the **Contents tab** (if it's not already selected), click the **Microsoft Access Help expand button** ⊞, click the **Tables expand button** ⊞, click the **Creating Tables expand button** ⊞, click **Create a table** in the Contents window, then click the **Create a table by using the Table Wizard link** on the Help page to expand that section of the page
   See Figure GS-13.

5. Click the **Show All link** on the Help page to show all sections and glossary words on the Help page

6. Click the **Answer Wizard tab**, type **How do I create a table?**, then click **Search**
   The topics that address that question are displayed in the Select topic to display list. You can click any entry in the list to show that page of the Help system.

7. Click the **Index tab**, type **table** in the Type keywords box, then click **Search**
   All the topics for this keyword are displayed in the Choose a topic list. You can click any entry in the list to show that page of the Help system.

8. Close the Microsoft Access Help window

Step 4
If the Contents, Answer Wizard, and Index tabs are not visible, click the Show button ⊟ on the Microsoft Access Help toolbar.

Figure GS-12: Using the Ask a Question box

Ask a Question box

About creating a table link

Figure GS-13: Using the Contents window to find information in the Help system

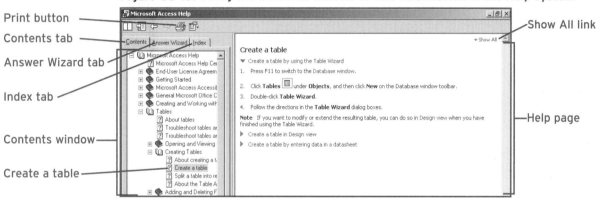

Print button
Contents tab
Answer Wizard tab
Index tab
Contents window
Create a table

Show All link

Help page

TABLE GS-5: Help menu options

Help menu option	description
Microsoft Access Help	Opens the Office Assistant, which prompts you for a keyword search of the Help manual
Show the Office Assistant	Displays the **Office Assistant**, an automated character that provides tips and interactive prompts while you are working
Hide the Office Assistant	Temporarily closes the Office Assistant for the working session
What's This	Changes the pointer to and provides a short description of an area, icon, or menu option that you click using this special pointer
Office on the Web	If you are connected to the Web, displays the Microsoft Web site, which provides additional Microsoft information and support articles
Sample Databases	Provides easy access to the sample databases installed with Access 2002
Detect and Repair	Analyzes a database for possible data corruption and attempts to repair problems
About Microsoft Access	Provides the version and product ID of Access

Close a Database and Exit Access

You can close a database and exit Access by clicking the Access Close button in the upper-right corner of the screen at any time. Since data is automatically saved in an Access database, you don't need to worry about saving data before you close a window or exit Access. However, if you make any structural or formatting changes to an object (such as add a new field to a table or change the font in a datasheet), you will be prompted to save those changes when you close the object. Therefore, it's a good idea to close each object window when you are finished working in it to make sure you've saved the changes you intend to save. When all object windows are closed, you are returned to the Database window. From there, you can close the database and exit Access.

Step 2
If your database is stored on a floppy disk, do not eject the floppy disk from the disk drive until the Access window (not just the Database window) is closed.

Activity Steps

 Employees01.mdb

1. Click the **Close button** ☒ on the Database window
   See Figure GS-14. When the Access window is open without an open database, you can still use the Access Help system and many Access tools (such as those used to compact or convert existing databases). You can also open a new database.

2. Click the **Close button** ☒ on the Access window

Figure GS-14: Access window Close button

Close button for
Access window

extra!

Compacting on Close

The **Compact on Close** feature compacts and repairs your database each time you close it. To activate the Compact on Close feature, click **Tools** on the menu bar, click **Options**, click the **General tab** in the Options dialog box, select the **Compact on Close check box,** and click **OK**. While the Compact on Close feature works well if your database is stored on a hard drive, it can cause problems if you are working from a floppy disk. This is because the Compact on Close process creates a temporary file that is just as large as the original database. This temporary file is deleted after the compact process finishes. If you are working on a floppy disk and do not have enough room on the disk to complete the compact process successfully, an error occurs that might result in an error message, or, in the worst case, a corruption of the database. Therefore, you shouldn't compact a database unless you know that you have plenty of room to accommodate the temporary file that is created during the process.

Getting Started

Getting Started with Access 2002

Target Your Skills

 Doctors01.mdb

1 Answer the following questions on a separate sheet of paper: What tables are stored in this database? How many fields and records are in each table? What queries are stored in this database? How many fields and records are in each query? What form is stored in this database? How many fields are displayed on the form? How many records are in the form? What reports are stored in this database? Open the Zips table, then display the subdatasheet as shown in Figure GS-15. What is the relationship between the Zips and Doctors tables?

Figure GS-15

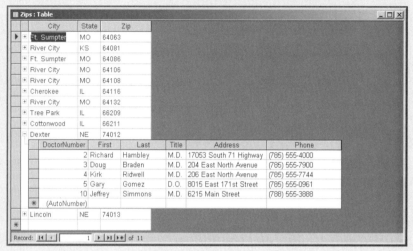

 Doctors01.mdb

2 Start Access, but do not open a database. Enter "toolbar" in the Ask a Question box, then click the Troubleshoot toolbars link to display the Help page shown in Figure GS-16.

Figure GS-16

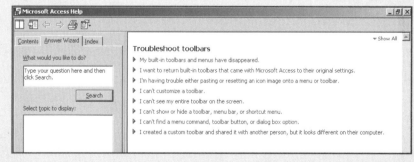

Skill List

1. Create Access databases
2. Open database objects in multiple views
3. Move among records
4. Format datasheets

In Skill Set 1, you will learn how to use an Access database wizard to build a database quickly, and you will explore many database objects, such as tables, queries, forms, and reports. You'll also learn how to navigate through a database to find information and how to format information to enhance your printouts.

Skill Set 1

Creating and Using Databases

Create Access Databases

Access provides many **templates**, or sample databases, such as inventory, event, contact, and expense management, which you can use to create your own database quickly. Some Access templates are also **database wizards**, which provide a series of dialog boxes that guide you through a process for creating a database. Whether you create a database using a template or a database wizard, you can further modify it to meet your needs.

Activity Steps

1. Start Access, then click **General Templates** in the task pane

2. Click the **Databases tab** in the Templates dialog box
   See Figure 1-1.

3. Click **Contact Management**, then click **OK**

4. Click **Create** to save the database with the name Contact Management1 in the My Documents folder
   If a database with the name Contact Management1 already exists, the new database will be named Contact Management2, and so on.

5. Click **Next**, click **Next** again to accept all of the suggested fields in the three sample tables, click **SandStone** for the screen display style, click **Next**, click **Soft Gray** for the printed report style, click **Next**, click **Next** again to accept "Contact Management" as the database title, then click **Finish** to instruct the wizard to build the database using these choices

6. Click the **Enter/View Contacts button**, click the **Close button** [X] on the Contacts form, then click other buttons on the Main Switchboard form to explore the Contact Management database
   See Figure 1-2.

7. When finished exploring, click the **Exit this database button** on the Main Switchboard form to close the Contact Management1 database

Step 1
If Access is running, but the task pane is not visible, click the New button [ ] on the Database toolbar.

Skill 1

Create Access Databases

Figure 1-1: Access database wizards and task pane

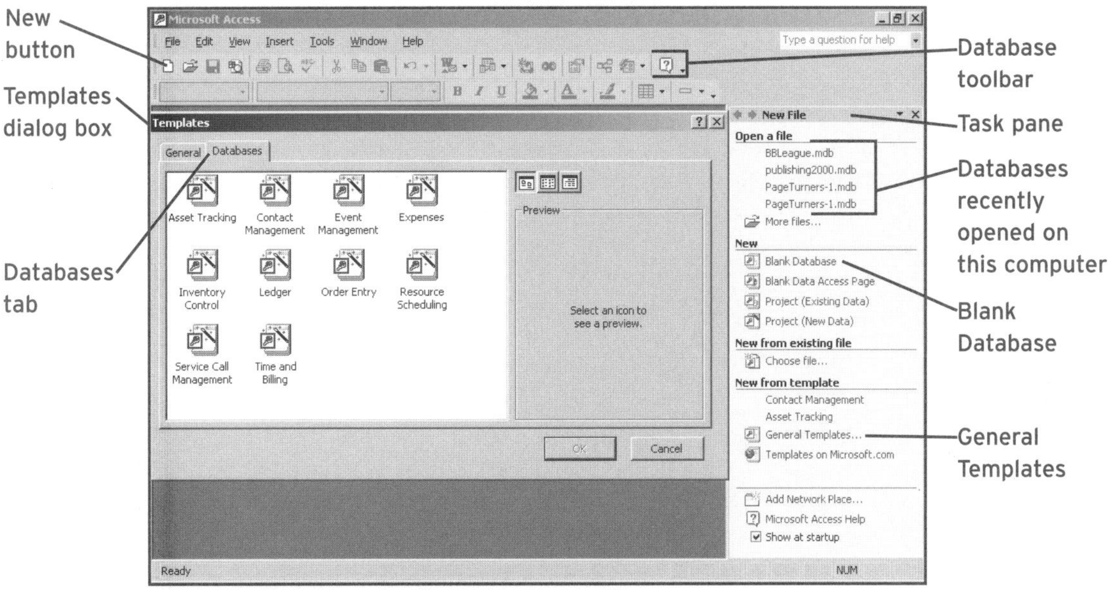

New button
Templates dialog box
Databases tab
Database toolbar
Task pane
Databases recently opened on this computer
Blank Database
General Templates

Figure 1-2: Contact Management database

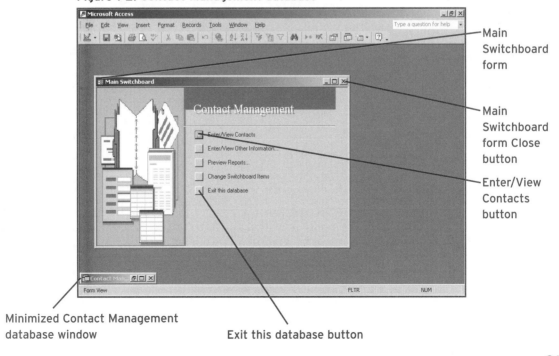

Main Switchboard form
Main Switchboard form Close button
Enter/View Contacts button
Minimized Contact Management database window
Exit this database button

Skill Set 1

Creating and Using Databases

Open Database Objects in Multiple Views

Database objects, such as tables, queries, forms, and reports, have different **views**, or presentations of an object that support different database activities. Every object has a **Design View**, which you use to modify the structure of the object. For example, in Table Design View, you add or delete fields; in Report Design View, you change the layout and format of the report. **Datasheet View** of a table and query displays data in a spreadsheet-like arrangement in which the fields are in columns and the records are in rows. You use Datasheet View to view, find, edit, and enter records. **Form View** of a form presents information in a layout that you create, and you use it to edit and enter data. **Preview** allows you to view a report on the screen before you print it.

Activity Steps

 PageTurners01.mdb

1. Click the **Tables button** ▥ Tables on the Objects bar (if it's not already selected), click **Employees**, then click the **Open button** ⬑Open on the Database window toolbar to open the table in Datasheet View
   See Figure 1-3.

2. Click the **View button** 🖾 to view Table Design View, then click the table's **Close button** ✕ to close the Employees table

3. Click the **Queries button** 🗗 Queries on the Objects bar, click **Sales List**, then click the **Open button** ⬑Open on the Database window toolbar to open the query in Datasheet View

4. Click the **View button** 🖾 to view Query Design View, then click the query's **Close button** ✕ to close the Sales List query

5. Click the **Forms button** 🖾 Forms on the Objects bar, click **Customer Orders**, then click the **Open button** ⬑Open on the Database window toolbar to open the form in Form View
   See Figure 1-4.

6. Click the **View button** 🖾 to view Form Design View, then click the form's **Close button** ✕ to close the Customer Orders form

7. Click the **Reports button** ▥ Reports on the Objects bar, click **Books by Category**, then click the **Preview button** 🔍Preview on the Database window toolbar to open the report in Preview

8. Click the **View button** 🖾 to view Report Design View, then click the report's **Close button** ✕ to close the Books by Category report

Step 1
Double-clicking an object in the Database window has the same effect as clicking an object in the Database window, then clicking the Open button on the Database window toolbar.

Figure 1-3: Employees Datasheet View

Employees table

Employees : Table

ID #	First Name	MI	Last Name	Address	City	State	ZIP	Phone	Start
108-47	Lillian	H.	Sanchez	5725 Somerset Drive	Cincinnati	OH	45208	(513) 555-8203	7/8/
109-45	Edwin	C.	Herrick	145 Vine St.	Lebanon	OH	45036	(513) 555-2401	8/12/
121-63	Isaak	O.	Matroin	65 Sheldon Ave.	Norwood	OH	45236	(513) 555-3886	7/15/
127-75	Paul	S.	Teague	4453 Tanbark Court	Fairfield	OH	45032	(513) 555-4884	3/10/
128-79	Martin	L.	Stowell	2313 Lakewood Drive	Cincinnati	OH	45224	(513) 555-9942	3/28/
133-09	Ronald	N.	Welling	3290 Teakwood Ave.	Covington	KY	44106	(606) 555-8563	5/19/
137-69	Bryan	J.	Dolgas	544 Harrison Ave.	West Chester	OH	45233	(513) 555-9116	2/11/
147-72	Chelsea	V.	Hanekamp	658 Stett Road	Lebanon	OH	45036	(513) 555-4391	6/21/
155-28	Francis	J.	Klajic	4922 Mound Ave.	Milford	OH	45068	(513) 555-9924	11/19/
159-92	Nancy	M.	Brusman	1445 Stella Ave.	Mt. Healthy	OH	45217	(513) 555-8020	7/17/
177-03	Gary	R.	Malott	394 Delhi Ave.	Cincinnati	OH	45229	(513) 555-3382	5/27/
190-47	Nelson	E.	Jasper	6703 Superior Drive	Fort Mitchell	KY	44573	(606) 555-4391	12/1/
202-14	Diana	B.	Widmeyer	1221 Maple Ave.	Covington	KY	44106	(606) 555-4299	1/30/
210-15	Shawna	E.	Ison	5786 Tall Oaks Drive	Cincinnati	OH	45217	(513) 555-7306	12/1/
210-44	Kirk	M.	Schneeman	1023 Maggie Ave.	Fairfield	OH	45032	(513) 555-6845	4/4/
213-33	Raymond	A.	Franklin	912 Wilma Court	Montgomery	OH	45244	(513) 555-7520	6/23/
227-59	Clifton	B.	Pross	383 Bayberry Drive	Cincinnati	OH	45233	(513) 555-3218	8/10/
227-85	Mary	R.	Neltner	177 Victory Pkwy.	Cincinnati	OH	45212	(513) 555-0446	9/15/
229-55	Sue	K.	Wiehe	9865 Colonial Drive	Milford	OH	45068	(513) 555-8474	2/21/
231-87	Joseph	L.	Gersper	2200 Augusta Blvd.	Cincinnati	OH	45228	(513) 555-0344	9/29/
256-81	Jessica	B.	Kindig	5417 Fairfax Ave.	Evanston	OH	45238	(513) 555-7743	10/17/

Record: 1 of 24

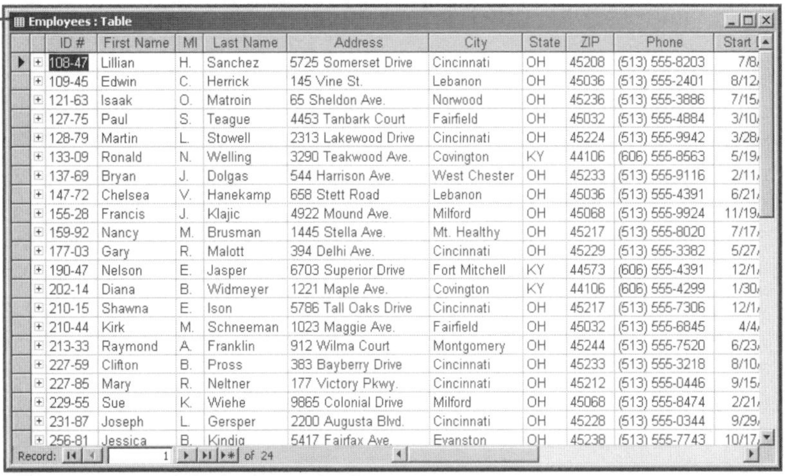

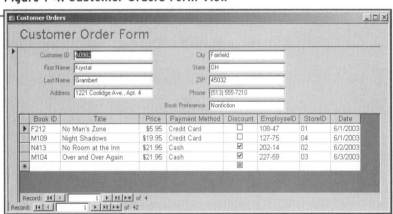

Figure 1-4: Customer Orders Form View

Customer Orders form

Customer Orders

Customer Order Form

Customer ID: A0982
First Name: Krystal
Last Name: Grambert
Address: 1221 Coolidge Ave., Apt. 4
City: Fairfield
State: OH
ZIP: 45032
Phone: (513) 555-7210
Book Preference: Nonfiction

Book ID	Title	Price	Payment Method	Discount	EmployeeID	StoreID	Date
F212	No Man's Zone	$5.95	Credit Card	☐	108-47	01	6/1/2003
M109	Night Shadows	$19.95	Credit Card	☐	127-75	04	6/1/2003
N413	No Room at the Inn	$21.95	Cash	☑	202-14	02	6/2/2003
M104	Over and Over Again	$21.95	Cash	☑	227-59	03	6/3/2003

Record: 1 of 4
Record: 1 of 42

Skill Set 1

Creating and Using Databases

Move Among Records
Navigate Through Datasheet View and Form View

To view or find specific records or to add or edit data, you must be able to move around in a database. You can use the navigation buttons on the **navigation toolbar** in the Database View and Form View windows to navigate through records. The navigation toolbar also displays the number of the current record and the total number of records. You can also use keys, such as [Tab] and [Up Arrow], to navigate through records and individual fields. Table 1-1 summarizes the navigation buttons and common navigation keys that you can use to navigate through data in Datasheet View or Form View.

Activity Steps

 PageTurners01.mdb

1. Click the **Tables button** 🔲 Tables on the Objects bar (if it's not already selected), then double-click **Inventory** to open the table in Datasheet View
   See Figure 1-5.

2. Press **[Enter]** or **[Tab]** as many times as it takes to move to the second record

3. Press **[Down Arrow]** twice, then press **[Up Arrow]** twice

4. Press **[Ctrl][End]** to move to the last field of the last record, then press **[Ctrl][Home]** to move to the first field of the first record

5. Click the **Next Record button** ▶ on the navigation toolbar, then click the **Last Record button** ▶| on the navigation toolbar

6. Click the **Previous Record button** ◀ on the navigation toolbar, then click the **First Record button** |◀ on the navigation toolbar

7. Close the Inventory table, click the **Forms button** 🔲 Forms on the Objects bar, then double-click **Inventory Entry** to open the form in Form View
   See Figure 1-6.

8. Repeat steps 2 through 6 to observe how the same quick keystrokes and navigation buttons work in Form View

9. Close the Inventory Entry form

Select the record number in the Specific Record box on the navigation toolbar, type any other record number, then press [Enter] to move directly to that record.

Figure 1-5: Navigating in Datasheet View

Inventory table

Navigation toolbar

Figure 1-6: Navigating in Form View

Inventory Entry form

Current record number

Specific Record box

Total number of records

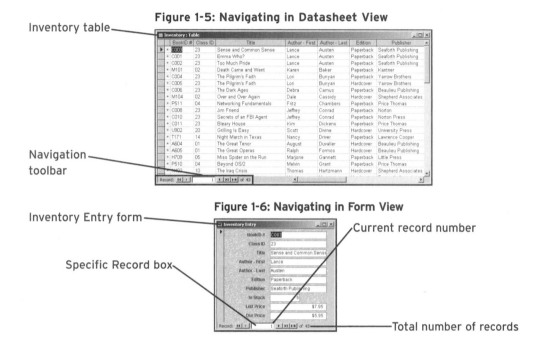

TABLE 1-1: Common navigation techniques

navigation button	navigation button name or key	moves to the following place
◄	First Record	first record
◄	Previous Record	previous record
►	Next Record	next record
►◄	Last Record	last record
►✱	New Record	new record (for data entry purposes)
	[Enter]	next field
	[Tab]	next field
	[Up Arrow]	previous record (Datasheet View)
	[Up Arrow]	previous field (Form View)
	[Down Arrow]	next record (Datasheet View)
	[Down Arrow]	next field (Form View)
	[Ctrl][Home]	first field of the first record
	[Ctrl][End]	last field of the last record

Skill Set 1
Creating and Using Databases

Move Among Records
Navigate Through Subdatasheets

A **subdatasheet** is a datasheet within a datasheet that contains records from a related table. Subdatasheets are available when a one-to-many relationship exists between two tables. For example, suppose that a one-to-many relationship exists between the tables Customers and Sales. If you expand a record in the Customers table datasheet, a subdatasheet (from the Sales table) containing records of what the customer purchased will appear. After you expand the subdatasheet, you navigate through a subdatasheet the same way you navigate through a datasheet.

Step 2
You can expand all subdatasheets at the same time by clicking the Selector button in the upper-left corner of the table in Datasheet View, then clicking any expand button.

Activity Steps

 PageTurners01.mdb

1. Click the **Tables button** 🔲 Tables on the Objects bar (if it's not already selected), then double-click **Customers**

2. Click the **expand button** ⊞ to the left of the first record
   See Figure 1-7.

3. Press **[Enter]** several times to move through the fields of the subdatasheet

4. Click the **expand button** ⊞ to the left of the second record, click the date entry in the first record of the second subdatasheet, then click the **Next Record button** ▶ on the navigation toolbar
   See Figure 1-8.

5. Click the **collapse button** ⊟ to the left of the first record, then click the **collapse button** ⊟ to the left of the second record

6. Close the Customers table

Figure 1-7: Navigating through a subdatasheet

Collapse button

Subdatasheet

Expand button

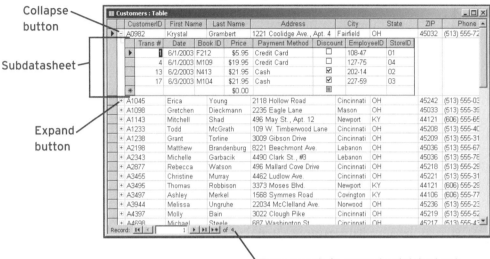

Four records in current subdatasheet

Figure 1-8: Navigating through a second subdatasheet

Selector button

Second subdatasheet

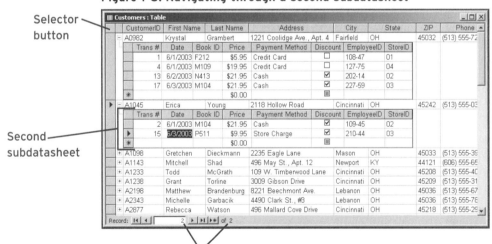

Record 2 of 2 in current subdatasheet

Skill Set 1
Creating and Using Databases

Format Datasheets

You can format datasheets in a variety of ways to enhance the presentation of information on the screen and on printouts. The most common formatting enhancement commands are represented as buttons on the Formatting (Datasheet) toolbar. You can use these buttons to change the type, size, and colors of a datasheet. These buttons are described in Table 1-2. You can access other formatting and datasheet modification commands, such as hiding, resizing, and renaming columns, from the Format menu.

Step 5
To unhide a column in a datasheet, click Format on the menu bar, click Unhide Columns, select the check boxes beside those columns (fields) that you want to unhide, then click Close.

Activity Steps

 PageTurners01.mdb

1. Click the **Tables button** ⊞ Tables on the Objects bar (if it's not already selected), then double-click **Inventory**

2. Click the **Font list arrow** |Arial ▼| on the Formatting (Datasheet) toolbar, press **[v]**, then click **Verdana**

3. Click the **Font/Fore Color button list arrow** 🔺▾ on the Formatting (Datasheet) toolbar, then click the **Blue box** in the sixth column in the second row

4. Click the **Gridlines button list arrow** ⊞▾ on the Formatting (Datasheet) toolbar, then click **Gridlines: Horizontal**

5. Click any entry in the Edition field, click **Format** on the menu bar, then click **Hide Columns**
See Figure 1-9.

6. Close the Inventory table without saving changes

Figure 1-9: Formatting a datasheet

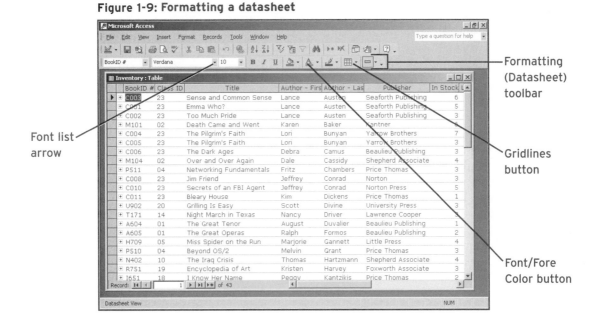

Formatting (Datasheet) toolbar

Font list arrow

Gridlines button

Font/Fore Color button

TABLE 1-2: Formatting buttons

button	name	description
Arial	Font	Applies a new font face
10	Font Size	Applies a new font size
B	Bold	Toggles the bold font style on and off
I	Italic	Toggles the italic font style on and off
U	Underline	Toggles the underline font style on and off
(Fill/Back Color icon)	Fill/Back Color	Changes the background color of the datasheet
(Font/Fore Color icon)	Font/Fore Color	Changes the text color of the datasheet
(Line/Border Color icon)	Line/Border Color	Changes the gridline color of the datasheet
(Gridlines icon)	Gridlines	Determines which gridlines appear on the datasheet
(Special Effect icon)	Special Effect	Changes the effect (flat, raised, or sunken) of the cells in a datasheet

Skill Set 1

Creating and Using Databases

Target Your Skills

 PageTurners01.mdb

1 Use Figure 1-10 as a guide to open the Datasheet View of the Stores table with one expanded sub-datasheet. Using the Next Record navigation button and keyboard, navigate to the field that is selected in the subdatasheet so that your datasheet matches the figure.

Figure 1-10

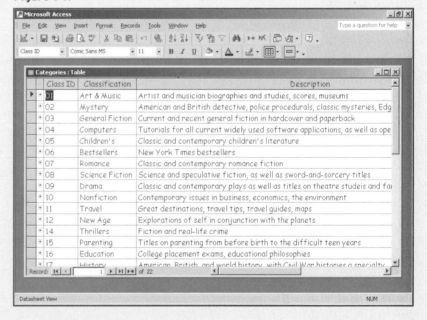

 PageTurners01.mdb

2 Use Figure 1-11 as a guide to format the Categories table datasheet. Use the information shown on the Formatting (Datasheet) toolbar to help you determine what formatting changes need to be applied.

Figure 1-11

Skill List

1. Create and modify tables
2. Add a pre-defined input mask to a field
3. Create lookup fields
4. Modify field properties

In Skill Set 2, you will learn how to create and modify tables. Tables are the most important object in the database because they store data. Access provides several different techniques and tools for creating tables. You can create a table by using Table Design View, by importing data from an external data source (such as a Microsoft Excel workbook), or by using the Table Wizard. The primary task in creating a table is defining **fields**, the categories of information that determine what data can be entered for each record. You can also add, delete, or modify fields within an existing table by using Table Design View.

Skill Set 2
Creating and Modifying Tables

Create and Modify Tables
Create Tables Using the Table Wizard

You can create a table by using the **Table Wizard**, which lists sample tables and fields that you can use to quickly build a new table. The Table Wizard also helps you choose a field that will make each record in the table unique (the primary key field) and helps you connect the new table to existing tables in the database.

Step 1
You can click the New button on the Database window toolbar to display the New Table dialog box, which provides several techniques for creating a new table (including the Table Wizard).

Activity Steps
📁 **MedSchool01.mdb**

1. Click the **Tables button** 🗔 Tables on the Objects bar (if it's not already selected), then double-click **Create table by using wizard**

2. Scroll down to the bottom of the Sample Tables list, then click **Students**
   See Figure 2-1.

3. Click the **Select All Fields button** >>

4. Click **ParentsNames** in the Fields in My New Table list, then click the **Remove Single Field button** <

5. Click **MiddleName** in the Fields in My New Table list, click **Rename Field**, type **MiddleInitial**, then click **OK**

6. Click **Next**, click **Next** to accept Students as the table name and to allow the wizard to set the primary key

7. Click **Next** to avoid setting any table relationships at this time, click the **Modify the table design option button**, then click **Finish** to open the table in Design View
   See Figure 2-2.

8. Close the Students table, then click **Yes** (if prompted) to save it

extra!

Choosing a primary key field
The **primary key field** contains data unique to each record. For example, if a table contains information about people, such as employees or students, the Social Security Number would be a good primary key field candidate, because the values in this field would be unique to each individual. Name fields do not make good primary key fields, because they often contain the same data for two different people.

Figure 2-1: Table Wizard dialog box

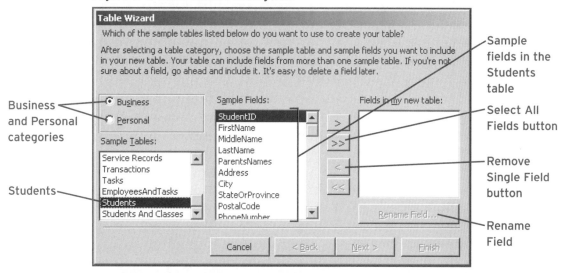

Sample fields in the Students table

Business and Personal categories

Students

Select All Fields button

Remove Single Field button

Rename Field

Figure 2-2: Students table in Design View

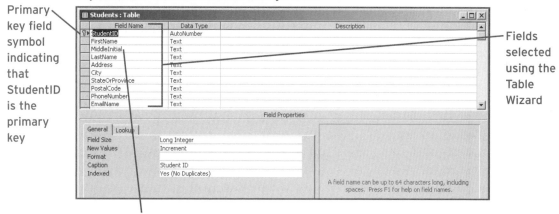

Primary key field symbol indicating that StudentID is the primary key

Fields selected using the Table Wizard

MiddleInitial field renamed using the Table Wizard

Skill Set 2
Creating and Modifying Tables

Create and Modify Tables
Create Tables Using Table Design View

You can use Table Design View to create a new table. Unlike the Table Wizard, which helps you make decisions about field names and other characteristics of a table, Table Design View requires that you plan and enter each new field by yourself. In Table Design View, you enter field names, field data types, and field **properties** (individual characteristics of a field, such as Field Size). The **data type** of the field determines what types of values you can enter into the field, such as numbers, dates, or text. (See Table 2-1 for more information on data types.) Regardless of the technique you use to build a table, you use Table Design View to add, delete, or modify the fields in an existing table.

Step 4

The Primary Key button works as a toggle, so if you set the wrong field as the primary key field, click the field, then click the Primary Key button to remove the primary key field designation from the incorrect field.

Activity Steps

 MedSchool01.mdb

1. Click the **Tables button** ▦ Tables on the Objects bar (if it's not already selected), then double-click **Create table in Design view**

2. Type **InstructorID**, press **[Down Arrow]**, type **InstructorFirst**, press **[Down Arrow]**, type **InstructorLast**, press **[Down Arrow]**, then type **Specialty**

3. Click **Text** in the Data Type cell for the InstructorID field, click the **list arrow**, then click **AutoNumber**

4. Click the **Primary Key button** on the Table Design toolbar to set the InstructorID field as the primary key field for this table

5. Click the **Save button** on the Table Design toolbar, type **Instructors** in the Table Name box, then click **OK**
   See Figure 2-3.

6. Close the Instructors table

Figure 2-3: Creating and Modifying the Instructors table in Design View

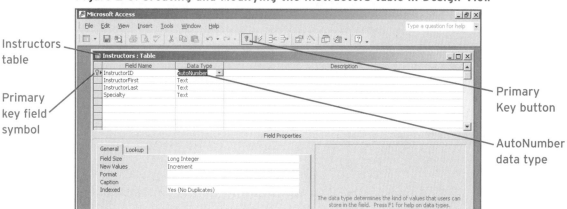

Instructors table

Primary key field symbol

Primary Key button

AutoNumber data type

TABLE 2-1: Data types

data type	description of data	field examples
Text	Text or combinations of text and numbers	FirstName, City
Memo	Lengthy text over 255 characters	Comments, Notes
Number	Numeric information used in calculations	Quantity, Rating
Date/Time	Dates and times	BirthDate, InvoiceDate
Currency	Monetary values	PurchasePrice, Salary
AutoNumber	Integers assigned by Access to sequentially order each record added to a table	InvoiceID, CustomerID
Yes/No	Only one of two values (Yes/No, On/Off, True/False)	Veteran, Tenured
OLE Object	Files created in other programs	Resume, Picture
Hyperlink	Web page addresses	HomePage, CompanyWebPage

Skill Set 2

Creating and Modifying Tables

Add a Pre-defined Input Mask to a Field

You can use the **Input Mask** property to specify the number and types of characters that can be entered into a field and to display a visual guide as data is entered. For example, you might apply an input mask to a Social Security Number field so that the only characters allowed are the numbers 0 through 9. You could also set the input mask to enter dashes automatically as the Social Security Number is entered (for example 123-12-1234). You can use the Input Mask property only with fields that have Text and Date/Time data types. You can use the **Input Mask Wizard** to enter Input Mask properties.

Activity Steps

file >| MedSchool01.mdb

1. Click the **Tables button** ⊞ Tables on the Objects bar (if it's not already selected), click **Physicians**, then click the **Design button** ⩊ Design on the Database window toolbar to open the table in Design View

2. Click the **Input Mask property box** (for the selected field, SocialSecurityNumber), click the **Build button** ..., then click **Yes** (if prompted) to save the table

3. Click **Social Security Number** in the Input Mask list, press **[Tab]**, then type **111223333** to test the new input mask
   See Figure 2-4.

4. Click **Next**, click **Next** to accept the suggested input mask (000-00-000) and the placeholder character (_)
   In the input mask 00-000-0000, 0 represents a required number, which means that only numbers (not letters or symbols) are allowed as valid characters for the SocialSecurityNumber field.

5. Click **Finish** to store the data without the symbols in the input mask
   See Figure 2-5.

6. Click the **Save button** 🖫 on the Table Design toolbar, click the **View button** ⊞ on the Table Design toolbar, type **333224444**, then press **[Tab]** to test the new Input Mask property
   The Input Mask property guides the entry of the numbers in the SocialSecurityNumber field.

7. **Close the Physicians table**

You can press F6 to switch between the upper and lower panes of Table Design View.

Figure 2-4: Input Mask Wizard dialog box

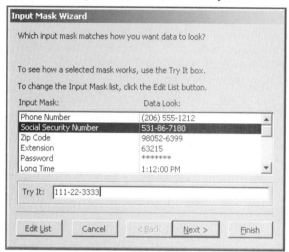

Figure 2-5: Input mask entry in Table Design View

SocialSecurity Number field

Selected field symbol

Build button

Input Mask property box displaying input mask

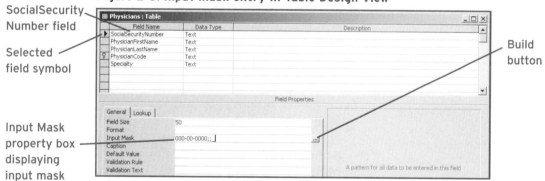

Skill Set 2

Creating and Modifying Tables

Create Lookup Fields

To make data entry easier, faster, and more accurate, you can provide a **lookup field**, a field that contains a list of values from which you can choose an entry. This data appears in a combo box (sometimes called a drop-down list) for a lookup field on either a datasheet or form. To create a lookup field, you must specify **Lookup properties**, which will provide the list of values for the field. You can use the **Lookup Wizard** to enter Lookup properties for a field.

Activity Steps

 MedSchool01.mdb

1. Click the **Tables button** [Tables] on the Objects bar (if it's not already selected), click **Insurance**, then click the **Design button** [Design] on the Database window toolbar to open the table in Design View

2. Click **Text** in the Data Type cell for the ZipCode field, click the **list arrow**, then click **Lookup Wizard**

3. Click **Next** to accept the option for the lookup column to look up values in a table or query

4. Click **Table: Zip** to choose the table that will provide the values for the combo box, then click **Next**

5. Double-click **ZipCode**, then double-click **City**
   See Figure 2-6.

6. Click **Next**, deselect the **Hide key column check box**
   A **key column** refers to the primary key field column.

7. Click **Next**, then Click **Next** to accept the option that the ZipCode field uniquely identifies each row, click **Finish** to accept "ZipCode" as the label for the lookup column, then click **Yes** when prompted to save the table

8. Click the **View button** [⊞] on the Table Design toolbar, click the **ZipCode** field for the first record, click the **list arrow**, then click **64014** in the combo box list

9. Close the Insurance table

You can click any property box to display a short description of it in the lower right corner of Table Design View. Click any property box, then press F1 to display a longer description of the property in the Help system.

Figure 2-6: Lookup Wizard dialog box

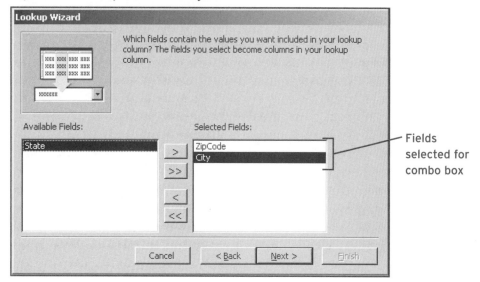

Skill Set 2

Creating and Modifying Tables

Modify Field Properties

You modify field properties in Table Design View. Field properties vary among field data types. For example, fields with a Text data type have a Field Size property that you can use to change the number of characters allowed for entries stored in that field. However, fields with a Date/Time data type do not have a Field Size property, because the size of a Date/Time field is controlled by Access. A list of common field properties for various data types is shown in Table 2-2.

Activity Steps

 MedSchool01.mdb

1. Click the **Tables button** [Tables] on the Objects bar (if it's not already selected), click **Zip**, then click the **Design button** [Design] on the Database window toolbar to open the table in Design View

2. Click the **State** field, double-click **50** in the Field Size property box, then type **2**

3. Click the **Format property box**, then type **>**

4. Click the **Validation Rule property box**, then type **CO or WY**

5. Click the **Validation Text property box**, then type **Must be CO or WY**
   See Figure 2-7.

6. Click the **Save button** [save icon] on the Table Design toolbar, click **Yes** when prompted to continue, click **Yes** when prompted to test the rules, then click the **View button** [view icon] on the Table Design toolbar

7. Press **[Tab]** to move to the State field, type **MDD** (note that the third character is not allowed), then press **[Down Arrow]**

8. Click **OK** when prompted with the Validation Text message, then press **[Esc]** to undo the edit to the current record

9. Close the Zip table

Step 4
Access automatically enters quotation marks around text typed into the Validation Rule property box.

Figure 2-7: Modifying other properties

State field is selected

Field Size property

Format property

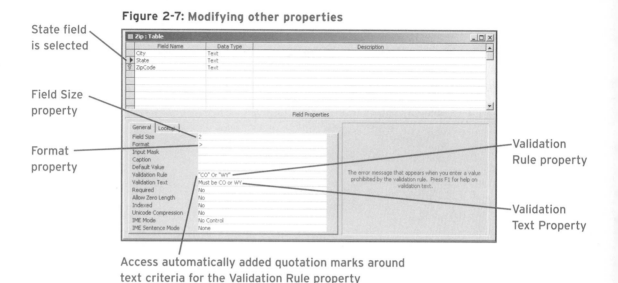

Validation Rule property

Validation Text Property

Access automatically added quotation marks around text criteria for the Validation Rule property

TABLE 2-2: Common Field Properties

property	description	typical value
Field Size (Text data type)	Determines how many characters can be entered into a field	1 through 255
Field Size (Number data type)	Determines the size and type of numbers that can be entered into a field	Integer
Format	Determines how data will appear on the datasheet	> (display values in uppercase) < (display values in lowercase)
Caption	Overwrites the actual field name in the first row of the datasheet	First Name (if the field name is FName, for example)
Default Value	Automatically provides a value for a field in a new record	CO (for a State field in which the majority of records contained the CO entry)
Validation Rule	Provides a list of valid entries for a field	"CO" OR "WY" or "MT"
Validation Text	Provides a descriptive message in case a user attempts to enter data into a field that doesn't meet the criteria specified in the Validation Rule property box	Valid entries are CO, WY, or MT
Decimal Places	Determines the number of digits that are displayed to the right of the decimal point	0, 2
Input Mask	Determines the number and type of characters that can be entered in a field and provides a visual guide for data entry	00000-9999;;_

Skill Set 2

Creating and Modifying Tables

Target Your Skills

 MedSchool01.mdb

1 Create a new table in Table Design View and save it with the name Hospitals. Use Figure 2-8 to determine the fields to create. Be sure to designate the HospitalNumber field as the primary key field. Use the Input Mask Wizard to apply the Input Mask property to the HospitalPhone field.

 MedSchool01.mdb

2 Open the Physicians table in Design View and add a new field named Title, as shown in Figure 2-9. Modify the Field Size, Format, Validation Rule, and Validation Text properties as shown in the figure.

Figure 2-8

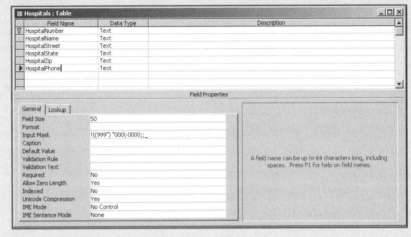

Figure 2-9

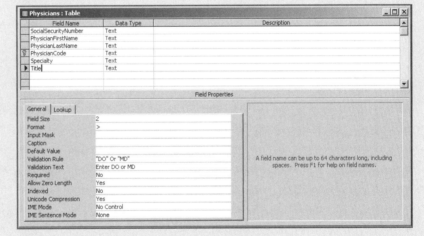

Skill List

1. **Create and modify select queries**
2. **Add calculated fields to select queries**

In Skill Set 3, you will work with the **select query**, a database object that collects fields from one or more tables into a single datasheet. You build a query when you have a question about the data. For example, you could use a query to determine which customers bought a particular product. You can build a select query by using either the Simple Query Wizard or Query Design View. Once a query is created, you open it in Datasheet View to find, filter, and edit data. You can also use a select query to create **calculated fields**, fields whose contents depend on the values in other fields. For example, you could multiply a numerical value in a field, such as Sales, by a percentage to obtain a numerical value for a different field, such as Tax.

Skill Set 3

Creating and Modifying Queries

Create and Modify Select Queries

Create Select Queries Using the Simple Query Wizard

You can use the **Simple Query Wizard** to build a select query. The Simple Query Wizard prompts you to choose the fields you want in the query, asks you how the final records should be presented (as individual or summarized records), and asks you to enter a title for the query. Your selections determine how the data is presented and organized in the final Datasheet View of the query.

Activity Steps

 Team01.mdb

1. Click the **Queries button** on the Objects bar (if it's not already selected), then double-click **Create query by using wizard**

2. Click the **Tables/Queries list arrow**, then click **Table: Players** (if it's not already selected)

3. Double-click **FName**, then double-click **LName**

4. Click the **Tables/Queries list arrow**, click **Table: Pledges**, double-click **Amount**, then double-click **Date**
   See Figure 3-1.

5. Click **Next**, then click **Next** again to accept the Detail option
   The Detail option will show every record.

6. Type **Pledges To Date** as the title for the query, then click **Finish** to view the query in Datasheet View
   See Figure 3-2.

7. Close the Pledges to Date query

Step 4
You can also use the Select Single Field button ![>], Select All Fields button ![>>], Remove Single Field button ![<], or Remove All Fields button ![<<] to add fields to or remove fields from the Selected Fields list.

Skill 1

Create and Modify Select Queries

Figure 3-1: Building a select query with the Simple Query Wizard

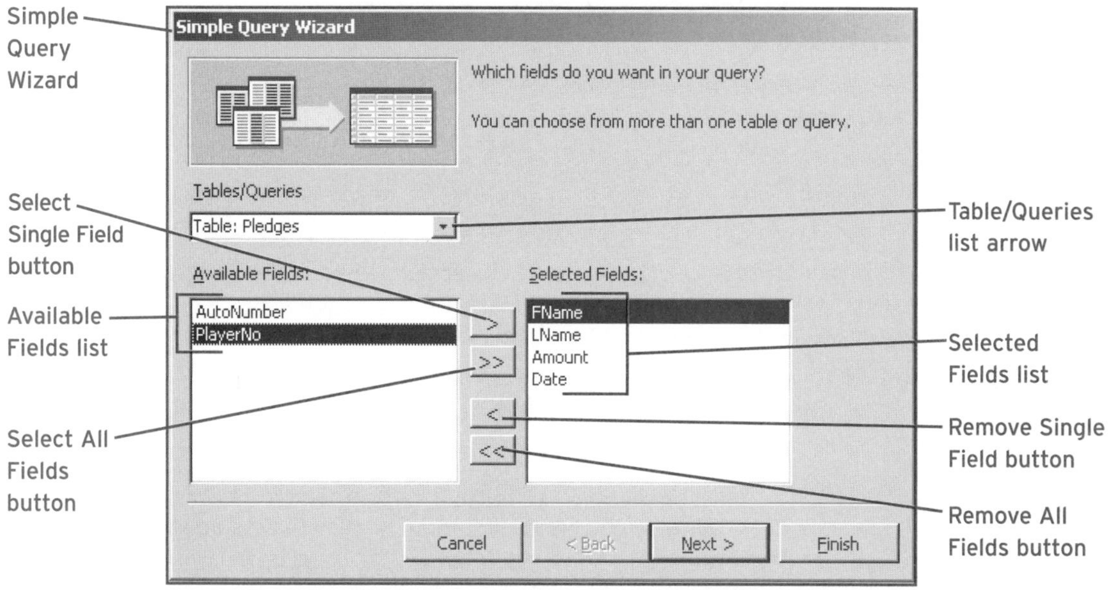
Simple Query Wizard
Simple Query Wizard
Which fields do you want in your query?
You can choose from more than one table or query.
Tables/Queries
Table: Pledges
Available Fields:
AutoNumber
PlayerNo
Selected Fields:
FName
LName
Amount
Date
>
>>
<
<<
Cancel
< Back
Next >
Finish
Select Single Field button
Available Fields list
Select All Fields button
Table/Queries list arrow
Selected Fields list
Remove Single Field button
Remove All Fields button

Figure 3-2: Datasheet View for the Pledges To Date query

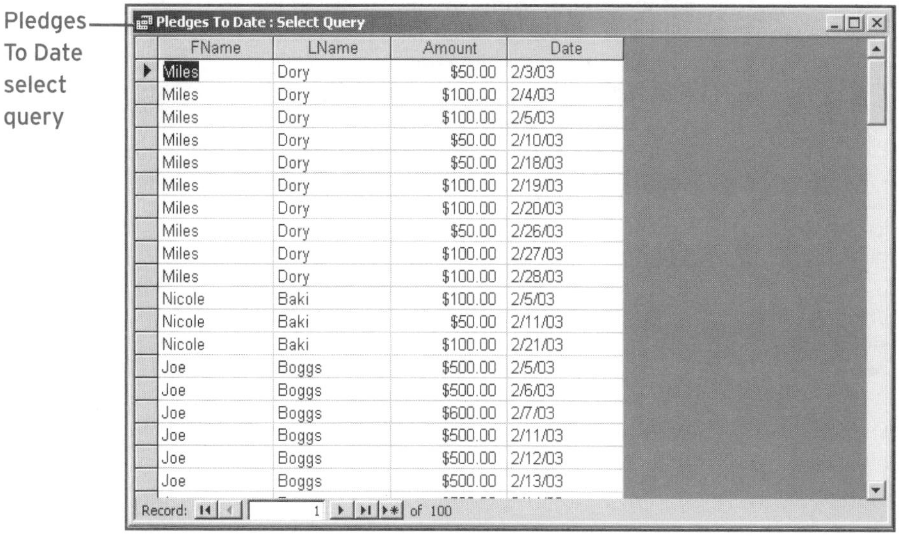
Pledges To Date select query
Pledges To Date : Select Query
FName
LName
Amount
Date
Miles Dory $50.00 2/3/03
Miles Dory $100.00 2/4/03
Miles Dory $100.00 2/5/03
Miles Dory $50.00 2/10/03
Miles Dory $50.00 2/18/03
Miles Dory $100.00 2/19/03
Miles Dory $100.00 2/20/03
Miles Dory $50.00 2/26/03
Miles Dory $100.00 2/27/03
Miles Dory $100.00 2/28/03
Nicole Baki $100.00 2/5/03
Nicole Baki $50.00 2/11/03
Nicole Baki $100.00 2/21/03
Joe Boggs $500.00 2/5/03
Joe Boggs $500.00 2/6/03
Joe Boggs $600.00 2/7/03
Joe Boggs $500.00 2/11/03
Joe Boggs $500.00 2/12/03
Joe Boggs $500.00 2/13/03
Record: 1 of 100

Skill Set 3
Creating and Modifying Queries

Create and Modify Select Queries
Create Select Queries Using Query Design View

You can use Query Design View to create or modify a select query. Query Design View is separated into two parts: the upper and lower panes. The upper pane displays table field lists, which show the fields available for the query. The lower pane displays the **query design grid**, which contains rows that you use to specify field name, table name, sort order, and **criteria**, rules that limit the number of records that will appear in Query Datasheet View. To create a query in Query Design View and to specify the order in which you want the fields to appear in Query Datasheet View, you can drag the desired field from a field list in the upper pane to a column in the query design grid.

Step 2
To add field lists to the upper pane of Query Design View, click the Show Table button on the Query Design toolbar, then double-click the desired table. To delete field lists, click the title bar of the extra list and press [Delete].

Activity Steps

 **Team01.mdb**

1. Click the **Queries button** ⊞ Queries on the Objects bar (if it's not already selected), then double-click **Create query in Design view**

2. Click **Players** (if it's not already selected), click **Add**, click **Teams**, click **Add**, then click **Close** in the Show Table dialog box

3. Drag **FName** from the Players field list to the first column in the query design grid, drag **LName** from the Players field list to the second column in the query design grid, then drag **TeamName** in the Teams field list to the third column of the query design grid
   You added three fields to the query design grid by dragging. You can also double-click a field to add it to the next available column.

4. Click the **Sort cell** for the Lname field, click the **list arrow**, then click **Ascending**

5. Click the **Criteria cell** for the TeamName field, then type **sharks**
   See Figure 3-3.

6. Click the **View button** ▦ on the Query Design toolbar to view the final datasheet
   See Figure 3-4.

7. Close the query without saving it

Figure 3-3: Building a select query with Query Design View

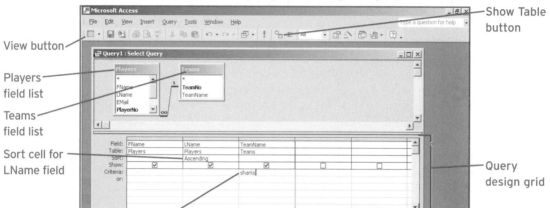

View button

Players
field list

Teams
field list

Sort cell for
LName field

Show Table
button

Query
design grid

Criteria cell for
TeamName

Figure 3-4: Query Datasheet View

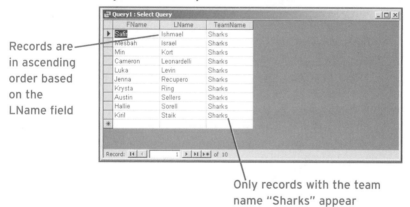

Records are
in ascending
order based
on the
LName field

Only records with the team
name "Sharks" appear

Skill Set 3

Creating and Modifying Queries

Add Calculated Fields to Select Queries

Add a Calculated Field Using Query Design View

A **calculated field's** contents are created by an **expression**: any combination of field names, **constants** (such as the number 5 or word "Page"), and **operators** (such as add, subtract, multiply, and divide) used to calculate a value. Table 3-1 shows examples of expressions you can use to define new calculated fields. A calculated field built in Query Design View will automatically calculate the field value, guaranteeing that the new field will always contain accurate, up-to-date information. Therefore, if you can calculate field values, you shouldn't define the field in Table Design View the way you'd define the other fields. Rather, build the field in Query Design View so that it will automatically calculate the correct value.

Activity Steps

 Team01.mdb

In an expression, field names need to be referenced (but not capitalized) exactly the same way they are defined in Table Design View.

1. Click the **Queries button** 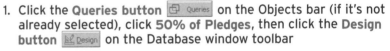 on the Objects bar (if it's not already selected), click **50% of Pledges**, then click the **Design button** on the Database window toolbar

2. Click in the fourth Field cell column in the query design grid, then type **Half:[Amount]*0.5** to create a calculated field named Half, whose values are created by multiplying the Amount field by 0.5. *See Figure 3-5.*

3. Click the **View button** on the Query Design toolbar to view the datasheet

4. Press **[Tab]** twice to move to the Amount field for the first record, type **150**, press **[Tab]** twice to move to the next record, then view the calculated value in the Half field *See Figure 3-6.*

5. Save and close the 50% of Pledges query

Figure 3-5: Creating a calculated field in Query Design View

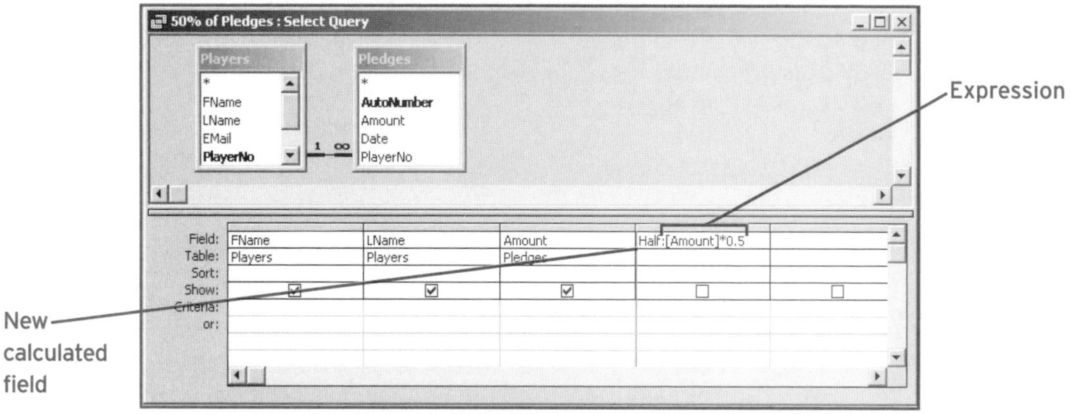

New calculated field

Expression

Figure 3-6: Viewing a calculated field in Datasheet View

Change in Amount value automatically updates the Half value

New calculated field name

Calculated values

TABLE 3-1: Common Access expressions

category	sample expression	description
Arithmetic	=[Retail]/[Wholesale]	Divides the Retail field by the Wholesale field to calculate the markup percentage
Page Number	="Page "&[Page]	Displays the word "Page," a space, and the current page number, such as Page 2, Page 6, or Page 10
Text	=[FirstName]&" "&[LastName]	Displays the value of the FirstName field and LastName field separated by a space

Skill Set 3

Creating and Modifying Queries

Add Calculated Fields to Select Queries
Format Values in a Calculated Field

Formatting a value means changing the way it appears but not changing the value itself. For example, you can format the number 5000 as $5,000, $5,000.00, or 5,000.0000, depending on how you want the value to appear on the screen and on printed reports. To format a calculated field, you change field properties, such as the Format or Decimal Places properties, using the Field Properties dialog box accessed from Query Design View.

Step 3
Choosing the Currency option for the Format property automatically displays values with two digits to the right of the decimal point. You can override this default by entering a specific value such as 0 in the Decimal Places property box.

Activity Steps

 Team01.mdb

1. Click the **Queries button** [Queries] on the Objects bar (if it's not already selected), then double-click the **Corporate Match** query to open it in Datasheet View
   View the formatting characteristics of the calculated field named Double.

2. Click the **View button** on the Query Datasheet toolbar, click the **Double** field name in the fourth column, then click the **Properties button** on the Query Design toolbar to open the field property sheet (if it's not already open)
   See Figure 3-7.

3. Click **General Number** in the Format property box, click the **Format property list arrow**, then click **Currency**

4. Click the **View button** on the Query Design toolbar to view the formatting change for the Double field
   See Figure 3-8.

5. Save and close the Corporate Match query

Figure 3-7: Formatting a calculated field

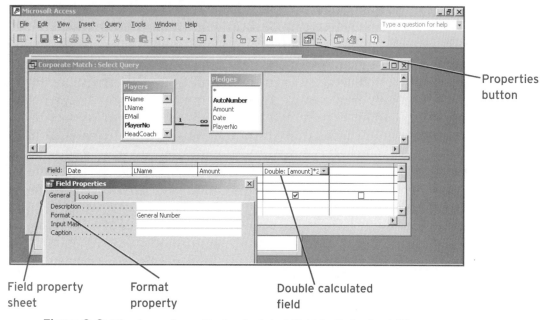

Properties button

Field property sheet

Format property

Double calculated field

Figure 3-8: Viewing a formatted calculated field in Datasheet View

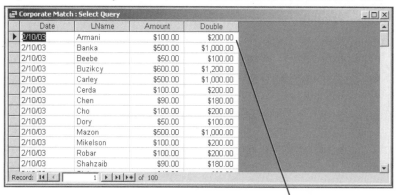

Calculated field values appear with currency symbols

Skill Set 3

Creating and Modifying Queries

Target Your Skills

 Team01.mdb

1 Use Figure 3-9 as a guide to create a new select query. The fields are provided by the Teams table and the Players table. The records are sorted in ascending order by the values in the TeamName field, followed by an ascending order by the values in the LName field.

Figure 3-9

TeamName	FName	LName	HeadCoach
Angels	Paige	Cahill	☐
Angels	Kelsey	Land	☐
Angels	Cici	Lapoint	☐
Angels	Ananias	Marcus	☐
Angels	Gina	Noack	☐
Angels	Marco	Polo	☐
Angels	Monserrat	Toby	☐
Angels	Riley	Toloza	☐
Angels	Tyler	Vandewalle	☑
Angels	Cornelius	Washington	☐
Eggheads	Sevana	Buzikcy	☑
Eggheads	Peter	Cerda	☐
Eggheads	Jimmy	Chen	☐

Record: 1 of 40

 Team01.mdb

2 Use Figure 3-10 as a guide to create a select query. The records are sorted in descending order by the values in the Amount field. The Points calculated field is created by dividing the Amount field by three, Points:[Amount]/3. The Points field is formatted with the Standard option for the Format property and 0 for the Decimal Places property. (Hint: If you're having trouble opening the property sheet for the Point field, switch to Datasheet View, then return to Query Design View.)

Figure 3-10

TeamName	LName	Date	Amount	Points
Angels	Cahill	2/17/03	$600.00	200
Sharks	Kort	2/13/03	$600.00	200
Sharks	Kort	2/14/03	$600.00	200
Eggheads	Merlo	2/11/03	$600.00	200
Sharks	Staik	2/11/03	$600.00	200
Angels	Cahill	2/13/03	$600.00	200
Sharks	Ring	2/14/03	$600.00	200
T-Bones	Boggs	2/25/03	$600.00	200
Eggheads	Buzikcy	2/10/03	$600.00	200
Angels	Marcus	2/13/03	$600.00	200
T-Bones	Boggs	2/7/03	$600.00	200
Angels	Marcus	2/17/03	$600.00	200
T-Bones	Boggs	2/11/03	$500.00	167
Angels	Vandewalle	2/17/03	$500.00	167
T-Bones	Boggs	2/6/03	$500.00	167
T-Bones	Boggs	2/13/03	$500.00	167

Record: 1 of 100

Skill List

1. Create and display forms
2. Modify form properties

In Skill Set 4, you will learn how to create, view, and modify forms. An Access database **form** provides an easy-to-use data entry screen. While you can also enter or edit data using the Datasheet View of a table or query, a datasheet is not always the fastest or easiest way to view, enter, or edit existing data. For example, if a record has many fields, you might not be able to see all the fields for one record on a datasheet without scrolling left or right. Using a form, however, you can rearrange the fields on the screen and present them in any layout that you design, or you can model an Access form after an existing paper form. You can also add graphical items, such as images and buttons, to forms to make your database easy to use.

Skill Set 4
Creating and Modifying Forms

Create and Display Forms
Create Forms Using AutoForms

You can use the AutoForm tool to create a new form quickly. First you need to choose a record source, a table or query upon which a form is to be based. After you select a record source, you start the AutoForm process by using the New Object: AutoForm button on the Database toolbar. The AutoForm process creates the new form using all the fields and records from the record source, organizes the fields in a Columnar layout, and automatically displays the new form in Form View. To apply form layouts other than the Columnar layout to a new form, you can use the Form Wizard or design the form yourself in Form Design View. Form layouts are described in Table 4-1.

Step 2
If the New Object button displays the AutoForm icon , you can click the button to create a form using the AutoForm tool instead of clicking the New Object button list arrow and clicking AutoForm.

Activity Steps
📁 Recycle01.mdb

1. Click the **Tables button** ⊞ Tables on the Objects bar (if it's not already selected), then click **Clubs**

2. Click the **New Object button list arrow** 📇▾ on the Database toolbar, then click **AutoForm**
   See Figure 4-1. The AutoForm tool automatically created a form in a Columnar layout using the Clubs table as the record source. Since the Clubs table is related to the Deposits table in a one-to-many relationship, associated records from the Deposits table also were added automatically. Deposits records appear as a subform in datasheet layout.

3. **Close the Clubs form without saving it**

Figure 4-1: Clubs form created by the AutoForm tool

Fields from the Clubs table

Fields and records from the Deposits table

Columnar layout

Datasheet layout

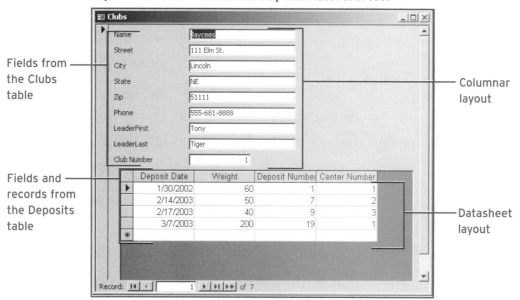

TABLE 4-1: Form layouts

layout	description
Columnar	Fields are positioned in a column (or multiple columns, if needed), each with a descriptive label to its left
Tabular	Fields are organized in columns with all the fields of one record on one row; descriptive field labels are positioned at the top of each column
Datasheet	Fields are organized in columns with all the fields of one record in one row just as they appear in the datasheet of a table or query; descriptive field labels are positioned at the top of each column
Justified	Fields are organized in columns, but if all the fields of one record do not fit on one row (as defined by the width of the screen), additional fields are positioned on a second (or third) row
PivotTable	Opens the form in PivotTable View; to add fields to the form, drag them from the Field List to the PivotTable field areas
PivotChart	Opens the form in PivotChart View; to add fields to the form, drag them from the Field List to the PivotChart field areas

Skill Set 4

Creating and Modifying Forms

Create and Display Forms
Create Forms Using the Form Wizard

You can use the **Form Wizard** to quickly create a form. The Form Wizard prompts you with several questions to specify many aspects of the final form, including the fields you want to use and the layout, style, and title of the form. If you want to modify a form that was created using the Form Wizard, you use Form Design View.

Step 4
Forms created with the Form Wizard are automatically saved as form objects within the database. They are given the same name as the form title specified in the last step of the Form Wizard.

Activity Steps

 Recycle01.mdb

1. Click the **Forms button** 🔲 Forms on the Objects bar (if it's not already selected), then double-click **Create form by using wizard**

2. Click the **Tables/Queries list arrow**, click **Table: Clubs**, then click the **Select All Fields button** >>
   See Figure 4-2.

3. Click **Next**, click the **Columnar option button** (if it's not already selected) for the layout, click **Next**, click **Blends** (if it's not already selected) for the style, click **Next**, then click **Finish** to accept "Clubs" as the form title
   See Figure 4-3. The form is created with the specific fields, layout, style, and name that you specified in the steps of the Form Wizard.

4. Close the Clubs form

Figure 4-2: Form Wizard dialog box

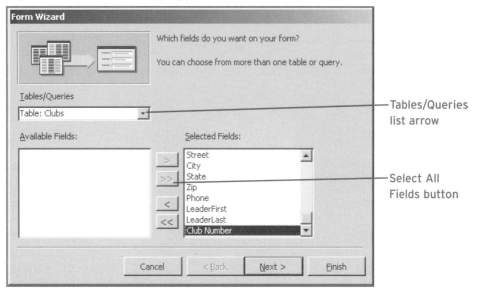

Tables/Queries list arrow

Select All Fields button

Figure 4-3: Clubs form created by the Form Wizard

Blends style

Fields from the Clubs table

Columnar layout

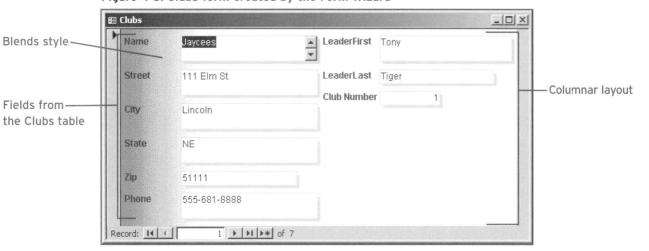

Skill Set 4

Creating and Modifying Forms

Modify Form Properties
Apply an AutoFormat to a Form

An **AutoFormat** is a collection of formatting characteristics and design elements, such as background colors and images, text color and styles, and border colors and styles, that you can quickly apply to a form. Access provides ten AutoFormats from which you can choose while using the Form Wizard, or you can apply an AutoFormat to any existing form in Form Design View using the AutoFormat dialog box.

Step 2
To create your own AutoFormat, click Customize in the AutoFormat dialog box. You will be given options to create your own AutoFormat, or update or delete the existing AutoFormat.

Activity Steps

 Recycle01.mdb

1. Click the **Forms button** 📧 Forms on the Objects bar (if it's not already selected), click **Center Contact Info,** then click the **Design button** 🔛 Design on the Database window toolbar

2. Click the **AutoFormat button** 📲 on the Form Design toolbar to display the AutoFormat dialog box
   See Figure 4-4.

3. Click **Industrial,** then click **OK**

4. Click the **View button** 📧 on the Form Design toolbar to display the Center Contact Info form with the new AutoFormat properties in Form View
   See Figure 4-5.

5. Save and close the Center Contact Info form

Figure 4-4: AutoFormat dialog box

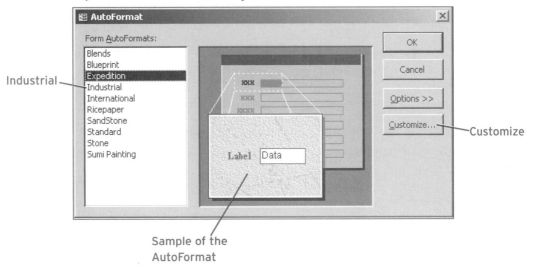

Sample of the
AutoFormat

Figure 4-5: Centers form with the Industrial AutoFormat

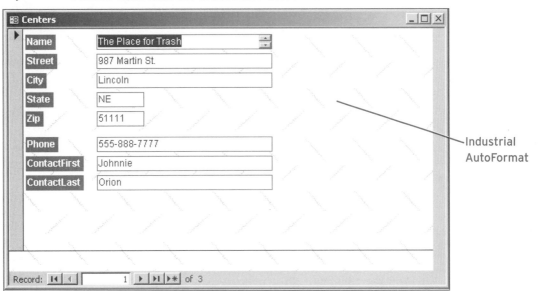

Skill Set 4
Creating and Modifying Forms

Modify Form Properties
Modify a Control on a Form

A **control** is any item on a form, such as a label, text box, or command button. You modify the properties of a control in Form Design View. **Properties** refer to all of the characteristics of the control including its color, size, and position. You can modify control properties in many ways. For example, you can apply a new formatting property (such as text color) to a selected control using the Formatting (Form/Report) toolbar. You can change a form's properties by using its **property sheet**, a window used to view and modify an object's properties. You can also modify a control's location and size properties by using pointers and dragging move or sizing handles. See Table 4-2 for information on pointers.

Activity Steps
 RecycleO1.mdb

1. Click the **Forms button** 🔲 Forms on the Objects bar (if it's not already selected), click **Center Designation**, then click the **Design button** 🔲 Design on the Database window toolbar

2. Click the 1-inch mark on the horizontal ruler to select all the labels in the first column, click the **Font Size list arrow** 10 ▾ on the Formatting (Form/Report) toolbar, then click **11**
   See Figure 4-6.

3. Click **Format** on the menu bar, point to **Vertical Spacing**, then click **Make Equal**

4. Point to any **sizing handle** of any of the selected labels so that the pointer changes to a double-headed arrow, then double-click to resize each label automatically to display all text

Step 5
You use the move handle in the upper-left corner of a selected control to move only that control.

5. Point to the edge of any selected control so that the pointer changes to 👋, then drag the controls to the right so that the right edge of the labels are positioned at about the 2-inch mark on the horizontal ruler

6. Click the **Designation text box**, click the **Properties button** 🔲 on the Form Design toolbar to display the property sheet, click the **Other tab**, scroll down, click the **ControlTip Text property box**, type **Federal size designation number**, then click the **Properties button** to toggle off the property sheet

7. Click the **View button** 🔲 on the Form Design toolbar, then point to the **Designation text box**
   See Figure 4-7.

8. Save and close the Center Designation form

Figure 4-6: Modifying control properties

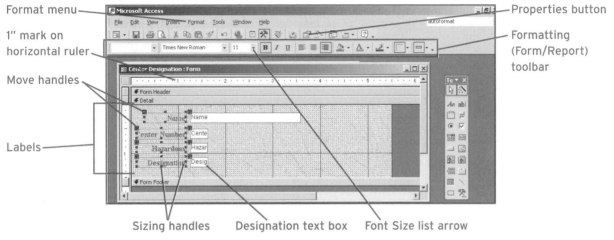

Format menu

1" mark on horizontal ruler

Move handles

Labels

Properties button

Formatting (Form/Report) toolbar

Sizing handles   Designation text box   Font Size list arrow

Figure 4-7: Final form

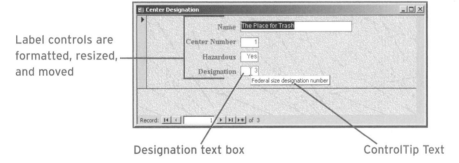

Label controls are formatted, resized, and moved

Designation text box   ControlTip Text

TABLE 4-2: Form Design View pointer shapes

shape	when does this shape appear?	action
⌖	When you point to any nonselected control on the form (the default pointer)	Single-clicking with this pointer *selects* a control
✋	When you point to the edge of a selected control (but not when you are pointing to a sizing handle or the move handle)	Dragging this pointer moves all selected controls
☝	When you point to the move handle in the upper-left corner of a selected control	Dragging this pointer *moves only the single control* where the pointer is currently positioned, not other controls that might also be selected
↔ ↕ ⤢ ⤡	When you point to any sizing handle	Dragging one of these pointers *resizes* the control; double-clicking one of these pointers *resizes* the control to be as large as required to display the text

Skill Set 4

Creating and Modifying Forms

Target Your Skills

 RecycleO1.mdb

 1 Use the Form Wizard to create a new form. Use all of the fields from the Centers table, apply a Columnar layout, apply a Ricepaper style, and title the form "Center Information." In Form Design View, change the font size for all labels to 11, then move and resize the controls as necessary to display all text. The final form is shown in Figure 4-8.

Figure 4-8

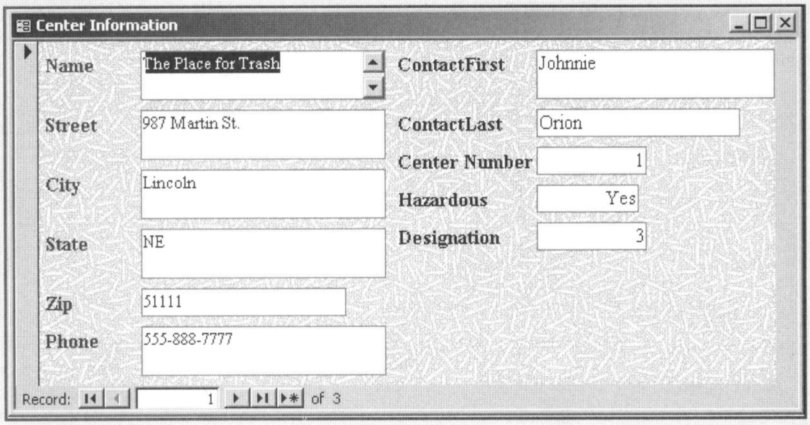

Center Information	
Name	The Place for Trash
Street	987 Martin St.
City	Lincoln
State	NE
Zip	51111
Phone	555-888-7777
ContactFirst	Johnnie
ContactLast	Orion
Center Number	1
Hazardous	Yes
Designation	3

Record: 1 of 3

RecycleO1.mdb

2 Use the AutoForm tool to create a form based on the Deposit List query. In Form Design View, apply a SandStone AutoFormat, then display the form in Form View as shown in Figure 4-9. Save the form with the name "Deposit List."

Figure 4-9

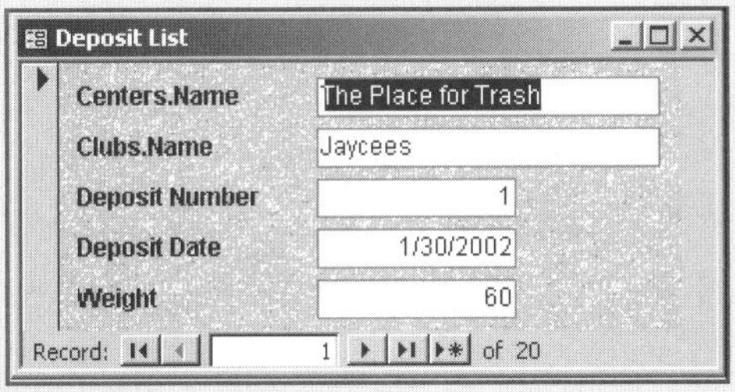

Deposit List	
Centers.Name	The Place for Trash
Clubs.Name	Jaycees
Deposit Number	1
Deposit Date	1/30/2002
Weight	60

Record: 1 of 20

Skill List

1. Enter, edit, and delete records
2. Create queries
3. Sort records
4. Filter records

In Skill Set 5, you will study ways to enter, edit, and delete information using the Datasheet View of a table or query and the Form View of a form. You'll use the Crosstab Query Wizard to create a datasheet that summarizes groups of records. You'll learn how to sort records in the Datasheet View of a table or query and how to specify multiple sort orders in Query Design View. Finally, you'll use two filter tools, Filter by Selection and Filter by Form, to display a subset of records within Datasheet View.

Skill Set 5
Viewing and Organizing Information

Enter, Edit, and Delete Records
Enter, Edit, and Delete Records in Datasheet View

In Datasheet View, you enter a new record by clicking the New Record button on either the Table (or Query) Datasheet toolbar or navigation toolbar, then typing the new data in the new record that opens as the last record in the datasheet. To delete a record, you click any value in the record that you want to delete, then click the Delete Record button on the Table (or Query) Datasheet toolbar. You edit a record by selecting the data that you want to change, then typing the new information. You can also use several special keystrokes to enter and edit data in a datasheet, as listed in Table 5-1.

Activity Steps
 Patients01.mbd

1. Click the **Tables button** [Tables] on the Objects bar (if it's not already selected), then double-click **Employees** to open it in Datasheet View

2. Click the **New Record button** [▶*] on the Table Datasheet toolbar

3. Type **Brothers**, press **[Tab]**, type **Gina**, press **[Tab]**, type **A**, press **[Tab]**, then type **17**
   See Figure 5-1. When you are editing a record, the edit record symbol [✎] appears in the **record selector**, the square button to the left of the record.

4. Click the **record selector** for the Jefferson, Sara record, click the **Delete Record button** [▶✕] on the Table Datasheet toolbar, then click **Yes** to confirm the deletion

5. Double-click **Cooper** in the Cooper, Paula record, then type **Langdon**

6. Double-click **Paula** in the Langdon, Paula record, then type **Jordan**

7. Press **Esc** once to undo the change to the current field, then press **Esc** again to undo all changes to the current record
   While you are editing a record, use the Esc key to undo changes. As soon as you move to a different record, however, the edits you made to the previous record are automatically saved to the database and the Esc key cannot undo them. To undo the changes to a saved record, click the Undo button [↻] on the Table (or Query) Datasheet toolbar. You can undo only your last action in Datasheet View.

8. Close the Employees table

Step 7
You cannot undo the deletion of a record.

Figure 5-1: Adding a new record to the Employees table using Datasheet View

Employees table

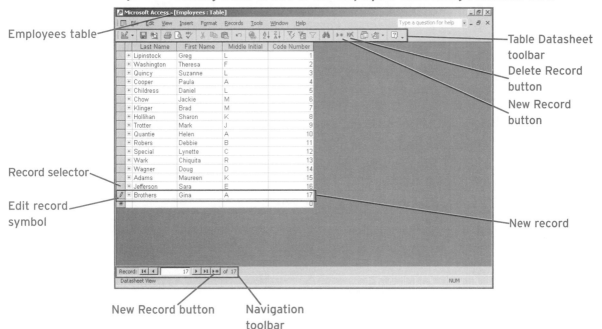

Table Datasheet toolbar

Delete Record button

New Record button

Record selector

Edit record symbol

New record

New Record button

Navigation toolbar

TABLE 5-1: Special keystrokes to enter and edit data

keystroke	action
[Backspace]	Deletes one character to the left of the insertion point
[Delete]	Deletes one character to the right of the insertion point
[F2]	Switches between Edit and Navigation mode
[Esc]	Undoes the change to the current field
[Esc][Esc]	Undoes all changes to the current record
[F7]	Starts the spell check feature
[Ctrl][']	Inserts the value from the same field in the previous record into the current field
[Ctrl][;]	Inserts the current date in a date field

Skill Set 5

Viewing and Organizing Information

Enter, Edit, and Delete Records
Enter, Edit, and Delete Records in Form View

You use the Form View of a form object to enter, edit, and delete records in a database. Since you can arrange fields in any layout on a form, using Form View is generally preferable to using the Datasheet View of a table or query object when entering, editing, or deleting data in a database. Because a form usually displays only one record at a time, you will use the navigation toolbar to move between the records of a form. The buttons on the navigation toolbar are listed in Table 5-2.

Activity Steps

 Patients01.mbd

1. Click the **Forms button** ⊞ Forms on the Objects bar (if it's not already selected), double-click **Patients** to open it in Form View, then maximize the Patients form

2. Click the **New Record button** ▶✱ on the Form View toolbar

3. Type **333224444**, press **[Tab]**, type **9/6/81**, press **[Tab]**, type **Winger**, press **[Tab]**, then type **Travis**
   See Figure 5-2. The **edit record symbol** 🖉 appears in the record selector, the button to the left of the record.

4. Click the **First Record button** ⏮ on the navigation toolbar to move to the first record for Alvin Patterson

5. Double-click **Alvin** to select it (if it's not already selected), then type **Aaron**

6. Click the **Next Record button** ▶ on the navigation toolbar to move to the second record for Andre Quantie

7. Click the **Delete Record button** ⌧ on the Form View toolbar, then click **OK** when notified that the record cannot be deleted
   By default, Access will not allow you to delete a record that has related records in another table.

8. Close the Patients form

Step 3
You can also press [Enter] to move between the fields of a record.

Figure 5-2: Adding a new record to the Patients table using Form View

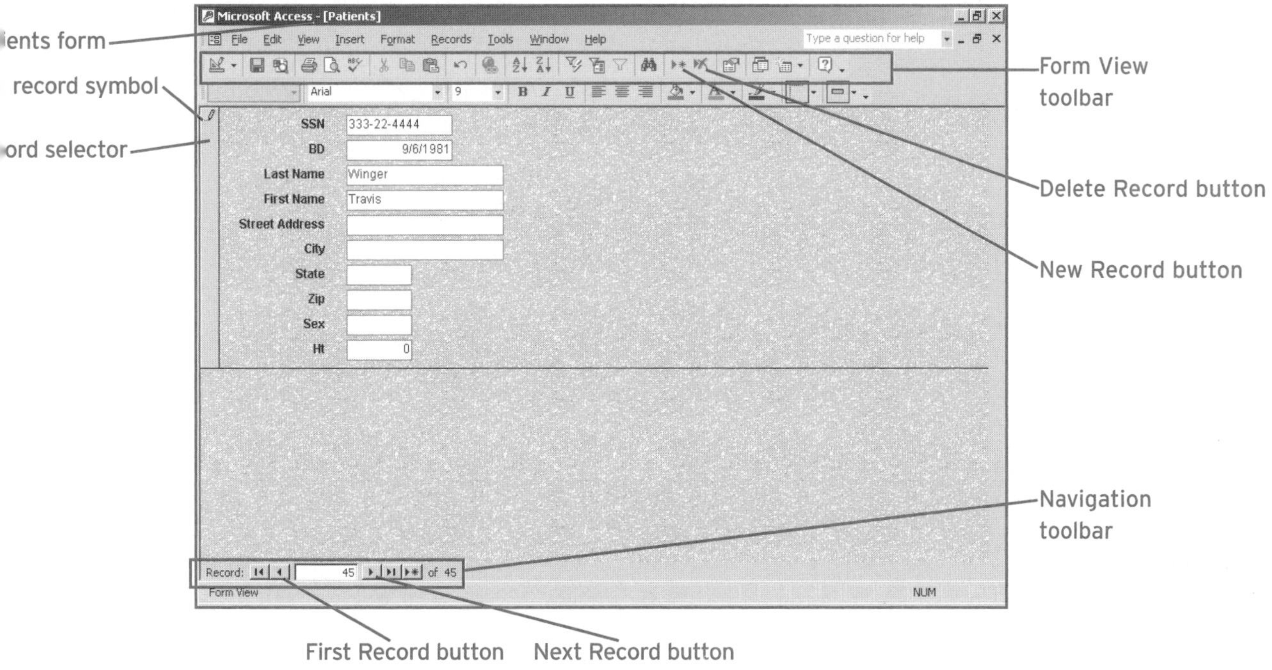

ents form

record symbol

ord selector

Form View toolbar

Delete Record button

New Record button

Navigation toolbar

First Record button   Next Record button

TABLE 5-2: Navigation toolbar buttons

button	name
I◀	First Record button
◀	Previous Record button
▶	Next Record button
▶I	Last Record button
▶✱	New Record button

Skill Set 5

Viewing and Organizing Information

Create Queries

A **crosstab query** calculates a sum, average, count, or other type of statistic for data that is grouped by at least two other fields. You use this type of query to obtain statistics on groups of records. A crosstab query typically uses three fields: one as a column heading, one as a row heading, and one to be summarized (that is, subtotaled, counted, or averaged) within the intersection of each column and row. For example, you might use a crosstab query to subtotal a company's sales values by product and by country. For this example you'd use the values in the Country field as row headings, the values in the ProductName field as column headings, and the summarized values in the Sales field as subtotals within the body of the crosstab query datasheet. You can create a crosstab query using the **Crosstab Query Wizard**.

Step 1
To start the Crosstab Query Wizard, you must click the New button on the Database window toolbar. If you double-click Create query by using wizard in the Database window, you'll start the Simple Query Wizard, which creates a select query rather than a crosstab query.

Activity Steps

Patients01.mbd

1. Click the **Queries button** Queries on the Objects bar (if it's not already selected), click the **New button** New on the Database window toolbar, then double-click **Crosstab Query Wizard** in the New Query dialog box

2. Click the **Queries option button**, click **Query: Visit Stats** to choose the Visit Stats query as the record source for the new crosstab query, then click **Next**

3. Double-click **Last Name** to choose the Last Name values as row headings, then click **Next**

4. Click the **Gender** field (if it's not already selected) to choose the Gender values as column headings, click **Next**, then click **Count** in the Functions list (if it's not already selected)
   See Figure 5-3.

5. Click **Next**, then click **Finish** to accept **Visit Stats_Crosstab** as the query name, and to create the query
   See Figure 5-4. The second column, the Total Of Visit Date column, calculates a total for each row. In this case, the Total Of Visit Date column totals the F and M values for each last name.

6. Close the Visit Stats_Crosstab query

Figure 5-3: Crosstab Query Wizard dialog box

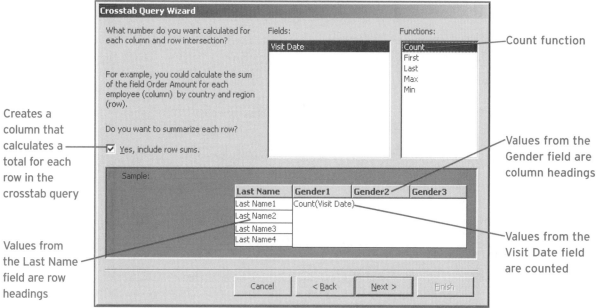

Creates a column that calculates a total for each row in the crosstab query

Values from the Last Name field are row headings

Count function

Values from the Gender field are column headings

Values from the Visit Date field are counted

Figure 5-4: Visit Stats_Crosstab query in Datasheet View

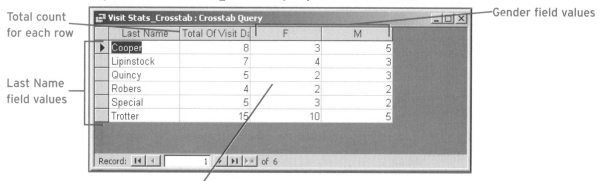

Total count for each row

Last Name field values

Gender field values

Count of all records with "F" in the Gender field and "Robers" in the Last Name field

Skill Set 5

Viewing and Organizing Information

Sort Records
Sort Records in Datasheet View

Sorting means arranging records in an ascending or descending order based on the values in a field. An ascending sort on a field with a Text data type arranges the values from A-Z, with numbers appearing before letters (for example, 1ABC appears before ABC). An ascending sort on fields with a Number or Currency data type arranges the values from smallest to largest. An ascending sort on a field with a Date/Time data type arranges the values from the past to the future. To sort records in Datasheet View, click any value for the field that you want to base the sort on, then click either the Sort Ascending button or the Sort Descending button on the Table Datasheet toolbar.

Step 3
When you sort in ascending order, null values (fields that contain nothing) appear before fields with any value, even the value of 0 in a Number field.

Activity Steps

 Patients01.mdb

1. Click the **Queries button** ⊞ Queries on the Objects bar (if it's not already selected), then double-click **Cholesterol Screenings** to open it in Datasheet View

2. Click any value in the Cholesterol field, then click the **Sort Descending button** on the Query Datasheet toolbar
See Figure 5-5.

3. Click the **Sort Ascending button** on the Query Datasheet toolbar

4. Click any value in the Last Name field, then click the **Sort Ascending button** on the Query Datasheet toolbar

5. Click any value in the BD field, then click the **Sort Ascending button** on the Query Datasheet toolbar
See Figure 5-6.

6. Close the Cholesterol Screenings query without saving changes

Figure 5-5: Sorting in descending order on a Number field

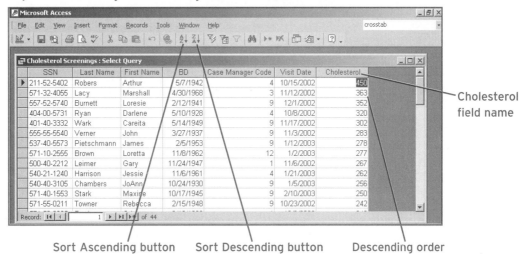

Cholesterol field name

Sort Ascending button   Sort Descending button   Descending order

Figure 5-6: Sorting in ascending order on a Date/Time field

Last Name field name

BD field name

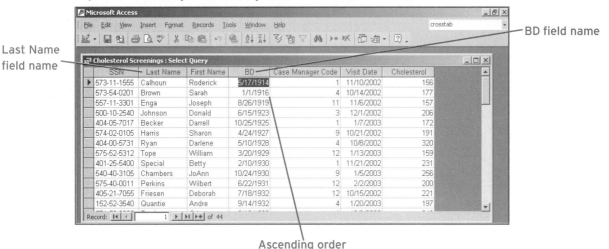

Ascending order

Skill Set 5

Viewing and Organizing Information

Sort Records
Sort Records in Query Design View

You use Query Design View to sort records using more than one sort field. For example, the records in a telephone book are sorted by at least three fields: LastName, FirstName, and MiddleInitial. The second sort field is not needed unless multiple records contain the same value in the first sort field. Using the telephone book as an example, if two records with the last name "Gomez" exist, the values of the FirstName field will determine which record appears first. If two records with the last name "Gomez" *and* the first name "Anthony" exist, the value in the third sort field, MiddleInitial, will determine which record appears first.

Activity Steps

 Patients01.mdb

1. Click the **Queries button** [Queries] on the Objects bar (if it's not already selected), click **Cholesterol Screenings**, then click the **Design button** [Design] on the Database window toolbar

2. Click the **Sort cell** for the Last Name field, click the **list arrow**, then click **Ascending**

3. Click the **Sort cell** for the First Name field, click the **list arrow**, then click **Ascending**
   See Figure 5-7. Sort orders entered in Query Design View are evaluated in a left-to-right order. Therefore, the Last Name field is the first sort order and the First Name field will not be used to sort the records unless the same value is in the Last Name field for more than one record.

4. Click the **View button** [icon] on the Query Design toolbar
   See Figure 5-8.

5. Close the Cholesterol Screenings query without saving changes

Step 3
Fields used to specify sort orders do not have to be side-by-side in the query design grid.

Figure 5-7: Using two sort fields in Query Design View

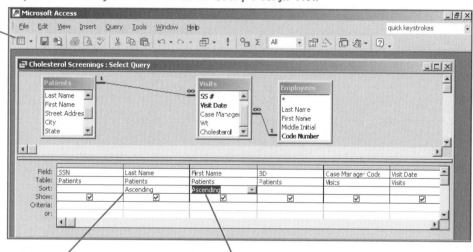

Ascending sort order
for Last Name field

Ascending sort order
for First Name field

Figure 5-8: Datasheet View of a query with two sort fields

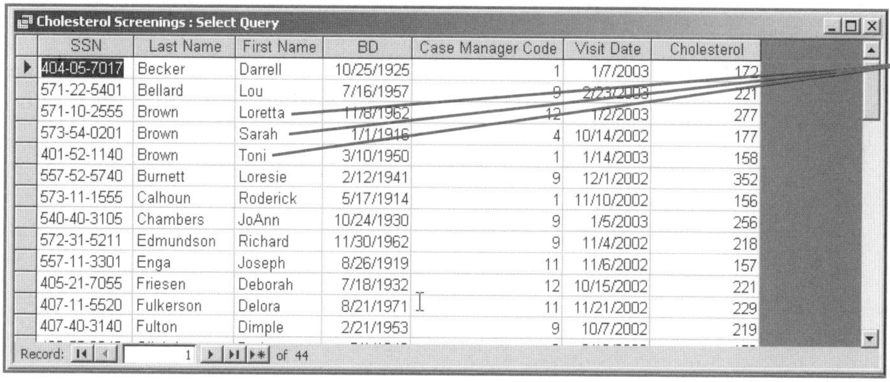

Records with
"Brown" in the
Last Name field
are ordered by
values in the
First Name
field: Loretta,
Sarah, Toni

Skill Set 5

Viewing and Organizing Information

Filter Records

Filter Records Using Filter by Selection

A **filter** is a tool you can use to temporarily isolate a subset of records that matches a limiting condition. For example, you could display only those records that contain the value "Madison" in the City field. The **Filter by Selection** tool lets you quickly display a subset of records that matches a value you choose in a single field. You can use the Filter by Selection tool in both Datasheet View and Form View. Since both filters and queries are used to show subsets of records, some similarities exist between these tools. Table 5-3 compares filters and queries.

Step 5

Filters are temporary and are not saved with the object, even if you click "Yes" to save the changes.

Activity Steps

 Patients01.mdb

1. Click the **Tables button** ⊞ Tables on the Objects bar (if it's not already selected), then double-click **Patients** to open it in Datasheet View

2. Click any **F** value in the Gender field, then click the **Filter By Selection button** ✦ on the Table Datasheet toolbar
   See Figure 5-9.

3. Click the **Remove Filter button** ▽ on the Table Datasheet toolbar to redisplay all records
   The Remove Filter button toggles between two buttons: Apply Filter and Remove Filter. Once the filter is removed, you can use the Apply Filter button to quickly reapply the last filter used on the datasheet.

4. Click the **Apply Filter button** ▽ on the Table Datasheet toolbar to reapply the filter that displays records with "F" in the Gender field

5. Close the Patients table without saving changes

Figure 5-9: Using the Filter by Selection tool

Filter By Selection button

Remove Filter/Apply Filter button

All Gender values are "F"

	SSN	BD	Last Name	First Name	Street Address	City	State	Zip	Gen	Ht
+	401-25-5400	2/10/1930	Special	Betty	6614 Park Rd.	Greenfield	WI	37132-	F	67
+	401-40-3332	5/14/1949	Wark	Careita	184 Garland Street	Leavenworth	IL	36078-	F	62
+	401-52-1140	3/10/1950	Brown	Toni	3131 Cypress Hills	Greenfield	WI	37128-	F	69
+	403-55-2040	5/1/1948	Gilchrist	Darlene	111 West 8th Street	Greenfield	WI	37117-	F	62
+	404-00-5731	5/10/1928	Ryan	Darlene	316 N. 73rd Street	Greenfield	WI	36109-	F	60
+	405-21-7055	7/18/1932	Friesen	Deborah	178 Bolger Rd.	Independenc	WI	37055-	F	64
+	407-11-5520	8/21/1971	Fulkerson	Delora	11 North Prairie St.	Liberty	WI	37068-	F	73
+	500-50-4053	8/6/1942	Wilson	Grace	114 West 83 rd Terrace	Raytown	WI	37138-	F	70
+	500-55-2020	9/26/1944	Stowe	Grace	136 Paseo Dr.	Greenfield	WI	37110-	F	69
+	500-55-5531	10/29/1939	Oliver	Hattie	3818 E 67 Terrace	Greenfield	WI	37132-	F	61
+	505-40-5311	6/13/1946	Parsons	Hillary	164 Denver Lane	Greenfield	WI	37127-	F	67
+	540-12-3012	12/9/1945	Williams	Janet	3144 Elmwood Rd.	Greenfield	WI	37128-	F	67
+	540-21-1240	11/6/1961	Harrison	Jessie	1134 West 1th Street	Independenc	WI	37053-	F	68
+	540-40-3105	10/24/1930	Chambers	JoAnn	194 E. 19th Dr.	Greenfield	WI	37130-	F	60
+	557-52-5740	2/12/1941	Burnett	Loresie	1131 E. 64nd Dr.	Raytown	WI	37133-	F	60
+	571-10-2555	11/8/1962	Brown	Loretta	336 Askew	Greenfield	WI	37128-	F	72
+	571-40-1553	10/17/1945	Stark	Maxine	13 Oat Circle Lane	Cherokee	WI	37016-	F	61
+	571-52-2205	9/16/1936	Parris	Odeana	819 E. 94nd Dr.	Greenfield	WI	37138-	F	67
+	571-55-0211	2/15/1948	Towner	Rebecca	3711 Montgall Street	Greenfield	WI	37128-	F	64
+	573-52-0405	11/19/1944	Tezon	Ruby	891 Oak Dr.	Greenfield	WI	37117-	F	63
+	573-54-0201	1/1/1916	Brown	Sarah	1111 Belmont	Greenfield	WI	37126-	F	59

Record: 1 of 24 (Filtered)

M or F or leave blank   FLTR   NUM

24 records are filtered

TABLE 5-3: Queries versus filters

characteristics	filters	queries
Are saved as an object in the database	No	Yes
Can be used to select a subset of records in a datasheet	Yes	Yes
Can be used to select a subset of fields in a datasheet	No	Yes
Its resulting datasheet can be used to enter, edit, and delete data	Yes	Yes
Its resulting datasheet can be used to sort, filter, and find records	Yes	Yes
Can be used as the record source for a form or report	No	Yes
Can calculate sums, averages, counts, and other types of summary statistics across records	No	Yes
Can be used to create calculated fields	No	Yes

Skill Set 5

Viewing and Organizing Information

Filter Records
Filter Records Using Filter by Form

You use the **Filter by Form** tool to specify more than one limiting condition within a filter. For example, you could display only those records that contain the value "Spain" in the Country field *and* the value "Barcelona" in the City field. Or you might want to use the Filter by Form tool to define the limiting condition using **comparison operators**, such as less than (<) or greater than (>). For example, you could filter for all orders with an OrderDate field entry greater than 1/1/2002. Common comparison operators are described in Table 5-4.

Activity Steps

file >> **Patients01.mdb**

1. Click the **Queries button**  on the Objects bar (if it's not already selected), then double-click **Cholesterol Screenings** to open it in Datasheet View

2. Click the **Filter By Form button** on the Query Datasheet toolbar

3. Click the **Cholesterol cell**, type **>300**, click the **Case Manager Code cell**, click the **list arrow**, then click **4**
   See Figure 5-10.

4. Click the **Apply Filter button** on the Filter/Sort toolbar
   See Figure 5-11. Two records matched the >300 and Case Manager Code equals 4 criteria for the Cholesterol field.

5. Close the Cholesterol Screenings query without saving changes

tip

Step 3
Click the Clear Grid button on the Filter/Sort toolbar to clear all entries in the Filter by Form window.

Figure 5-10: Filter by Form window

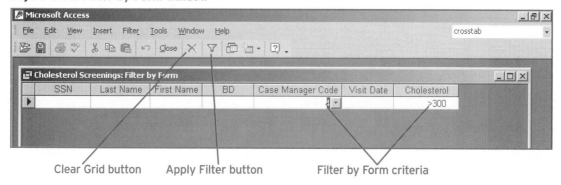

Clear Grid button   Apply Filter button   Filter by Form criteria

Figure 5-11: Filtered datasheet

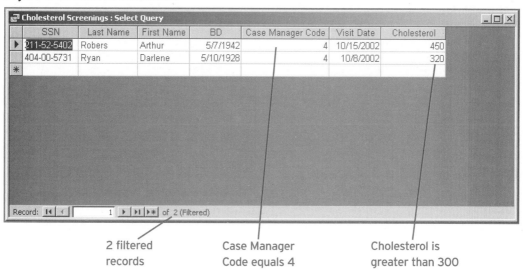

2 filtered records   Case Manager Code equals 4   Cholesterol is greater than 300

TABLE 5-4: Comparison operators

operator	description	expression	meaning
>	Greater than	>500	Numbers greater than 500
>=	Greater than or equal to	>=500	Numbers greater than or equal to 500
<	Less than	<"Braveheart"	Names from A through Braveheart, but not Braveheart
<=	Less than or equal to	<="Bridgewater"	Names from A through, and including, Bridgewater
<>	Not equal to	<>"Cyclone"	Any name except for Cyclone

Skill Set 5

Viewing and Organizing Information

Target Your Skills

 Patients01.mdb

1 Open the Cholesterol Screenings query in Datasheet View. Filter for all records with a Visit Date earlier than 1/1/2003, then sort the records in descending order based on the value in the Cholesterol field. The resulting datasheet should look like Figure 5-12.

Figure 5-12

SSN	Last Name	First Name	BD	Case Manager (	Visit Date	Cholesterol
211-52-5402	Robers	Arthur	5/7/1942	4	10/15/2002	450
571-32-4055	Lacy	Marshall	4/30/1968	3	11/12/2002	363
557-52-5740	Burnett	Loresie	2/12/1941	9	12/1/2002	352
404-00-5731	Ryan	Darlene	5/10/1928	4	10/8/2002	320
401-40-3332	Wark	Careita	5/14/1949	9	11/17/2002	302
555-55-5540	Verner	John	3/27/1937	9	11/3/2002	283
500-40-2212	Leimer	Gary	11/24/1947	1	11/6/2002	267
571-55-0211	Towner	Rebecca	2/15/1948	9	10/23/2002	242
571-52-2205	Parris	Odeana	9/16/1936	1	12/8/2002	240
401-25-5400	Special	Betty	2/10/1930	1	11/21/2002	231
407-11-5520	Fulkerson	Delora	8/21/1971	11	11/21/2002	229
405-21-7055	Friesen	Deborah	7/18/1932	12	10/15/2002	221
407-40-3140	Fulton	Dimple	2/21/1953	9	10/7/2002	219

Record: |◄ ◄ | 1 | ► ►I ►* | of 25 (Filtered)

 Patients01.mdb

2 Open the Employees form in Form View. Enter a new record with the following data:
Last Name: Quincy
First Name: Kia
Middle Initial: A
Code Number: 20
Use the Filter by Selection tool to filter all records with the last name equal to Quincy, and sort by first name in ascending order as shown in Figure 5-13.

Figure 5-13

Employees

Last Name	Quincy
First Name	Kia
Middle Initial	A
Code Number	20

Record: |◄ ◄ | 1 | ► ►I ►* | of 2 (Filtered)

Skill List

1. Create one-to-many relationships
2. Enforce referential integrity

In Skill Set 6, you will use the Relationships window to create one-to-many relationships between two database tables. A **one-to-many relationship** ties or relates one table to another. By using multiple tables to store your data, you can minimize redundant data in your database. For example, suppose you enter all the information for a customer purchase into a single table. One problem with this scenario becomes apparent when the customer makes a second purchase; you must reenter all the customer fields, such as name and address, into a second record of the same table. Duplicating data in a single table is unproductive and can cause data entry errors. If you put the customer fields in a Customers table and the fields that are determined at the time of the purchase in a Purchases table, you won't need to reenter all the customer information a second time. Instead, you can create a one-to-many relationship between the Customers and Purchases tables to tie "one" customer to "many" purchases. You'll also learn about referential integrity, a set of rules that, when applied to a one-to-many relationship, helps maintain the integrity of the data in the database.

Skill Set 6

Defining Relationships

Create One-To-Many Relationships

A one-to-many relationship between two tables in an Access database ties the tables together; a one-to-many relationship lets a record in one table look up information in another. To create a one-to-many relationship, the same field must be present in both tables so that "one" record in the first table knows how to connect or relate to "many" records in the second table. The field common to both tables is called the **linking field**, and is often the primary key field for the table on the "one" side of the relationship. The linking field is called the **foreign key field** in the table on the "many" side of the relationship. You create one-to-many relationships using the Relationships window.

Activity Steps

 Clients01.mdb

1. Click the **Relationships button** 🖳 on the Database toolbar to open the Relationships window

2. Click the **Show Table button** 🖳 on the Relationship toolbar, click **ZipCodes**, click **Add**, click **Contacts**, click **Add**, then click **Close** in the Show Table dialog box

3. Drag the **bottom border** of the Contacts field list down so that all fields are visible

4. Drag the **ZIPCODE** field from the ZipCodes field list to the ZipCode field in the Contacts field list
See Figure 6-1.

5. Click **Create**
See Figure 6-2. The bold field in a field list is the primary key field for a table.

6. Click the **Save button** 🖫 on the Relationship toolbar, then close the Relationships window

7. Click the **Tables button** 🖾 Tables on the Objects bar (if it's not already selected), then double-click **ZipCodes** to open it in Datasheet View
When a one-to-many relationship is established between two tables, the datasheet for the table on the "one" side of the relationship will display expand buttons to the left of each record in Datasheet View. You click an expand button to see a subdatasheet of related records from the table on the "many" side of the relationship.

8. Click the **expand button** ⊞ to the left of the first record to show related records from the Contacts table
See Figure 6-3.

9. Close the ZipCodes table

Step 5
To edit a relationship, double-click the relationship line to open the Edit Relationships dialog box and make desired changes. To delete a relationship, right-click the line, then click Delete on the shortcut menu.

Figure 6-1: Edit Relationships dialog box

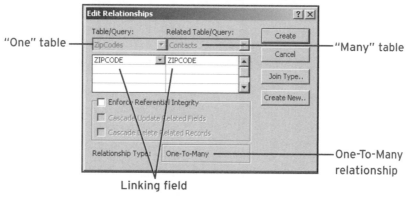

"One" table — Linking field — "Many" table — One-To-Many relationship

Figure 6-2: Final Relationships window

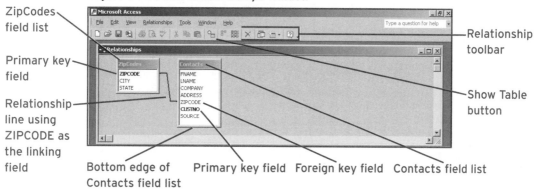

ZipCodes field list

Primary key field

Relationship line using ZIPCODE as the linking field

Relationship toolbar

Show Table button

Contacts field list

Bottom edge of Contacts field list

Primary key field

Foreign key field

Figure 6-3: Datasheet View and subdatasheet showing one-to-many relationship between the ZipCodes table and Contacts table

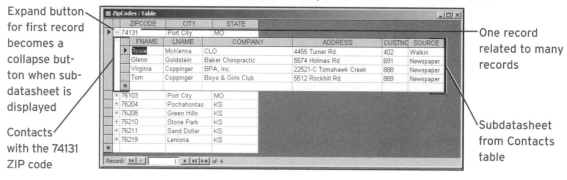

Expand button for first record becomes a collapse button when sub-datasheet is displayed

Contacts with the 74131 ZIP code

One record related to many records

Subdatasheet from Contacts table

Skill Set 6

Defining Relationships

Enforce Referential Integrity

Referential integrity is a set of rules imposed on a one-to-many relationship. The rules help to ensure that no orphan records are entered or created in a database. An **orphan record** is a record in the "many" table that doesn't have a matching entry in the linking field of the "one" table. For example, if you apply referential integrity to the link between a Sales and Customers table, all records entered in the Sales table must have a matching record in the Customers table. In this scenario, applying referential integrity will prevent you from entering a customer's order without first entering important customer information, such as a billing and shipping address. When you apply referential integrity to a one-to-many relationship, a one (1) symbol will appear next to the table on the "one" side of the relationship, and an infinity (∞) symbol will appear next to the table on the "many" side of the relationship.

Activity Steps

 Clients02.mdb

1. Click the **Relationships button** ⊞ on the Database toolbar to open the Relationships window
2. Click the **Show Table button** ⊞ on the Relationship toolbar, click **Contacts**, click **Add**, click **Seminars**, click **Add**, then click **Close** in the Show Table dialog box
3. Drag the **bottom border** of the Contacts field list down so that all fields are visible
4. Drag the **CUSTNO** field from the Contacts field list to the CUSTNO field in the Seminars field list, then select the **Enforce Referential Integrity check box** in the Edit Relationships dialog box
   See Figure 6-4.
5. Click **Create**
   See Figure 6-5.
6. Click the **Save button** 🖫 on the Relationship toolbar, then close the Relationships window
   When referential integrity is enforced on a relationship, Access will not allow you to enter or create an orphan record in the table on the "many" side of the relationship.
7. Click the **Tables button** ⊞ Tables on the Objects bar (if it's not already selected), then double-click **Seminars** to open it in Datasheet View
8. Type **222** as the CUSTNO entry for the first record, then press the down arrow key
   An alert box appears indicating that there is no related record in the Contacts table. (There is no record in the Contacts table with 222 in the CUSTNO field.) *See Figure 6-6.*
9. Click **OK**, press **Esc** to undo the last edit, then close the Seminars table

To create a report that shows the table relationships, click File on the menu bar in the Relationships window, then click Print Relationships.

Figure 6-4: Enforcing referential integrity

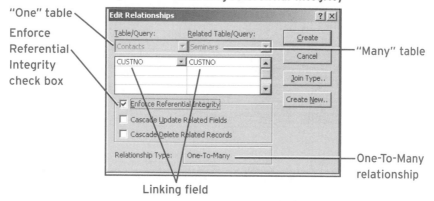

"One" table

Enforce Referential Integrity check box

"Many" table

Linking field

One-To-Many relationship

Figure 6-5: Final Relationships window with referential integrity enforced

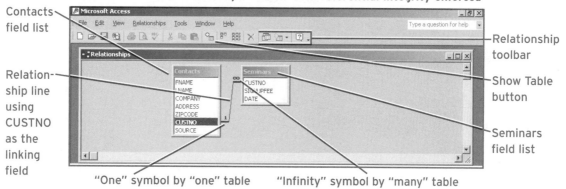

Contacts field list

Relationship line using CUSTNO as the linking field

Relationship toolbar

Show Table button

Seminars field list

"One" symbol by "one" table   "Infinity" symbol by "many" table

Figure 6-6: Referential integrity alert box

Skill Set 6

Defining Relationships

Target Your Skills

 Members01.mdb

1 Build one-to-many relationships between the Activities, Names, and Zips tables as shown in Figure 6-7.

Figure 6-7

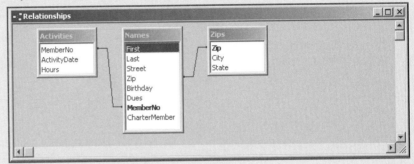

 Members02.mdb

2 Build one-to-many relationships with referential integrity enforced between the Activities, Names, and Zips tables as shown in Figure 6-8.

Figure 6-8

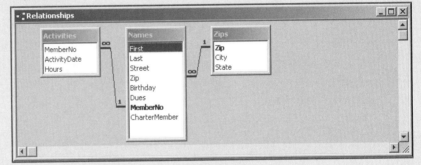

Skill List

1. Create and format reports
2. Add calculated controls to reports
3. Preview and print reports

In Skill Set 7, you will work with **reports**, the Access object used to create professional printouts. While you can print the Datasheet View of a table or query, the report object provides important printing benefits. For example, you can customize the header and footer on a report to include any type of information, but you cannot modify the header or footer of a datasheet printout. Also, a report allows you to show both detail and summary information in one printout, which is not possible on a datasheet printout. For example, you might want to show all the individual sales records as well as the subtotaled sales for each customer. Finally, with a report, you can specify many formatting options, such as multiple colors, graphics, and font choices for different fields and sections of the report. You cannot choose different formats for different areas of a datasheet, nor can you add graphics, such as logos, lines, or clip art, to a datasheet printout.

Skill Set 7

Producing Reports

Create and Format Reports
Create Reports Using the Report Wizard

The **Report Wizard** is a tool you can use to quickly create a report. Using the wizard, you can specify several aspects of a report, such as the fields you want to use and how you want to group and sort the report's records. You can also use the wizard to specify the layout, style, and title of a report. You can later modify a report created by the Report Wizard using **Report Design View**, the view in which you modify or format the items on the report or the report itself.

Step 6

Reports created with the Report Wizard are automatically saved as report objects in the database. They are given the name that you entered as the report title while using the Report Wizard.

Activity Steps

 Clinic01.mdb

1. Click the **Reports button** [Reports] on the Objects bar (if it's not already selected), then double-click **Create report by using wizard**

2. Click the **Tables/Queries list arrow**, click **Table: Patients**, click the **Select All Fields button** [>>], then click **Next**
   See Figure 7-1.

3. Click **Next** to accept the Doctor field as the grouping field, click the first sort order **list arrow**, click **PtLastName** as the first sort field, then click **Next**
   The **grouping field** determines the primary sort order of the records on the report. The sort fields determine the order of records *within* each group. In this case, the records are sorted by the values in the PtLastName field (the sort field) within the Doctor field (the grouping field).

4. Click the **Outline 2 option button** for the layout, click **Next**, click **Corporate** for the style, click **Next**, type **Patient Visits by Doctor** as the title for the report, then click **Finish**

5. Maximize the report, then scroll to view information for the first three doctors
   See Figure 7-2.

6. Close the Patient Visits by Doctor report

Figure 7-1: Report Wizard dialog box

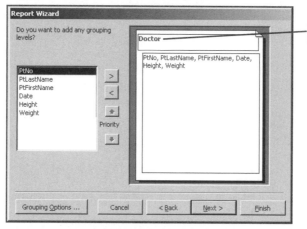

Records will be grouped
by the Doctor field

Figure 7-2: Patient Visits by Doctor report

Records are
grouped by the
Doctor field

Within each
Doctor field
value, records
are in ascend-
ing order based
on PtLastName

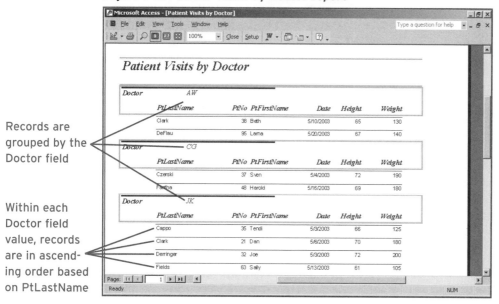

Skill Set 7

Producing Reports

Create and Format Reports
Format Reports Using Report Design View

Formatting a report means to customize its appearance by changing the fonts, colors, or borders of the controls on the report. A **control** is any item on a report, such as a label, line, or text box. Report controls are placed in report **sections**, which determine where and how often controls print. See Table 7-1 for more information on report sections. You make all formatting changes to a report in Report Design View. To format a control in Report Design View, you first select the control(s) you want to change, then make the formatting change using the buttons on the Formatting (Form/Report) toolbar.

Step 3

If you make a mistake, click the Undo button on the Report Design toolbar to undo your last action. You can undo up to 20 actions in Report Design View.

Activity Steps

file > **Clinic01.mdb**

1. Click the **Reports button** [📄 Reports] on the Objects bar (if it's not al-ready selected), click **Patient Activity Report**, click the **Design button** [📐 Design] on the Database window toolbar, maximize Report Design View (if it's not already maximized), then click the **Patient Activity Report label** in the Report Header section
   See Figure 7-3.

2. Click the **Font list arrow** [Times New Roman ▾] on the Formatting (Form/Report) toolbar, press [i], then click **Impact**

3. Point to the **middle-right sizing handle** of the Patient Activity Report label so that the pointer changes to ◀▬▶, then drag the sizing handle to the right about 0.5 inches to ensure that the control is wide enough to display the label's text

4. Click the **line** above the label in the Report Header section, click the **Line/Border Color button list arrow** [✏▾] on the Formatting (Form/Report) toolbar, click the **Red box** (in the first column, third row), click the **Line/Border Width button list arrow** [▭▾], then click **4**

5. Click the **vertical ruler** to the left of the controls in the Page Header section to select all the labels in the section, click the **Font/Fore Color button list arrow** [A▾] on the Formatting (Form/Report) toolbar, then click the **Red box** (in the first column, third row)

6. Click the **View button** [🔍] on the Report Design toolbar
   See Figure 7-4.

7. Save and close the Patient Activity Report

Figure 7-3: Formatting the Patient Activity Report in Report Design View

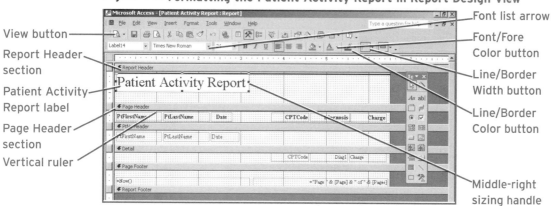

View button
Report Header section
Patient Activity Report label
Page Header section
Vertical ruler

Font list arrow
Font/Fore Color button
Line/Border Width button
Line/Border Color button
Middle-right sizing handle

Figure 7-4: Formatted Patient Activity Report

Thick red line
Impact font

Patient Activity Report

PtFirstName	PtLastName	Date	CPTCode	Diagnosis	Charge
Greta	Garbo	5/5/2003			
			11750	703.0	$294.00
			99202	703.0	$42.00
Dan	Clark	5/6/2003			
			L3020	838.04	$148.00
			L3020	838.04	$148.00

Red text

TABLE 7-1: Report sections

section	where does this section print?	what type of information does this section typically display?
Report Header	At the top of the first page of the report	Report title
Page Header	At the top of every page (but below the report header on page one)	Page number, current date, clip art
Group Header	Before every group of records	Value of the current group
Detail	Once for every record	Values for the rest of the fields in the report
Group Footer	After every group of records	Subtotal or count of the records in that group
Page Footer	At the bottom of every page	Page number or current date
Report Footer	At the end of the entire report	Grand total or count for all of the records in the entire report

Skill Set 7

Producing Reports

Add Calculated Controls to Reports
Add Subtotals for Groups of Records

To produce a subtotal for a group of records, you create a calculated control. A **calculated control** is a text box control that contains an expression that calculates a value. Expressions can contain **functions**, built-in formulas that help you build an expression quickly. Not all expressions contain functions, but the Sum, Avg, and Count functions are commonly used to create subtotals for groups of records. See Table 7-2 for more examples of common Access expressions used with reports. To make a calculated control work as a subtotal, you add it to the Group Footer section of the report. When you preview or print the report, a subtotal will appear immediately after each group of records. To add controls to a report, you use Report Design View.

Activity Steps

 Clinic01.mdb

1. Click the **Reports button** ⬛ Reports on the Objects bar (if it's not already selected), click **Doctor Activity Report**, click the **Design button** ⬿ Design on the Database window toolbar, then maximize Report Design View

2. Click the **Sorting and Grouping button** 匡 on the Report Design toolbar
   See Figure 7-5.

3. Click **No** in the Group Footer property box, click the **list arrow**, then click **Yes** to display the Group Footer section for the DocCode field

4. Click the **Sorting and Grouping button** 匡 to close the Sorting and Grouping window

5. Click the **Text Box button** abl on the Toolbox toolbar, then click in the DocCode Footer section just below the Charge text box

6. Click **Unbound** in the new text box, then type **=Sum([Charge])**
   In expressions, the arguments for a function (the pieces of information expressions need to calculate a value) are always surrounded by parentheses. When an argument is a field name, the name is surrounded by brackets. In the =Sum([Charge]) expression, the Sum function will subtotal the values in the Charge field.

7. Click **Text16** in the label to the left of the new text box to edit the text, double-click **Text16** to select it, type **Subtotal**, click the vertical ruler to the left of the label to select it, double-click one of the label's sizing handles to automatically resize it to display all text, then click the **View button** ▣
   See Figure 7-6.

8. Save and close the Doctor Activity Report

Step 7
If you double-click the edge of the label instead of the text within a selected label, you'll open the label's property sheet instead of selecting the label's text.

Figure 7-5: Sorting and Grouping window

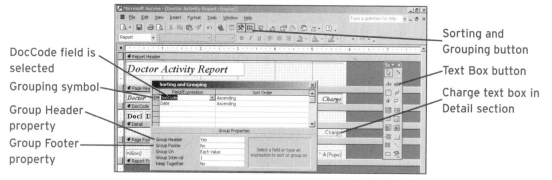

DocCode field is selected

Grouping symbol

Group Header property

Group Footer property

Sorting and Grouping button

Text Box button

Charge text box in Detail section

Figure 7-6: Final Doctor Activity Report with subtotal calculation

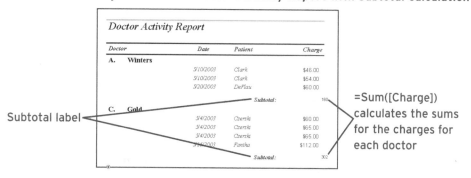

Subtotal label

=Sum([Charge]) calculates the sums for the charges for each doctor

TABLE 7-2: Sample expressions

sample expression	description
=[Price]*1.05	Multiplies the Price field by 1.05 (adds 5% to the Price field)
=[Subtotal]+[Shipping]	Adds the value of the Subtotal field to the value of the Shipping field
=[Page]	Displays the current page number, such as 5, 6, or 10
="Page "&[Page]	Displays the word Page, a space, and the current page number, such as Page 5, Page 6, or Page 10
=[FirstName]& " "&[LastName]	Displays the value of the FirstName and LastName fields separated by a space
=Avg([Freight])	Uses the **Avg** function to display an average of the values in the Freight field
=Count([FirstName])	Uses the **Count** function to display the number of records that contain an entry in the FirstName field
=Sum([Tracks])	Uses the **Sum** function to display the total value from the Tracks field
=Date()	Uses the **Date** function to display the current date in the form of m/d/yyyy, such as 10/23/2002 or 11/14/2003

Skill Set 7

Producing Reports

Add Calculated Controls to Reports
Add Date Calculated Controls

A **date calculated control** is a text box control that uses an Access function to calculate and display today's date on a report. Two date functions are commonly used: Date and Now. The **Date function** displays today's date in the m/d/yyyy format, for example, 6/15/2003. The **Now function** displays both today's date as well as the current time, for example, 6/15/2003 2:37:22 PM. You can add a date calculated control to any report section, but they are most commonly added to the Report Header, Page Header, or Page Footer sections. To add controls to a report, you use Report Design View.

Step 3
In an expression, the function name is not case-sensitive, so =date() is the same as =Date().

Activity Steps

 Clinic01.mdb

1. Click the **Reports button** 🔲 Reports on the Objects bar (if it's not already selected), click **Doctor List**, click the **Design button** 🔍 Design on the Database window toolbar, then maximize Report Design View (if it's not already maximized)

2. Click the **Text Box button** abl on the Toolbox toolbar, then click in the middle of the Report Header section

3. Click **Unbound** in the new text box, then type **=Date()**
   See Figure 7-7. The Date function does not have any arguments, but the parentheses are still required.

4. Click **Text11** in the label to the left of the new text box, double-click **Text11**, type **Today's Date**, then click the **View button** 🔍
   See Figure 7-8. The date calculated control reads the current date from your computer's battery, so if you open this report tomorrow, the date will automatically change to tomorrow's date.

5. Save and close the Doctor List report

Figure 7-7: Adding a date calculated control to the Report Header section

New label ⸻

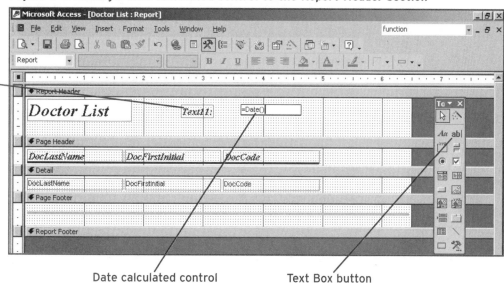

Date calculated control
in new text box

Text Box button

**Figure 7-8: Final Doctor List report with today's date
created from a calculated control**

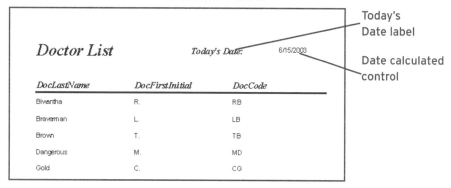

Today's
Date label

Date calculated
control

Skill Set 7

Producing Reports

Preview and Print Reports

You use **Print Preview** to see how your report will appear before you actually print it. This gives you an opportunity to fix printing problems (crowded data, for example) or change the layout of a report (add or modify a footer, for example) before printing. You use the buttons on the Print Preview toolbar to change the magnification of the report on the screen (called zooming) so that you can see more or less text or more or fewer pages. Any object view that you can print, such as Table Datasheet, Query Datasheet, or Form View, has an associated Print Preview window. However, Print Preview is most commonly used to preview reports, because reports are specifically created for the purpose of producing printouts.

Step 2
In Print Preview, the navigation buttons are not available when all pages of a report are currently displayed.

Activity Steps

ClinicO1.mdb

1. Click the **Reports button**  on the Objects bar (if it's not already selected), double-click **Patient List**, then maximize Report Preview (if it's not already maximized)
   See Figure 7-9.

2. Click the **Two Pages button** on the Print Preview toolbar

3. Click the last record on the second page with the Zoom In pointer to zoom in to read that record
   The pointer changes to a Zoom Out pointer.

4. Click the last record with the Zoom Out pointer to restore the two-page view

5. Click the **Zoom button list arrow** , click **200%** to magnify the printout to twice as large as it'll appear on the printout, scroll to view various parts of the report, click the **Zoom button list arrow**, then click **Fit,** which "fits" full pieces of paper in the Print Preview window

6. Click the **Print button** on the Print Preview toolbar

7. Close the Patient List report

Figure 7-9: Patient List report in Print Preview

Two Pages button

Setup button

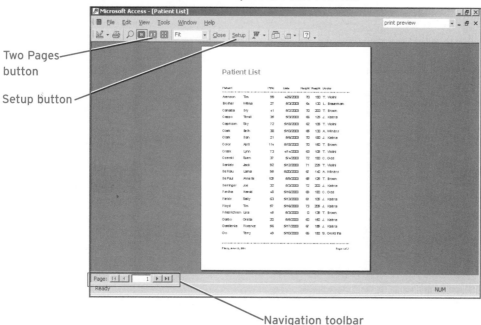

Navigation toolbar

extra!

Using the Page Setup dialog box

You use the Page Setup dialog box to change margins, paper orientation (portrait versus landscape), and number of columns. Click the **Setup button** on the Print Preview toolbar to open the Page Setup dialog box, then make desired changes.

Target Your Skills

 Seminar01.mdb

1 In Report Design View of the Attendee List report, create the report shown in Figure 7-10. Format the labels in the Page Header section with an Arial, bold, italic, 12-point font. Set the line below the labels in the Page Header section to a 1 line/border width. Format the Attendee List label in the Report Header section with an Arial, red, 24-point font.

Figure 7-10

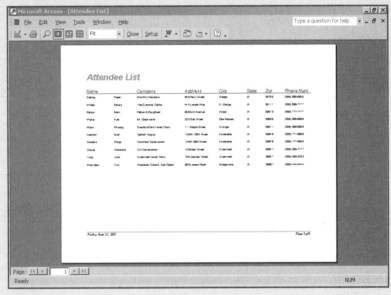

 Seminar01.mdb

2 Add calculated controls to the Event Registration Report to create the report shown in Figure 7-11. Open the EventID Footer section, then add a calculated control to this section to subtotal the RegistrationFee field. (Use the expression =Sum([RegistrationFee]).) Change the label to the left of the calculated control in the EventID Footer section to "Subtotal:". Add a date calculated control to the Report Header section. (Use the expression =Date().) Delete the date calculated control's label.

Figure 7-11

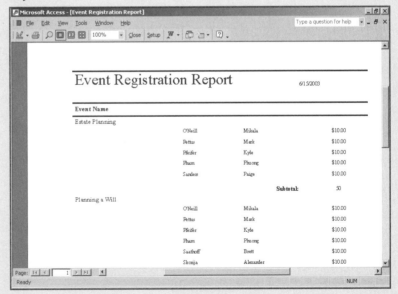

Skill List

1. Import data to Access
2. Export data from Access
3. Create a simple data access page

In Skill Set 8, you will work with other software programs, including Microsoft Excel and Internet Explorer, to import data into and export data out of an Access database. **Import** means to convert data from an external data source, such as an Excel workbook, into an Access database. **Export** means to convert data from an Access database to an external file, such as a Word document. Both processes are fast ways to copy data from one file format to another without having to reenter the data. Another way to make Access data available to others who prefer a different file format is to create a data access page. A **data access page** is a special type of Web page that maintains a connection with the database and gives other users the ability to edit and view up-to-date Access data using Internet Explorer.

Skill Set 8

Integrating with Other Applications

Import Data to Access
Import Data from an Excel Workbook

You can import data into an Access database from several file formats, including an Excel workbook or another Access, FoxPro, dBase, or Paradox database. It is not uncommon for a user to enter a list of data into Excel and later decide to convert that data into an Access database, because the user wants to use Access's extensive form or report capabilities or wants multiple people to be able to use the data at the same time. (An Access database is inherently **multi-user**; many people can enter and update data at the same time.) Since the data in an Excel workbook is structured similarly to data in an Access table datasheet, you can easily import data from an Excel workbook into an Access database by using the **Import Spreadsheet Wizard**.

Activity Steps

 Classes01.mdb

1. Click **File** on the menu bar, point to **Get External Data**, then click **Import**

2. Navigate to the drive and folder where your Project Files are stored, click the **Files of type list arrow**, click **Microsoft Excel**, click **Instructors**, then click **Import** to start the Import Spreadsheet Wizard
   See Figure 8-1.

3. Select the **First Row Contains Column Headings check box**, then click **Next**

4. Click **Next** to indicate that you want to create a new table, then click **Next** to not specify field changes

5. Click the **Choose my own primary key option button** to set InstructorID as the primary key field, then click **Next**

6. Type **Instructors** in the Import to Table box, click **Finish**, then click **OK**

7. Double-click **Instructors** to open it in Datasheet View
   See Figure 8-2. Imported data works the same way as any other table of data in a database.

8. Close the Instructors table

Step 4

You can also import Excel workbook data into an existing table if the field names used in the Excel workbook match the field names in the Access table.

Figure 8-1: Import Spreadsheet Wizard dialog box

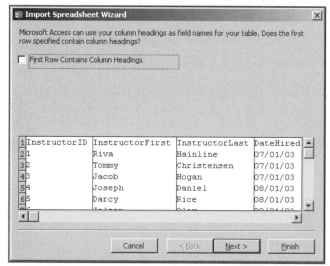

Figure 8-2: Imported Instructors table in Datasheet View

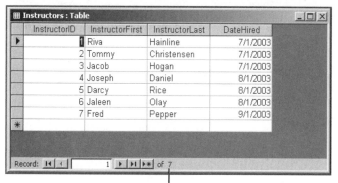

Seven records were imported

extra!

Using delimited text files

You can import data from a **delimited text file**, a file of unformatted data where each field value is delimited (separated) by a common character, such as a comma or a tab. Each record is further delimited by a common character, such as a paragraph mark. A delimited text file usually has a **txt** (for text) file extension. You can use delimited text files to convert data from a proprietary software system (such as an accounting, inventory, or scheduling software system) into a format that other programs can import. For example, most accounting software programs won't export data directly into an Access database, but they can export data to a delimited text file, which can then be imported by Access.

Skill Set 8

Integrating with Other Applications

Import Data to Access
Import Objects from Another Access Database

As a **database developer**, one who creates new database objects such as queries, forms, and reports, you should know how to import objects from one Access database to another. This skill will allow you to do your development work in a test database (often called the **development database**). When you're finished testing the new objects and are ready to make them accessible to others, you can import them into the database that's used on a regular basis by database users (often called the **production database**). (A **database user** is anyone who enters, edits, views, or uses database information, but doesn't design or create new database objects.) For example, you might use the development database to create and test a new data entry form that accommodates sales entries for a new product. Then you could import the new form into the production database on the day the new product is officially announced.

Step 4
To select all objects of the same type, click the Select All button in the Import Objects dialog box.

Activity Steps

 ClassesO1.mdb

1. Click the **Queries button** ⊞ Queries on the Objects bar (if it's not already selected), then click the **Reports button** ▣ Reports on the Objects bar to view the existing queries and reports

2. Click **File** on the menu bar, point to **Get External Data**, then click **Import**

3. Navigate to the drive and folder where your Project Files are stored, click the **Files of type list arrow**, click **Microsoft Access**, click **ClassesDevel01**, then click **Import** to display the Import Objects dialog box

4. Click the **Queries tab**, click **Class Rosters Query** to select it, click the **Reports tab**, then click **Class Rosters Report** to select it
   See Figure 8-3.

5. Click **OK** to import the Class Rosters query and the Class Rosters report from the ClassesDevel01 database
   You imported both the query and the report because a report cannot be displayed without a data source (in this case, the query defines what data from the tables are displayed in the report).

6. Click the **Queries button** ⊞ Queries on the Objects bar to see that the Class Rosters Query was imported successfully, then click the **Reports button** ▣ Reports on the Objects bar to see that the Class Rosters Report was also imported successfully

7. Double-click the **Class Rosters Report**, maximize the Print Preview window, then click the report to zoom to 100% magnification
   See Figure 8-4.

8. Close the Class Rosters Report

Figure 8-3: Import Objects dialog box

Queries
tab

Reports
tab

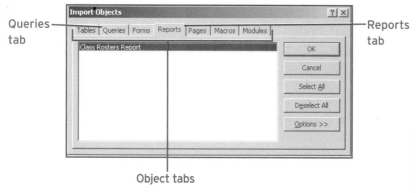

Object tabs

Figure 8-4: Previewing the imported Class Rosters Report

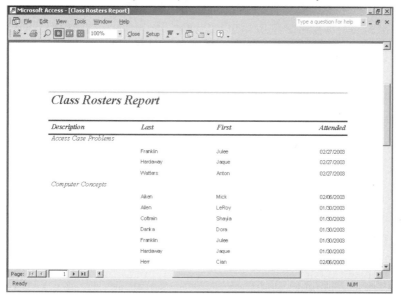

extra!

Creating a development database

If you want to develop a database outside the office, one way is to copy the production database, then delete all but a few records in each table. (Leaving some data helps you know what data is typically entered in each field in case the field names are not self-explanatory. It also gives you some sample data from which to create new forms and reports.) These steps create a development database that contains all the table definitions that you need to develop new queries, forms, and reports (which will later be imported back into the production database). These steps also minimize problems associated with copying and moving large amounts of sensitive data, which isn't required for development work.

Skill Set 8

Integrating with Other Applications

Export Data from Access
Export Data to an Excel Workbook

You can export data from an Access database to a variety of file formats, including a Word document, an Excel workbook, or another Access database. Access provides a special tool called **Analyze It with Microsoft Excel** to export the set of records defined by an Access table, query, form, or report to an Excel workbook. The Analyze It with Microsoft Excel feature is one of three special **OfficeLinks** tools for exporting Access data to other Microsoft Office file formats. The OfficeLinks tools are described in Table 8-1

Activity Steps

 Step 2
If an OfficeLink tool doesn't work with the selected object, the button and text for that option will be dim.

 Classes01.mdb

1. Click the **Tables button** 🖽 Tables on the Objects bar (if it's not already selected), then click **Courses**

2. Click the **OfficeLinks button list arrow** 🔽 on the Database toolbar, then click **Analyze It with Microsoft Excel**
   This process automatically creates an Excel workbook with the name Courses in the C:\My Documents folder. If a file with this name is already stored in that location, you'll be prompted to replace it.

3. If prompted to replace an existing file, click **Yes**
   See Figure 8-5.

4. Close the Courses workbook, then exit Excel

Skill 2

Export Data from Access

Figure 8-5: Courses Excel workbook

Courses.xls

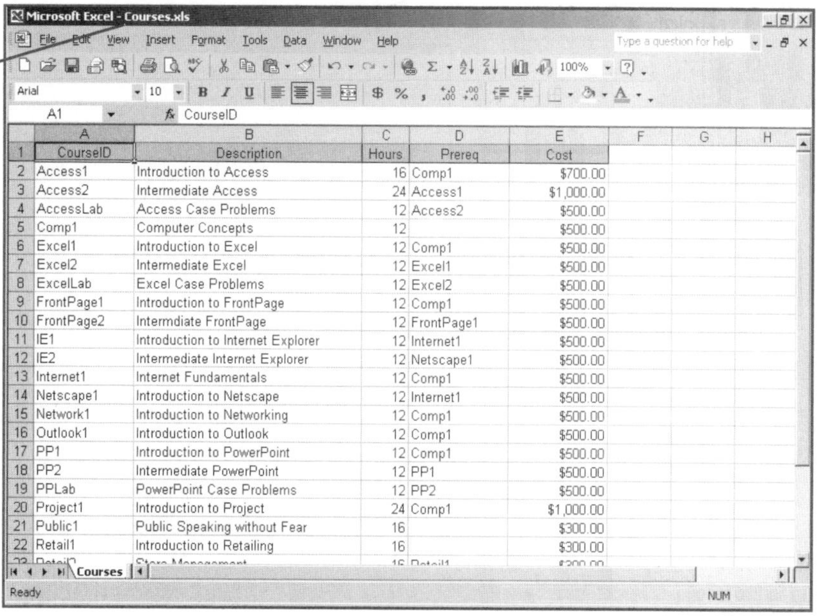

	A	B	C	D	E
1	CourseID	Description	Hours	Prereq	Cost
2	Access1	Introduction to Access	16	Comp1	$700.00
3	Access2	Intermediate Access	24	Access1	$1,000.00
4	AccessLab	Access Case Problems	12	Access2	$500.00
5	Comp1	Computer Concepts	12		$500.00
6	Excel1	Introduction to Excel	12	Comp1	$500.00
7	Excel2	Intermediate Excel	12	Excel1	$500.00
8	ExcelLab	Excel Case Problems	12	Excel2	$500.00
9	FrontPage1	Introduction to FrontPage	12	Comp1	$500.00
10	FrontPage2	Intermdiate FrontPage	12	FrontPage1	$500.00
11	IE1	Introduction to Internet Explorer	12	Internet1	$500.00
12	IE2	Intermediate Internet Explorer	12	Netscape1	$500.00
13	Internet1	Internet Fundamentals	12	Comp1	$500.00
14	Netscape1	Introduction to Netscape	12	Internet1	$500.00
15	Network1	Introduction to Networking	12	Comp1	$500.00
16	Outlook1	Introduction to Outlook	12	Comp1	$500.00
17	PP1	Introduction to PowerPoint	12	Comp1	$500.00
18	PP2	Intermediate PowerPoint	12	PP1	$500.00
19	PPLab	PowerPoint Case Problems	12	PP2	$500.00
20	Project1	Introduction to Project	24	Comp1	$1,000.00
21	Public1	Public Speaking without Fear	16		$300.00
22	Retail1	Introduction to Retailing	16		$300.00

TABLE 8-1: OfficeLinks tools

name	icon	description
Analyze It with Microsoft Excel		Sends a selected table, query, form, or report object's records to Excel
Publish It with Microsoft Word		Sends a selected table, query, form, or report object's records to Word
Merge It with Microsoft Word		Helps merge the selected table or query with a Word document

Skill Set 8
Integrating with Other Applications

Export Data from Access
Export Data to a Web Page

You can export data from Access tables, queries, forms, and reports to a variety of file formats, including Microsoft Office files, text files, and **Hypertext Markup Language** (**HTML**) documents, commonly called Web pages. Because Web pages can be distributed using the Internet, information provided on a Web page is more accessible to a larger audience than information provided as an Access report. Like all exported data, the data you export to an HTML document is no longer connected to the Access database, so the data is only as up-to-date as it was the moment you exported it.

Step 3
An HTML template contains formatting characteristics, such as font sizes and colors, that you can apply to Web pages to give them a consistent appearance.

Activity Steps

 Classes01.mdb

1. Click the **Reports button** Reports on the Objects bar (if it's not already selected), then click **Progress Report**

2. Click **File** on the menu bar, click **Export**, navigate to the drive and folder where your Project Files are stored, click the **Save as type list arrow**, click **HTML Documents**, then click **Export**

3. Click **OK** in the HTML Output Options dialog box
The export process finishes but doesn't automatically open the Progress Report Web page. You can open the Progress Report Web page from Windows Explorer.

4. Click **Start** on the taskbar, point to **Programs**, then click **Internet Explorer**

5. Maximize the Internet Explorer window (if it's not already maximized), click **File** on the menu bar, click **Open**, click **Browse**, navigate to the drive and folder where your Project Files are stored, click **Progress Report**, click **Open**, then click **OK**
See Figure 8-6. The Progress Report Web page opens in Internet Explorer. The export progress created eight Web pages from the report and linked them with **hyperlinks** (text or images that, when clicked, open another Web page). Four hyperlinks appear in the bottom-left corner of the Web page.

6. Scroll to the bottom of the Progress Report Web page, then click the **Last** hyperlink
See Figure 8-7. The last page of the report, converted into the Web page Progress Report8, opens in Internet Explorer.

7. Close Internet Explorer

Figure 8-6: First page of Progress Report, Progress Report.html

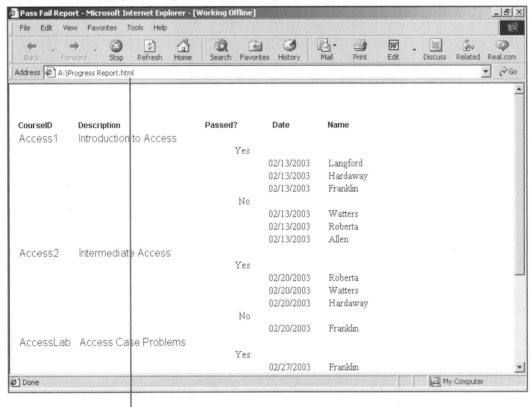

Progress Report.html

Figure 8-7: Last page of Progress Report, Progress Report8.html

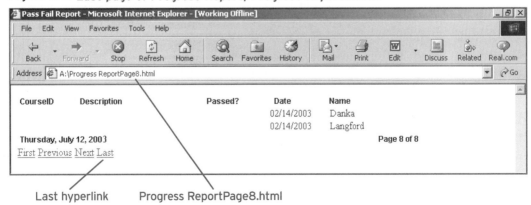

Last hyperlink   Progress ReportPage8.html

Skill Set 8
Integrating with Other Applications

Create a Simple Data Access Page
Create a Data Access Page for Data Entry

You use the **page** object, also called a **data access page** (**DAP**), to create a dynamic Web page. **Dynamic** means that the Web page is automatically linked to the database; every time the Web page is opened or refreshed, it reconnects with the database to display up-to-date data. You can use data access pages to enter and edit data in the database (like a form) or display current data in a Web page format (like a report). You can use the **Page Wizard** to create a data access page or build one by yourself using **Page Design View**. You view a data access page in **Page View**, which displays the final Web page just as it will appear in Internet Explorer. You modify a data access page in Page Design View.

Activity Steps

 Classes01.mdb

1. Click the **Pages button** on the Objects bar (if it's not already selected), then double-click **Create data access page by using wizard**

2. Click the **Tables/Queries list arrow**, click **Table: Courses**, click the **Select All Fields button** ⏵⏵, then click **Next**

3. Click **Next** to not specify any grouping levels, click the first sort order list arrow, click **CourseID**, then click **Next**

4. Type **Course Entry Form** as the title for the page, click the **Open the page option button**, then click **Finish**
   See Figure 8-8. You can enter and edit data using a data access page opened in Page View or in Internet Explorer, and it will automatically update the database just as if you were using a database form object. You use the buttons on the navigation toolbar to move through the data access page.

5. Double-click **$700.00** in the Cost box, then type **750**

6. Click the **Sort Descending button** ⬇ on the navigation toolbar to sort the records in descending order based on the Cost values, then click the **Next button** ▶ twice to move to the third record for the Access1 CourseID to make sure that the records were sorted correctly

7. Click the **Save button** 🖫 on the Page View toolbar, navigate to the drive and folder where your Project Files are stored, type **cform** in the File name box, click **Save**, then click **OK** when notified about the connection string

8. Close the Course Entry Form

Step 6
The Sort Ascending, Sort Descending, and Filter by Selection buttons work the same way on the navigation toolbar as they do on the Form View, Table Datasheet, or Query Datasheet toolbars.

Figure 8-8: Course Entry Form in Page View

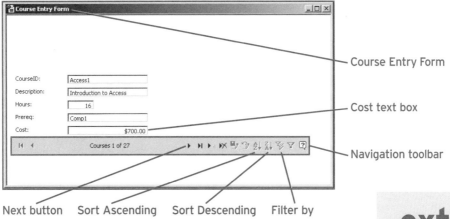

Course Entry Form

Cost text box

Navigation toolbar

Next button   Sort Ascending   Sort Descending   Filter by
button   button   Selection button

Figure 8-9: Deleting a data access page

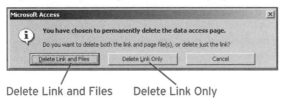

Delete Link and Files   Delete Link Only

extra!

Understanding the two parts of a data access page

When you create a data access page, you really create two things: the Web page itself (which is saved and given a filename with an HTML extension) and the link to the Web page (which is displayed as a page object in the Database window). If you click a page object icon in the Database window, then press **[Delete]**, the message shown in Figure 8-9 will appear. This message helps clarify that a data access page is really composed of two parts, and also points out that you can delete the link in the Access database and the associated Web page files, or just the link within the Access database.

Skill Set 8

Integrating with Other Applications

Create a Simple Data Access Page
Create a Data Access Page for Data Reporting

The two main purposes for building a data access page are to allow users to enter and edit data from a Web page, and to dynamically report up-to-date database activity through a report on a Web page. Your data access page will function as either a form or a report, depending on the choices you make while using the Page Wizard. All data access pages are automatically connected to the original database, so they will display up-to-date data when the Web page is opened or refreshed in the browser.

Activity Steps

 Classes01.mdb

1. Click the **Pages button** 🔲 Pages on the Objects bar (if it's not already selected), then double-click **Create data access page by using wizard**

2. Click the **Tables/Queries list arrow**, click **Table: Courses**, click **Description**, then click the **Select Single Field button** >

3. Click the **Tables/Queries list arrow**, click **Table: Customers**, click **First**, click the **Select Single Field button** >, click **Last**, click the **Select Single Field button** >, then click **Next**

4. Click **Description**, click the **Select Single Field button** > to use the Description field as the grouping level, then click **Next**

5. Click **Next** to bypass the sort order options and not specify a particular sort order, type **Course Attendee Report** as the title for the page, click the **Open the page option button**, then click **Finish**
   See Figure 8-10. As specified in the Page Wizard, the records are grouped by the Description field.

6. Click the **expand button** ⊞ to the left of the Description label
   See Figure 8-11. The Web page expands to show you the First and Last field values for each person who took that course. The upper navigation toolbar tells you that there are three records within this course description (three people have taken this course).

7. Click the upper navigation bar's **Next button** ▶ twice to move to the third record for Anton Watters
   You use the upper navigation toolbar to work with the records within each group and the lower navigation toolbar to work with the groups themselves.

8. Double-click **Watters**, then try to type **Winters**
   If you group records on a data access page, the Web page can be used only for data reporting, not for data entry.

9. Close the data access page without saving it

Step 1
If you open the page in Page Design View instead of Page View, click the View button 🖭 on the Page Design toolbar to switch to Page View.

Figure 8-10: Course Attendee Report in Page View

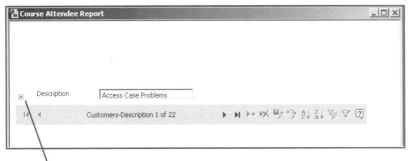

Expand button

Figure 8-11: Expanding records on a data access page

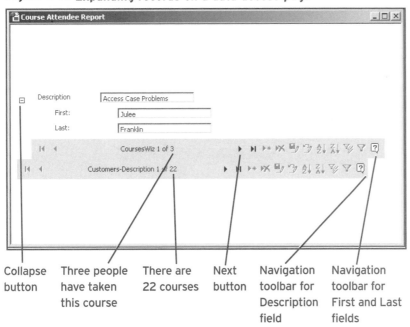

Collapse button

Three people have taken this course

There are 22 courses

Next button

Navigation toolbar for Description field

Navigation toolbar for First and Last fields

extra!

Understanding data access page browser requirements

When you create a data access page, special codes are added to the Web page to connect to the Access database, query the database for the latest data, and return that information to the Web page. You use **browser software** to find, download, and display Web pages. Because the codes placed in data access pages contain proprietary Microsoft technologies, the only browser that will display a data access page successfully is Microsoft's Internet Explorer version 5.0 or later. This means that data access pages are most useful in environments where you control users' browser software, such as corporate intranets or local area networks.

Skill Set 8

Integrating with Other Applications

Target Your Skills

 Classes01.mdb

1 Export the Customers table as an HTML document to the drive and folder where your Project Files are stored. Use the default name, Customers, as the file-name, and do not apply an HTML tem-plate if given the choice to do so. Open the Customers file in Internet Explorer as shown in Figure 8-12.

 Classes01.mdb

2 Create a data access page based on the fields in the Customers table. Do not add grouping levels or sort orders, and title the page Customer Entry Form. Navigate to the second record, then change the last name from Langford to Adams. Sort the records in ascending order based on the value in the Last field as shown in Figure 8-13. Close the page without saving it.

Figure 8-12

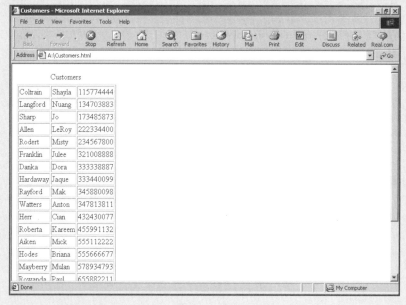

Figure 8-13

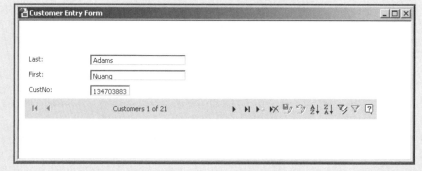

110 Certification Circle

Skill List

1. Use data validation
2. Link tables
3. Create lookup fields and modify Lookup field properties
4. Create and modify input masks

In Skill Set 9, you will use advanced tools to modify tables and fields to maximize fast and accurate data entry. Specifically, you will learn how to link tables to make use of data that is stored and maintained in another Access database. You'll also use the Field Validation and Input Mask properties, which help prevent inaccurate data from being accepted into the database. In addition, you will create and modify lookup fields, which support fast, easy, and accurate data entry.

Skill Set 9

Creating and Modifying Tables

Use Data Validation

Data validation is a process that compares a field entry with criteria that define a set or range of acceptable entries for a field. For example, you might limit a Gender field to only two possible entries, "Female" or "Male." However, for a DateofService field, you might allow any date after the date a business started. You use the **Validation Rule** property to set the criteria for data entry. You use the **Validation Text** property to display a message if a user attempts to enter a value that is outside the acceptable entries. By using the Validation Rule and Validation Text properties, you can minimize some types of data entry errors.

Step 3

If you enter a Validation Rule property but not a Validation Text property, Access still displays an error message if you attempt to enter data outside the criteria defined by the Validation Rule. By using the Validation Text property, though, you can customize the error message.

Activity Steps

 Basketball01.mdb

1. Click the **Tables button** ▦ Tables on the Objects bar (if it's not already selected), click **Games**, then click the **Design button** ☒ Design on the Database window toolbar

2. Click the **Home-Away** field, click the **Validation Rule property box**, type **A or H**, then click the **Validation Text property box**
   See Figure 9-1. Access helps you make a valid criteria entry in the Validation Rule property box by adding quotation marks around the possible text entries and by automatically capitalizing the word *Or*.

3. Type **Enter A for Away or H for Home** in the Validation Text property box

4. Click the **Date** field, click the **Validation Rule property box**, type **>=11/1/03**, then click the **Validation Text property box**
   This validation rule will require that all entries in the Date field are November 1, 2003 or later.

5. Type **Season starts November 1, 2003** in the Validation Text property box

6. Click the **Save button** 🖫 on the Table Design toolbar, click **Yes** when prompted to test the existing data against the new rules, then click the **View button** ▦ on the Table Design toolbar

7. Press **[Tab]** three times to select the value in the Home-Away field, type **B**, then press **[Tab]**
   See Figure 9-2. The text that you entered in the Validation Text property appears in an alert box.

8. Click **OK**, press **[Esc]** to undo the unacceptable "B" entry in the Home-Away field, press **[Tab]** three times to select the value in the Date field, type **10/1/03**, then press **[Tab]**

9. Click **OK**, press **[Esc]** to undo the unacceptable 10/1/30 entry in the Date field, then close the Games table

Figure 9-1: Entering a Validation Rule property

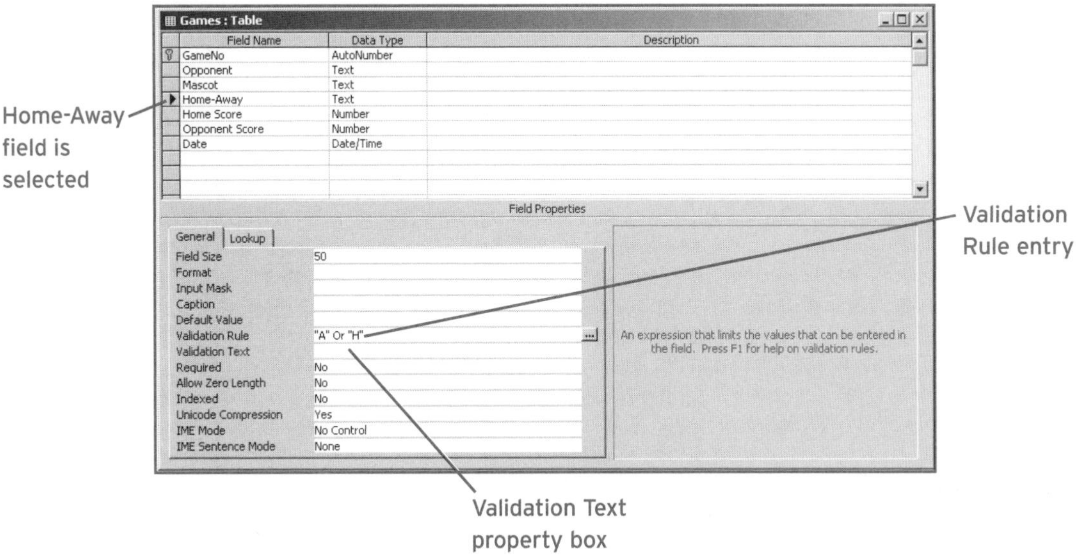

Home-Away field is selected

Validation Rule entry

Validation Text property box

Figure 9-2: Testing the Validation Text property

B entry

Validation Text property entry

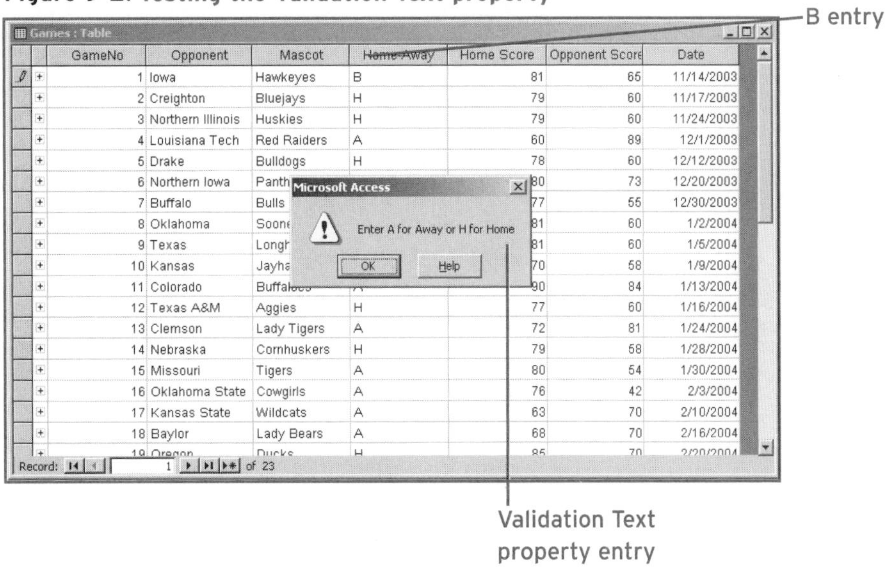

Skill Set 9

Creating and Modifying Tables

Link Tables

If you have a table that you can use in two or more databases, you don't need to create a copy of the table for each database. Instead, you can use a **linked table**, which is a link to data stored in a "real" table in another database. The advantage of using a linked table is that updates made in either database are automatically reflected in both databases. For example, if you have a database that tracks employee projects and another that tracks employee benefits, both databases could use a single table containing employee information. To ensure that changes to the employee data made from one database are automatically updated in the other, you would create the employee table in one database and use a linked table in the other. You can use a linked table to enter, modify, or delete data (just like you would in the original table), but you cannot save any changes in Table Design View of a linked table.

Step 2
You can link to data in multiple file formats including dBASE, Excel, Outlook, and HTML files. Click the Files of type list arrow in the Link dialog box to view a list of files that an Access database will link to.

Activity Steps

  Benefits01.mdb
Projects01.mdb

1. In the Benefits01 database, click the **Tables button** [Tables] on the Objects bar (if it's not already selected), click **File** on the menu bar, point to **Get External Data**, then click **Link Tables**

2. Click the **Look in list arrow**, navigate to the drive and folder where the Projects01 database is stored, click **Projects01**, then click **Link**

3. Click **Employees** in the Link Tables dialog box
   See Figure 9-3. The Link Tables dialog box shows all the tables that you can link to from the Projects01 database.

4. Click **OK**
   The Employees table appears as an object in the tables list with a linking table icon.

5. Double-click **Employees** to open the table in Datasheet View

6. Double-click **Jeff** in the First field of the second record, then type **Jeffrey**

7. Click the **View button** [icon] on the Table Datasheet toolbar, then click **Yes** after reading the message about linked table limitations

8. Read the message in the lower-right corner of the Field Properties pane that clarifies that you are working in a linked table and therefore cannot modify the current property, then close the Employees table

Figure 9-3: Link Tables dialog box

extra!

Using the Linked Table Manager

You use the Linked Table Manager to change the path between an original and linked table if one of the databases is moved. You also use the Linked Table Manager to refresh the linked copy of the table if the original table's structure (field names and properties) has been modified. While a linked table contains no data, it does store a copy of the structure of the original table, so you should refresh the linked table after you add or modify field properties in the original table. To access the Linked Table Manager, right-click a linked table, then click **Linked Table Manager** on the shortcut menu to open the Linked Table Manager dialog box.

Skill Set 9
Creating and Modifying Tables

Create Lookup Fields and Modify Lookup Field Properties
Create Lookup Fields

You create a lookup field by entering Lookup properties directly into Table Design View or by using the Lookup Wizard. A **lookup field** uses a combo box (sometimes called a drop-down list), which displays values for a field in either Datasheet View (of a table or query) or Form View of a form. A **combo box** is a "combination" of a list and a text box, so it allows you to choose a value from a drop-down list or type a value into a field. Choosing from a list of common entries improves data entry ease-of-use, speed, and accuracy. To create the combo box's list of values, you can enter your own values or use an existing list of values from a table in the database.

Activity Steps

 Basketball01.mdb

1. Click the **Tables button** ⊞ Tables on the Objects bar (if it's not already selected), click **Players** (if it's not already selected), then click the **Design button** ☑ Design on the Database window toolbar

2. Click **Text** in the Data Type cell for the Year field, click the **list arrow**, then click **Lookup Wizard**

3. Click the **I will type in the values that I want option button**, then click **Next**

4. Click the first cell for the **Col1** column, type **Fr**, press [Tab], type **So**, press [Tab], type **Jr**, press [Tab], type **Sr**, then press [Tab]
   See Figure 9-4. These values will appear in the combo box list for the Year field.

5. Click **Next**, then click **Finish** to accept Year as the label for the lookup column

6. Click the **View button** ⊞ on the Table Design toolbar, click **Yes** to save the table, click the **Year** field for the first record, then click the **list arrow**
   See Figure 9-5. The values that you entered in the Lookup Wizard are displayed in the combo box list, and can be used to enter and edit data in the Year field.

7. Close the Players table

Step 2
The Lookup Wizard isn't a data type even though it's listed in the Data Type list. After using the Lookup Wizard, the data type will return to Text because the field values are text entries.

Figure 9-4: Creating a list of values for a lookup field

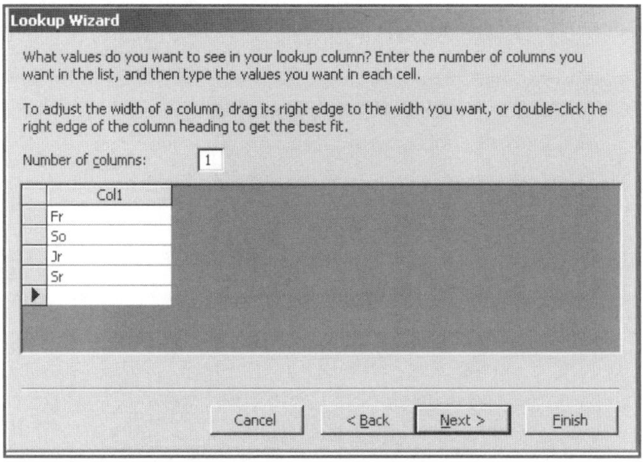

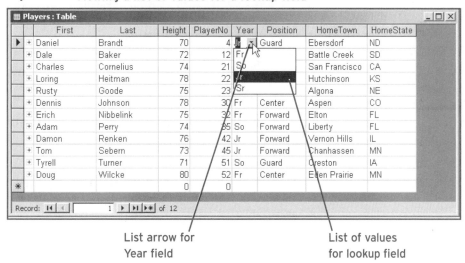

Figure 9-5: Viewing a list of values for a lookup field

List arrow for
Year field

List of values
for lookup field

Skill Set 9

Creating and Modifying Tables

Create Lookup Fields and Modify Lookup Field Properties

Modify Lookup Properties

You can modify a lookup field by using the Lookup Wizard or by changing the Lookup properties in Table Design View. While the Lookup Wizard is an excellent tool for creating a new lookup field, modifying a lookup by directly changing individual Lookup field properties can be faster. You modify Lookup properties using Table Design View, as you would modify any other properties.

Activity Steps

 Basketball01.mdb

1. Click the **Tables button** Tables on the Objects bar (if it's not already selected), click **Players** (if it's not already selected), then click the **Design button** Design on the Database window toolbar

2. Click the **Position** field, then click the **Lookup tab** in the Field Properties pane

3. Click the **Row Source property box**, then modify the entry to display the following text: "Point Guard";"Off Guard";"Forward";"Center"
   See Figure 9-6. These will appear in the combo box list for the Position field.

4. Click the **View button** on the Table Design toolbar, click **Yes** to save the table, click the **Position** field for the first record, then click the **list arrow**
   See Figure 9-7. Even though the existing value in the field, "Guard," isn't in the current drop-down list, it's still an acceptable entry for this field. By default, lookup fields give you a list of values to choose from, but they don't limit your ability to store or enter another value that is not in the list.

5. Close the Players table

Step 3
If you want to limit the choices for a lookup field to those in the list, change the Limit To List lookup property to Yes in the Field Properties pane in Table Design View.

Figure 9-6: Modifying a list of values for a lookup field

Position field is selected

Lookup tab

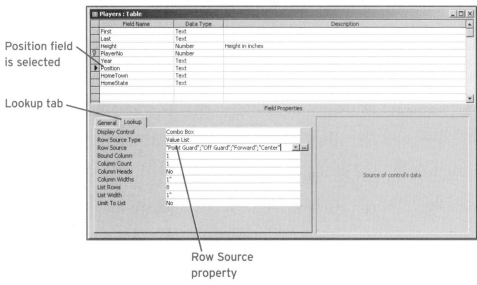

Row Source property

Figure 9-7: Using a list of modified values for a lookup field

List arrow for Position field

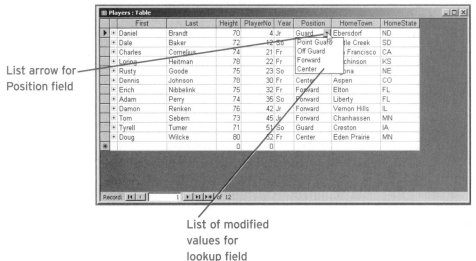

List of modified values for lookup field

Skill Set 9

Creating and Modifying Tables

Create and Modify Input Masks

You can use the Input Mask property to specify the number and types of characters that can be entered into a field, and also to display a visual guide as data is entered into a field. For example, you could apply an input mask to a Telephone field that allows only 10 digits and automatically enters dashes at the appropriate places as a user types the entry. You can use the Input Mask property only with fields that have Text and Date/Time data types. A complete Input Mask property has three parts (separated by semicolons) as described in Table 9-1. You can use the Input Mask Wizard to apply existing or create custom Input Mask properties, or you can modify Input Mask properties in Table Design View.

Activity Steps

 Basketball01.mdb

1. Click the **Tables button** 🔲 Tables on the Objects bar (if it's not already selected), click **Games**, then click the **Design button** 🗹 Design on the Database window toolbar

2. Click the **Date** field, click the **Input Mask property box** in the Field Properties pane, click the **Build button** ⸱⸱⸱, then click **Yes** if prompted to save the table

   By default, the Input Mask Wizard lists five common input masks for a field with a Date/Time data type. You will create an input mask that requires a two-digit month, two-digit day, and four-digit year entry, each separated by dashes. Since none of the existing input mask options meets this requirement, you'll create a custom input mask.

Step 4

If you use only two digits for the year, numbers you enter from 0 to 29 are assumed to be 2000 through 2029 and numbers from 30 to 99 are assumed to be 1930 through 1999.

3. Click **Edit List**, type **Two-Two-Four** in the Description box, press **[Tab]**, type **00/00/0000**, press **[Tab]**, type ***** (an asterisk), press **[Tab]**, type **11/22/2004**, click the **Mask Type list arrow**, and then click **Date-Time**

   See Figure 9-8. This custom input mask will be available each time you use the Input Mask Wizard.

4. Click **Close**, click **Two-Two-Four**, click **Next**, click **Next** to accept the input mask options, then click **Finish**

5. Click the **View button** 🔲 on the Table Design toolbar, click **Yes** when prompted to save the table, then press **[Tab]** six times to select the Date value for the first record

6. Type **1114**

   See Figure 9-9. The Input Mask property guides your entry by displaying asterisks for each number of the date. The slashes are automatically entered for you. Without the Input Mask property, you would have to type the slashes.

7. Type **2003** to finish the entry, then close the Games table

Figure 9-8: Customize Input Mask Wizard dialog box

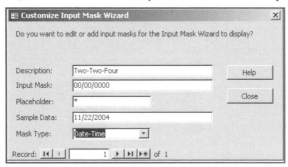

Figure 9-9: Entering a date in a field with a custom input mask

Entering a date using an input mask

TABLE 9-1: The parts of the input mask entry

part	description	options	examples (parts appear in bold)	how a sample entry appears in Datasheet View or Form View
first	Controls what type of data can be entered and how it will be displayed.	**9** represents an optional number **0** represents a required number **?** represents an optional letter **L** represents a required letter **** causes the next character to be displayed as entered	Telephone Number \\(999\\)\\-000\\-0000;1;*	(123)-456-7899
second	Determines whether all displayed characters (such as dashes in the SSN field) are stored in a field, or just the part you enter.	**0** stores all characters **1** stores only the entered characters	ZIP Code 00000\\-9999;0;_	12345 or 12345-7777
third	Determines which character Access will display as a placeholder for the space where a character will be typed in a field.	* (asterisk) _ (underscore) # (pound sign)	Social Security Number 000\\-00\\-0000;0;#	987-65-4321

Skill Set 9

Creating and Modifying Tables

Target Your Skills

 Basketball01.mdb
States01.mdb

1 In the Basketball01 database, create a linked table that links to the States table in the States01 database. In the Players table, create a new field using "Major" as the field name. Use the Lookup Wizard to add the values shown in Figure 9-10 to the Major field. Then use the combo box in the Major field to add the value "Business" to the first record in the Players table.

 Projects01.mdb

2 Set the Validation Rule property of the DateHired field in the Employees table so that values must be on or after 1/1/1997. Set the Validation Text property of the DateHired field to display the message shown in Figure 9-11. Create an input mask for the SSN field. Specify that all nine digits are required and separated by dashes in a 3-2-4 digit pattern. Use the asterisk (*) character for the place-holder, and store only the digits in the field.

Figure 9-10

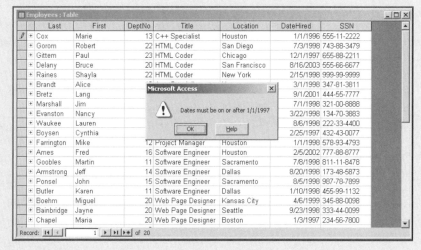

Figure 9-11

Certification Circle

Skill Set 10

Skill List

1. Create a form in Design View
2. Create a switchboard and set startup options
3. Add subform controls to Access forms

In Skill Set 10, you will use advanced tools to create and modify forms. For example, you'll use Form Design View to modify a form using a property sheet, and you'll work with advanced controls such as subforms. You will also create a special type of form called a **switchboard**, which is used to help users navigate through a database rather than help them enter or edit data (which is the purpose of most forms). Finally, you'll learn about Access startup options that help make your database easy to use and more secure.

Skill Set 10

Creating and Modifying Forms

Create a Form in Design View

You can use Form Design View to create a new form without the aid of a form creation tool, such as AutoForm or the Form Wizard. You also use Form Design View to modify an existing form. When you create a form in Form Design View, you need to set the **Record Source property** for the form, which determines which fields and records the form will display. You select either a table or a query as the Record Source property for the form. After you set the Record Source property, you specify where you want each field to appear on the form.

Activity Steps

 Jobs01.mdb

1. Click the **Forms button** on the Objects bar (if it's not already selected), then double-click **Create form in Design view**

2. Click the **Properties button** on the Form Design toolbar to open the Form property sheet (if it's not already open), click the **Data tab** (if it's not already selected), click the **Record Source list arrow**, then click **Project Summary**
   See Figure 10-1. Project Summary is a query in this database that contains five fields from three different tables. When you choose a table or query for the Record Source property, the **field list** opens, which displays the fields from the record source that you specify.

3. Click the **Properties button** to toggle off the Form property sheet

4. Double-click the **title bar** of the field list to select all the fields, then drag the selected fields to the middle of the form
   You can drag an individual field or several selected fields to a specific location on the form. You can also move, resize, and format fields after they have been added to a form.

5. Click the **View button** on the Form Design toolbar
   See Figure 10-2. This form shows the five fields of the Project Summary query. The navigation toolbar indicates that there are 13 records in this query.

6. Close the new form without saving it

tip

Step 2
If the field list doesn't open when you set the Record Source property, click the Field List button on the Form Design toolbar to toggle it on. Drag a border of the Field List to expand it to see all the fields or view the entire query or table name on the title bar.

Figure 10-1: Setting the Record Source property

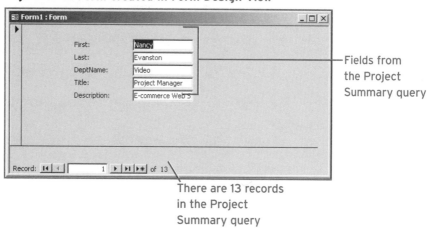

Properties
button

Field list

Field List
button

Form
property
sheet

Record
Source
property

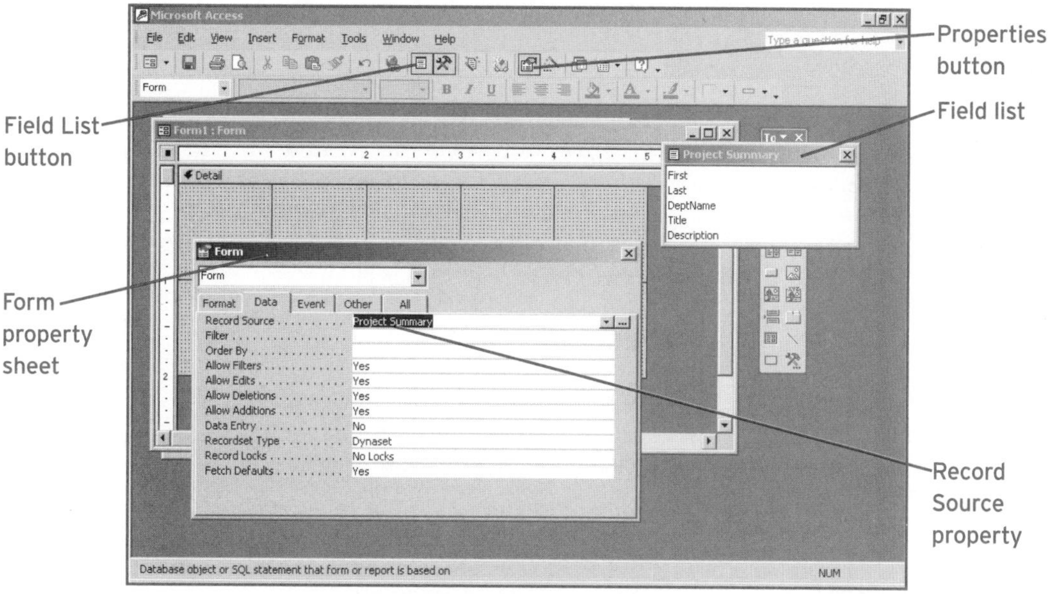

Figure 10-2: Form created in Form Design View

Fields from
the Project
Summary query

There are 13 records
in the Project
Summary query

Skill Set 10
Creating and Modifying Forms

Create a Switchboard and Set Startup Options
Create a Switchboard

You can create a special form called a **switchboard**, which is used to find, open, and use various parts of the database. A switchboard displays one command button for each object so that users don't have to use the Database window to find the parts of the database that they need. If you create more than one switchboard, you must designate a switchboard as the **default switchboard**. Typically, you add command buttons to the default switchboard to open the other switchboards. You use the **Switchboard Manager** to create all switchboards.

Activity Steps

 Jobs01.mdb

1. Click **Tools** on the menu bar, point to **Database Utilities**, then click **Switchboard Manager**

2. Click **Yes** when prompted to create a switchboard, click **Edit** in the Switchboard Manager dialog box, double-click **Main** and type **Jobs** in the Switchboard Name box to name the switchboard "Jobs Switchboard," then click **New** in the Edit Switchboard Page dialog box

3. Type **Open Employees Form** in the Text box, click the **Command list arrow**, click **Open Form in Edit Mode**, click the **Form list arrow**, then click **Employees**
   See Figure 10-3. The Edit Switchboard Item dialog box identifies the text and command for each button on the final switchboard.

4. Click **OK**
   The Edit Switchboard Page dialog box lists the existing commands on the switchboard.

5. Click **New**, type **Preview Assignments Report** in the Text box, click the **Command list arrow**, click **Open Report**, click the **Report list arrow**, click **Assignments**, then click **OK**

6. Click **Close** in the Edit Switchboard Page dialog box, click **Close** in the Switchboard Manager dialog box, click the **Forms button** 📇 **Forms** on the Objects bar (if it's not already selected), then double-click **Switchboard**
   See Figure 10-4. The Jobs Switchboard form displays the two command buttons you specified in the Switchboard Manager.

7. Click the **Open Employees Form button**, close the Employees form, click the **Preview Assignments Report button**, close the Assignments report, then close the Jobs Switchboard

If you delete a switchboard form, you must also delete the Switchboard Items table (which is automatically created by the Switchboard Manager) before you can create a new switchboard form.

Figure 10-3: Using the Switchboard Manager

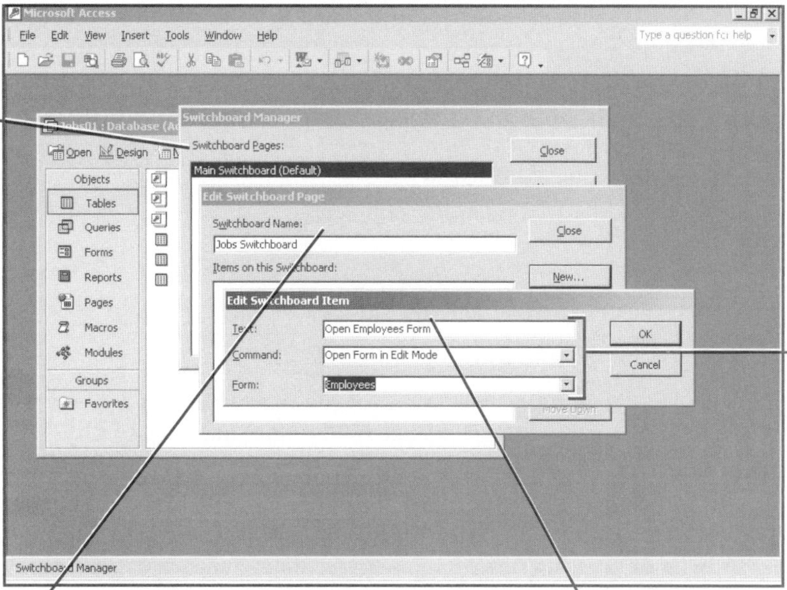

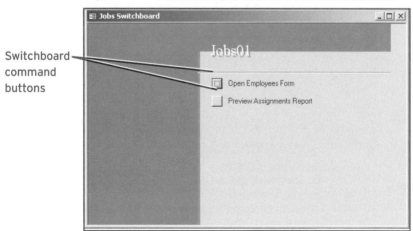

Switchboard Manager dialog box

These options define the command button

Edit Switchboard Page dialog box

Edit Switchboard Item dialog box

Figure 10-4: A switchboard with two command buttons

Switchboard command buttons

Skill Set 10
Creating and Modifying Forms

Create a Switchboard and Set Startup Options
Modify a Switchboard

After you create a switchboard form, you might want to modify it by adding, deleting, or changing the existing command buttons, or by formatting the form. To modify the command buttons (or the text to the right of the command buttons), you must use the Switchboard Manager. To format or modify any control other than the command buttons (for example, labels or clip art), you use Form Design View.

Step 5
The default teal color on a switchboard is created with two teal-colored rectangles. To change this color, click a rectangle, then choose a new color using the Fill/Back Color button in Form Design View.

Activity Steps
 Health01.mdb

1. Click **Tools** on the menu bar, point to **Database Utilities**, click **Switchboard Manager**, then click **Edit**

2. Click **View Activity Report**, then click the **Move Up button** three times to change the command button from the last position to the first position

3. Click **Edit**, change "View" to "Preview" in the Text box, then click **OK**
   See Figure 10-5. Any change to the command buttons or command button text of a switchboard *should* be made using the Switchboard Manager.

4. Click **Close** in the Edit Switchboard Page dialog box, click **Close** in the Switchboard Manager dialog box, click the **Forms button** on the Objects bar (if it's not already selected), click **Switchboard** in the Database window, then click the **Design button** on the Database window toolbar to open the Switchboard form in Design View

5. Click the **Medical Associates label**, click the **Font Size list arrow**, click **20**, then click the **View button** on the Form Design toolbar to display the switchboard in Form View
   See Figure 10-6. Changes to any control *other* than the command buttons can be made in Form Design View.

6. Save and close the Main Switchboard form

Figure 10-5: Modifying switchboard command buttons with the Switchboard Manager

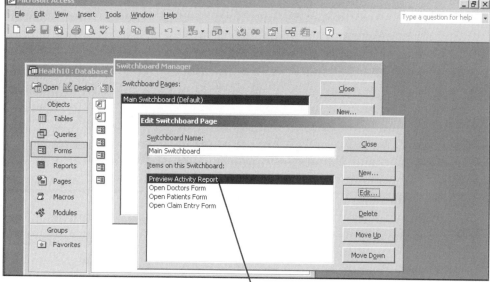

Item moved up and "View" is
changed to "Preview"

Figure 10-6: Switchboard formatted in Form Design View

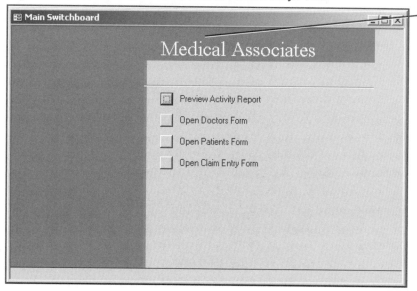

Font size
of label
has been
increased

Skill Set 10

Creating and Modifying Forms

Create a Switchboard and Set Startup Options
Set Startup Options

Startup options are commands that are automatically applied to the database when you open it. Some startup options help make the database easier to use. For example, you can use the Display Form/Page startup option to display a form or page object as soon as the database is opened. (If your database includes a switchboard form, you can use the Display Form/Page startup option to automatically display the switchboard when the database is opened.) You can also use startup options to increase database security. For example, some startup options allow you to disable the user's ability to modify Access toolbars and menus or hide the database window. Table 10-1 describes many popular startup options.

Activity Steps

 Health01.mdb

1. Click **Tools** on the menu bar, then click **Startup**

2. Click the **Display Form/Page list arrow**, then click **Switchboard**

3. Deselect the **Display Database Window check box**, then deselect the **Allow Toolbar/Menu Changes check box**
   See Figure 10-7.

4. Click **OK**, Close the Health01 database, then reopen the Health01 database
   The Main Switchboard form is automatically opened when you open the Health01 database. The Database window is hidden.

5. Right-click any toolbar or menu bar
   Since the startup options specify that you are not allowed to modify toolbars and menu bars, nothing happens when you right-click a toolbar or menu bar.

6. Close the Main Switchboard form and exit Access

Step 4
To bypass the startup options, press and hold [Shift] while opening a database.

Figure 10-7: Startup dialog box

Startup dialog box —

Display Form/Page option

Display Database Window check box

Allow Toolbar/Menu Changes check box

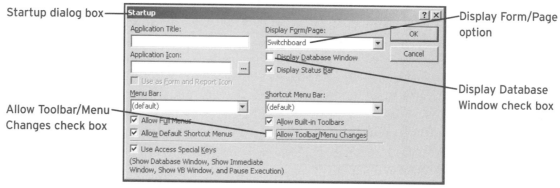

TABLE 10-1: Startup options

option	description
Application Title	Displays text (that you specify) on the Database title bar instead of the name of the database
Application Icon	Displays a bitmap or an icon file (that you specify) to the left of the text on the Database and application title bars
Menu Bar	Specifies which menu bar appears when the database is opened
Allow Full Menus	Toggles on or off the ability to work with full menus
Allow Default Shortcut Menus	Toggles on or off the ability to work with shortcut menus
Use Access Special Keys	Toggles on or off the ability to work with Access special keys such as F11, which opens the Database window
Display Form/Page	Specifies which form or page object automatically opens when you open the database
Display Database Window	Works as a toggle to hide or display the Database window when you open a database
Display Status Bar	Toggles on or off the ability to display the status bar
Shortcut Menu Bar	Specifies which shortcut menu bar appears when you right-click a menu bar
Allow Built-in Toolbars	Toggles on or off the ability to display Access toolbars
Allow Toolbar/Menu Changes	Toggles on or off the ability to modify Access toolbars and menu bars

Skill Set 10

Creating and Modifying Forms

Add Subform Controls to Access Forms

A **subform** is a form within a form. The form that contains the subform is called the **main form**. If two tables are joined in a one-to-many relationship, you can create a form and a subform by using data from the tables. For example, if you have two tables, Customers and Sales, that are joined in a one-to-many relationship, you can use a form and a subform to show information for one customer in the main form and the many related records of what the customer purchased in the subform.

Activity Steps

 Jobs01.mdb

1. Click the **Forms button** on the Objects bar (if it's not already selected), click **Employees**, click the **Design button** on the Database window toolbar, then maximize the Employees form in Form Design View

2. Click the **Toolbox button** on the Form Design toolbar to toggle it on (if it's not already visible), click the **Subform/Subreport button** on the Toolbox toolbar, then click under the **Dept No label** on the form
   The SubForm Wizard appears and assists you with the process of adding a subform. Each employee is related to many projects, so the subform should contain fields from the Projects table. You can also use an existing query or form as the source of data for the subform control.

3. Click **Next** to accept the option to use existing tables or queries, click the **Tables/Queries list arrow**, click **Table: Projects**, click the **Select All Fields button**, click **Next**, click **Next** to accept the suggested link between the main form and subform, then click **Finish** to accept the name "Projects subform" for the subform

4. Maximize the Employees form, point to the **lower-right sizing handle** of the subform so that the resize pointer appears, then drag down and to the right to expand the size of the subform to fill the screen
   See Figure 10-8.

5. Click the **View button** on the Form Design toolbar to display the Employees form with the new subform in Form View, then click the **Next Record button** on the main form navigation toolbar several times to display the record for Marie Cox
   See Figure 10-9.

6. Save and close the Employees form

Step 2
If the SubForm Wizard doesn't automatically appear, delete the subform control, make sure that the Control Wizards button on the Toolbox toolbar is selected, then repeat Step 2.

Figure 10-8: Adding a subform to a main form in Form Design View

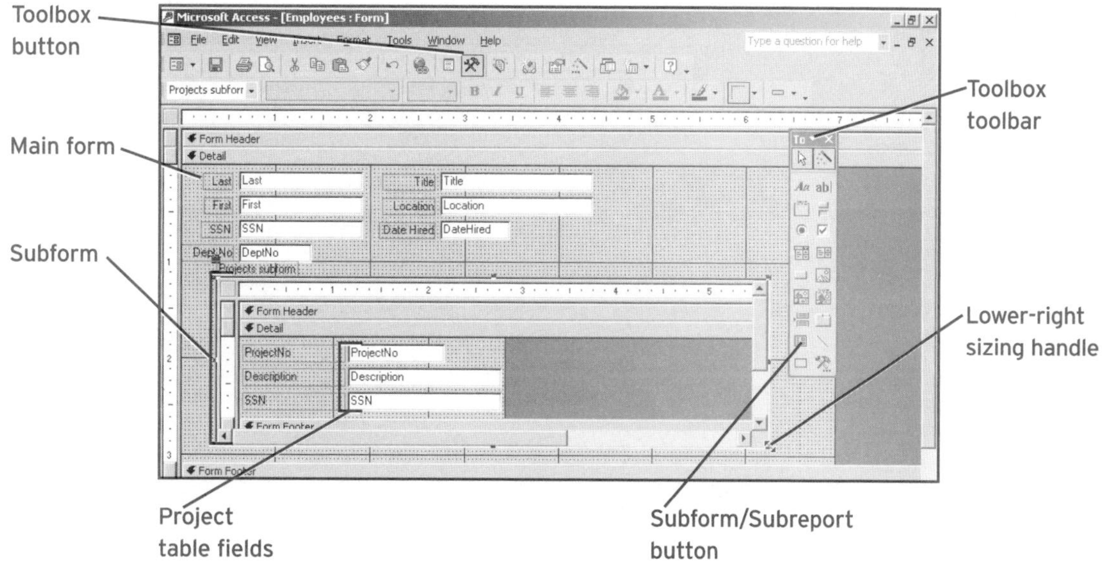

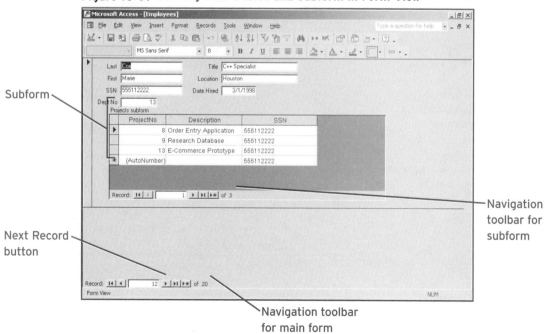

Toolbox button

Main form

Subform

Project table fields

Toolbox toolbar

Lower-right sizing handle

Subform/Subreport button

Figure 10-9: Working with a form and subform in Form View

Subform

Next Record button

Navigation toolbar for subform

Navigation toolbar for main form

Skill Set 10

Creating and Modifying Forms

Target Your Skills

 Jobs01.mdb

1 Use Form Design View to create the form and subform displayed in Figure 10-10. Use the Departments table for the main form's Record Source property, and use all the fields of the Employees table for the subform. Use the DeptNo field to link the main form and subform. Adjust the subform's columns in Form View.

Figure 10-10

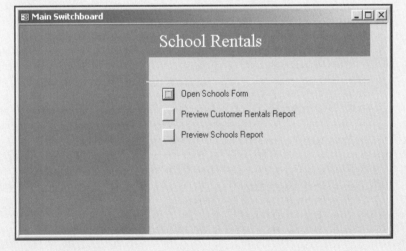

 Rentals01.mdb

2 Create the Switchboard form shown in Figure 10-11. The first button opens the Schools form in edit mode, the second opens the Customer Rentals report, and the third opens the Schools report. In Form Design View, change the "Rentals01" label to "School Rentals," move it up, and delete the gray "Rentals01" label. Set the switchboard to automatically open when you open the database.

Figure 10-11

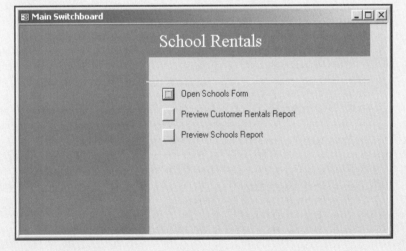

Skill List

1. Specify multiple query criteria
2. Create and apply advanced filters
3. Create and run parameter queries
4. Create and run action queries
5. Use aggregate functions in queries

In Skill Set 11, you will use advanced query functions that help you find, display, and analyze data. For example, you will apply advanced filters to quickly find and display specific data. You will use parameter criteria to customize a query to prompt a user to enter criteria. You'll also use action queries that change data, including the make-table, append, update, and delete queries. Finally, you'll use aggregate functions to help you analyze data by creating summary statistics for groups of records.

Skill Set 11

Refining Queries

Specify Multiple Query Criteria
Use AND Conditions

An **AND condition** consists of two or more criteria entered in Query Design View, where *each* criterion must be true for a record to appear in Query Datasheet View. For example, in a personnel database, you could create a query to show employees who are from a particular department *and* have a particular job code. In this example, both conditions must be true for a record to appear. Adding more AND conditions to a query decreases the number of records in a resulting datasheet. You enter AND conditions in the same row of the query design grid.

Activity Steps

Computers01.mdb

1. Click the **Queries button**  on the Objects bar (if it's not already selected), then double-click **Create query in Design view**

2. Click **Categories**, click **Add**, click **Equipment**, click **Add**, then click **Close**

3. Drag **CategoryDesc** from the Categories field list to the first column of the query design grid, then double-click **Description**, **PurchaseDate**, and **InitialValue** in the Equipment field list to add them to the query design grid

4. Click the **View button** on the Query Design toolbar to view the datasheet before adding criteria to the query design grid
   53 records appear in the datasheet.

Step 5
Text criterion is not case sensitive, so "laptop," "Laptop," and "LAPTOP" all work the same way.

5. Click the **View button** on the Query Datasheet toolbar to return to Query Design View, click the **Criteria cell** for the CategoryDesc field, type **laptop**, then click the **View button** on the Query Design toolbar
   17 records match the criterion.

6. Click the **View button** on the Query Datasheet toolbar, click the **Criteria cell** for the InitialValue field, then type **>2000**
   See Figure 11-1. Access automatically applied quotation marks around the criterion for the CategoryDesc field because it is a Text field.

7. Click the **View button** on the Query Design toolbar
   See Figure 11-2. 10 records appear in the datasheet. Each record has both "laptop" in the CategoryDesc field and a value greater than 2000 in the InitialValue field.

8. Close the query without saving changes

Figure 11-1: AND condition in Query Design View

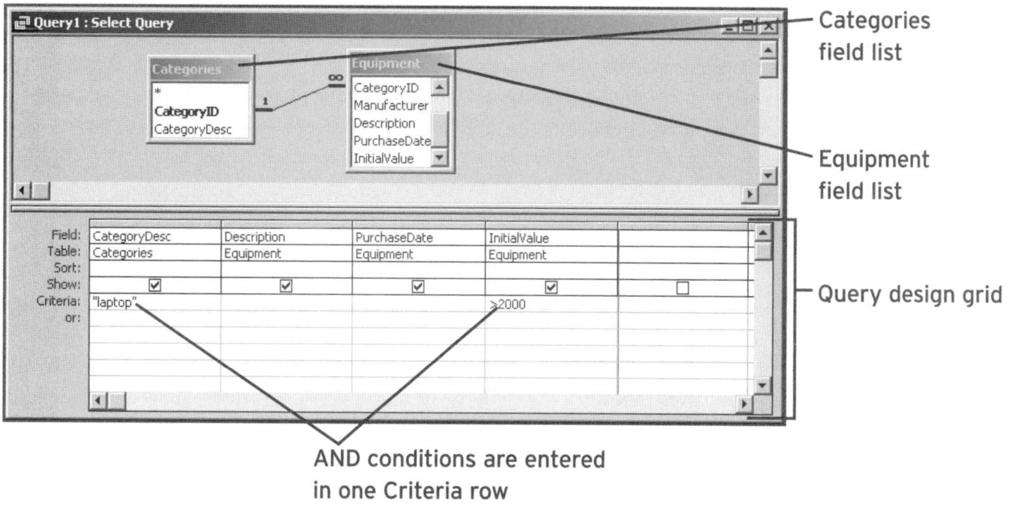

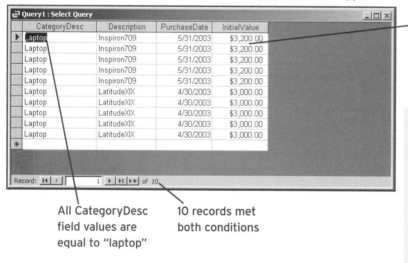

Categories field list

Equipment field list

Query design grid

AND conditions are entered in one Criteria row

Figure 11-2: Query Datasheet View with an AND condition applied

All InitialValue field values are greater than 2000

All CategoryDesc field values are equal to "laptop"

10 records met both conditions

Skill Set 11

Refining Queries

Specify Multiple Query Criteria
Use OR Conditions

An **OR condition** consists of two or more criteria entered in Query Design View, where only *one* criterion must be true for a record to appear in Query Datasheet View. For example, in a product inventory database, you could create a query to show records for all products that are categorized as fragile *or* those that require refrigeration. In this example, *either* criterion needs to be true for a record to appear. Because only one criterion in an OR condition must be true for a record to appear in a datasheet, adding more OR conditions to a query increases the number of records in a resulting datasheet. You enter OR conditions in different rows of the query design grid.

Activity Steps

 Computers01.mdb

1. Click the **Queries button** [🗗 Queries] on the Objects bar (if it's not already selected), then double-click **Create query in Design view**

2. Click **Categories**, click **Add**, click **Equipment**, click **Add**, then click **Close**

3. Drag **CategoryDesc** from the Categories field list to the first column of the query design grid, then double-click **Description**, **PurchaseDate**, and **InitialValue** in the Equipment field list to add each field to the query design grid

4. Click the **View button** [▦] on the Query Design toolbar to view the datasheet before adding criteria to the query design grid
   53 records appear in the datasheet.

5. Click the **View button** [◿] on the Query Datasheet toolbar to return to Query Design View, click the **Criteria cell** for the CategoryDesc field, type **laptop**, then click the **View button** [▦] on the Query Design toolbar
   17 records match the criterion.

6. Click the **View button** [◿] on the Query Datasheet toolbar, click the **or cell** for the InitialValue field, then type **>2000**
   See Figure 11-3. Access automatically applied quotation marks around the criterion for the CategoryDesc field because it is a Text field.

7. Click the **View button** [▦] on the Query Design toolbar, then press **[Ctrl][End]** to quickly navigate to the last field of the last record
   See Figure 11-4. 19 records appear in the datasheet. Each record has either "laptop" in the CategoryDesc field, a value greater than 2000 in the InitialValue field, or both.

8. Close the query without saving changes

Step 6
You can add as many OR conditions as desired by using additional rows of the query design grid. If you run out of rows, click Insert on the menu bar, then click Rows.

Figure 11-3: OR condition in Query Design View

Equipment field list

Categories field list

or row

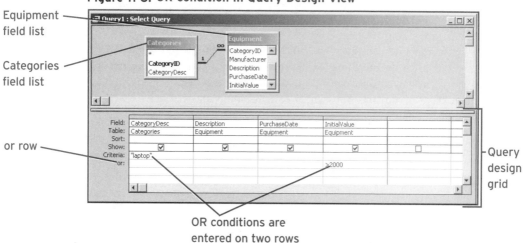

Query design grid

OR conditions are entered on two rows

Figure 11-4: Query Datasheet View with an OR condition applied

Record appears if "laptop" is entered in the CategoryDesc field or if the InitialValue field is greater than 2000

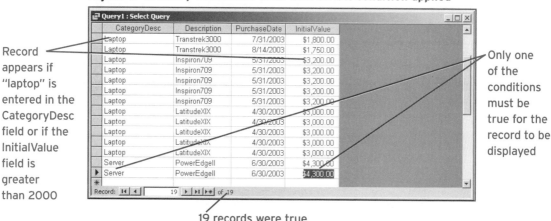

Only one of the conditions must be true for the record to be displayed

19 records were true for at least one of the conditions

Skill Set 11

Refining Queries

Create and Apply Advanced Filters

You can apply filters in Table Datasheet View, Query Datasheet View, or Form View to isolate a subset of records based on criteria that you specify. Advanced filters are similar to queries, because both are used to answer questions about the data in your database, and both use a design grid to enter criteria. Unlike queries, filters are not automatically saved as an object in the database, so they are typically applied for one-time questions that arise while working with data. However, if you build a filter and decide that you want to save the criteria you specified, you can save the filter as a query object in the database.

Activity Steps

 Computers01.mdb

1. Click the **Tables button** 🔲 Tables on the Objects bar (if it's not already selected), then double-click **Equipment** to open it in Datasheet View

2. Click **Records** on the menu bar, point to **Filter**, then click **Advanced Filter/Sort**

3. In the Equipment field list, double-click **Manufacturer**, **PurchaseDate**, and **InitialValue** to add each field to the filter design grid

4. Click the **Criteria cell** for the Manufacturer field, then type **Micron**

Step 5
You can enter more AND conditions to the same Criteria row or more OR conditions to multiple rows of the filter design grid just as you can in Query Design View.

5. Click the **Sort cell** for the PurchaseDate field, click the **list arrow**, click **Ascending**, click the **Sort cell** for the InitialValue field, click the **list arrow**, then click **Ascending**
   See Figure 11-5. Access automatically surrounds criteria in a Text field with quotation marks just as it does in Query Design View. Sort orders are evaluated left-to-right just as they are in Query Design View.

6. Click the **Apply Filter button** 🔽 on the Filter/Sort toolbar
   See Figure 11-6. 15 records match the criteria.

7. Click **Records** on the menu bar, point to **Filter**, then click **Advanced Filter/Sort**

8. Click the **Save As Query button** 💾 on the Filter/Sort toolbar, type **Micron equipment** in the Query Name box, then click **OK**

9. Close the Filter window, close the Equipment table without saving changes, then click **Queries button** 🔲 Queries on the Database window toolbar to confirm that the filter has been saved as a query

Figure 11-5: Filter Design View

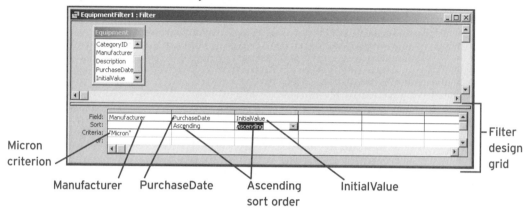

Micron criterion — Manufacturer — PurchaseDate — Ascending sort order — InitialValue — Filter design grid

Figure 11-6: Table Datasheet View with filter applied

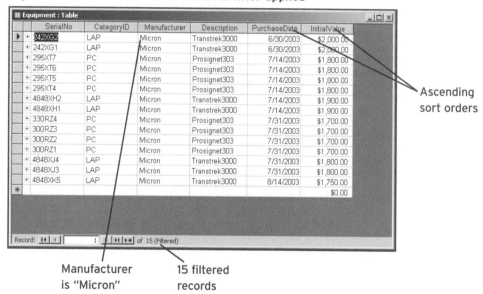

Ascending sort orders

Manufacturer is "Micron"   15 filtered records

Skill Set 11

Refining Queries

Create and Run Parameter Queries

A **parameter query** is a query that contains parameter criteria. **Parameter criteria** prompt you to enter actual criteria each time you run the query. (You **run** a query by opening it in Query Datasheet View.) For example, if you create a query based on an Employees table and enter parameter criteria for the table's Department field, the parameter criteria will prompt you to enter a department name each time you run the query. The department name that you enter determines the records that appear in Query Datasheet View. If you base a form or report on a parameter query, each time you open the form or report, the parameter query will run, prompting you for criteria. You create a parameter query by entering parameter criteria in the Criteria row of the query design grid. You create parameter criteria by typing the text that you want to use as a prompt inside brackets. The text you enter in the brackets appears in a dialog box each time you run the query. You enter the actual criteria entry into a dialog box.

Activity Steps

 Computers01.mdb

1. Click the **Queries button** Queries on the Objects bar (if it's not already selected), click **Inventory Parameter**, then click the **Design button** Design on the Database window toolbar

2. Click the **Criteria cell** for the CategoryDesc field, then type **[Enter category:]**
   See Figure 11-7.

3. Click the **View button** on the Query Design toolbar
   See Figure 11-8. The same text you entered in the Criteria cell is displayed in the dialog box.

4. Type **server** in the Enter Parameter Value dialog box, then click **OK**
   See Figure 11-9. Only two records appear (records with "Server" in the CategoryDesc field).

5. Save and close the Inventory Parameter query

6. Click the **Reports button** Reports on the Objects bar, double-click **Inventory Listing**, type **laptop** in the Enter Parameter Value dialog box, click **OK**, then zoom in as necessary to read the category value
   The Inventory Listing report was previously created from the Inventory Parameter query. Therefore, when you open the Inventory Listing report, you also run the Inventory Parameter query, which prompts you to specify a criterion for the CategoryDesc field.

7. Close the Inventory Listing report

Step 4
If you enter more than one parameter criterion in the query design grid, an Enter Parameter Value dialog box will appear for each parameter criterion entry you add.

Figure 11-7: Entering parameter criteria in the query design grid

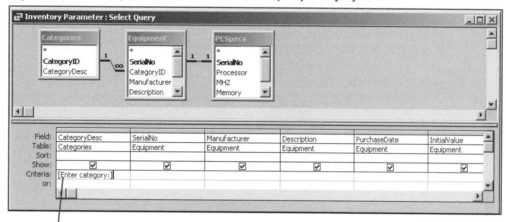

Parameter criteria

Figure 11-8: Enter Parameter Value dialog box

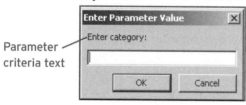

Parameter criteria text

Figure 11-9: Query Datasheet View

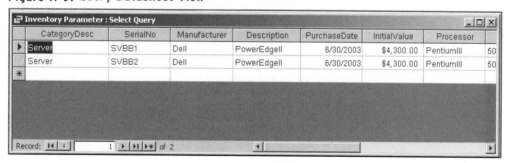

Skill Set 11

Refining Queries

Create and Run Action Queries

An **action query** helps you create, update, or delete data in the database. Unlike a select query, which simply displays a customized view of records in the database, an **action query** actually changes data in the database. There are four types of action queries: **make-table**, **append**, **delete**, and **update**. Table 11-1 provides more information on action queries. You can change an existing select query to an action query or create a new action query. You use the Query Type button on the Query Design toolbar to choose the action query you want, and then you use the query design grid to specify how you want data to be modified when you run the query.

Activity Steps

 Instruments01.mdb

1. Click the **Queries button** on the Objects bar (if it's not already selected), verify that Sales Log is selected, then click the **Design button** on the Database window toolbar

2. Click the **Query Type button list arrow** on the Query Design toolbar, click **Make-Table Query**, type **1Qtr Sales Log** in the Table Name box, then click **OK**
   You will create a table called 1Qtr Sales Log based on the data defined by the Sales Log query, which selects records from the Sales table.

3. Click the **Criteria cell** for the Date field, type **Between 1/1/03 and 3/31/03**, then click the **Run button** on the Query Design toolbar
   See Figure 11-10. Notice that Access added pound signs around the criteria in the Date field. The alert box tells you that you are about to create a table that contains 6 rows and that you cannot undo this.

4. Click **Yes** in the alert box
   You created a table that stores the first quarter sales records, so you no longer need those records in the Sales table. You can run a delete query using the same criteria you used for the make-table query to delete the records between 1/1/03 and 3/31/03 in the Sales table.

5. Click the **Query Type button list arrow**, then click **Delete Query**

6. Click the **Run button** on the Query Design toolbar, then click **Yes** when prompted that you are about to delete 6 rows

7. Close the Sales Log query without saving changes, then click the **Tables button** on the Objects bar

8. Verify that six records appear in the 1Qtr Sales Log table and that these six records were deleted from the Sales table, then close the tables

tip

Step 3
To display a long criteria entry in its entirety, position the pointer on the right edge of a column in the query design grid so that a resize pointer ‹+› appears, then drag the column to widen it. You can also double-click the right edge of the column while the resize pointer ‹+› is displayed to automatically widen the column to the width of the widest entry.

Figure 11-10: Creating a Make-Table query

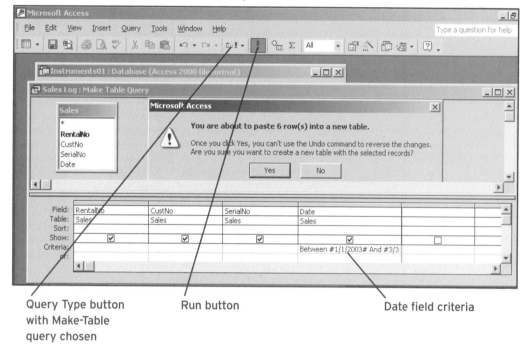

Query Type button
with Make-Table
query chosen

Run button

Date field criteria

TABLE 11-1: Action queries

type of action query	query icon	description	example
Delete		Deletes a group of records from one or more tables	Remove products that are discontinued
Update		Makes global changes to a group of records in one or more tables	Raise prices by 10 percent for all products
Append		Adds a group of records from one or more tables to the end of a table	Add an employee address table from one company to an address table for another
Make-Table		Creates a new table from data in one or more tables	Export records to another Access database or make a backup copy of a table

Skill Set 11
Refining Queries

Use Aggregate Functions in Queries

You use **aggregate functions**, such as Sum, Count, and Avg (average) to calculate summary statistics on groups of records. For example, suppose your database tracks sales. You could use an aggregate function to subtotal the revenue for each country, region, or product, or you could calculate the total sales for each sales representative. See Table 11-2 for a list of aggregate functions that you can use. You specify aggregate functions in Query Design View.

Activity Steps

 Computers01.mdb

1. Click the **Queries button** [⊞ Queries] on the Objects bar (if it's not already selected), double-click **Create query in Design view**, click **Equipment**, click **Add**, then click **Close**

2. Click the **Totals button** Σ on the Query Design toolbar to display the Total row in the query design grid, double-click **InitialValue** in the Equipment field list to add it to the query design grid, click **Group By** in the Total row for the InitialValue field, click the **list arrow**, then click **Sum**

3. Click the **View button** on the Query Design toolbar
   All the values in the InitialValue field for each record have been summed into a single value, $110,450.00. However, when using an aggregate function such as Sum, another field is usually used as the Group By field so that you can view subtotals for groups of records rather than a grand total for all records.

4. Click the **View button** on the Query Datasheet toolbar

5. Click the **Show Table button** on the Query Design toolbar, verify that Categories is selected, click **Add**, then click **Close**
   You'll group the records by the values in the CategoryDesc field so that you can view subtotals for each category.

6. Drag **CategoryDesc** from the Categories field list to the first column, double-click **InitialValue** in the Equipment field list twice, click **Group By** in the Total row for the second InitialValue field, click the **list arrow**, click **Count**, click **Group By** in the Total row for the third InitialValue field, click the **list arrow**, then click **Avg**
   See Figure 11-11.

7. Click the **View button** on the Query Design toolbar, then widen each column in Query Datasheet View to display all the text in the field names
   See Figure 11-12. The InitialValue field is summed, counted, and averaged for each group of records.

8. Close the query without saving it

Step 7
The field names created by aggregate functions that appear at the top of each column in Datasheet View are somewhat long. To create a new field name, insert the desired name followed by a colon in front of the existing entry in the Field cell of the query design grid.

Figure 11-11: Entering an aggregate function in Query Design View

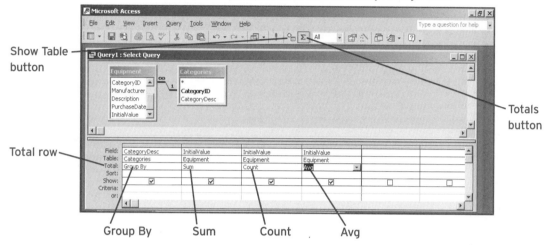

Show Table button

Totals button

Total row

Group By   Sum   Count   Avg

Figure 11-12: Summarized records grouped by CategoryDesc

Group By
CategoryDesc
field values

Sum of
InitialValue
field values

Average of
InitialValue
field values

Count of
InitialValue
field values

TABLE 11-2: Aggregate functions	
aggregate function	**calculates**
Sum	Total of values in a field
Avg	Average of values in a field
Min	Minimum value in a field
Max	Maximum value in a field
Count	Number of values in a field (not counting null values)
StDev	Standard deviation of values in a field
Var	Variance of values in a field
First	Field value from the first record in a table or query
Last	Field value from the last record in a table or query

Skill Set 11

Refining Queries

Target Your Skills

 Computers01.mdb

1 Create a query to select the fields and records shown in Figure 11-13. The query's fields come from the Categories and Equipment tables. Use an OR criteria in the CategoryDesc field to select only the printer and server records.

 Computers01.mdb

2 Create a query using aggregate functions to select the fields and records shown in Figure 11-14. Base the query on the Equipment table. Group the records by the Manufacturer field and apply both the Sum and Count statistics to the InitialValue field.

Figure 11-13

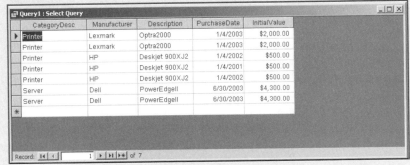

CategoryDesc	Manufacturer	Description	PurchaseDate	InitialValue
Printer	Lexmark	Optra2000	1/4/2003	$2,000.00
Printer	Lexmark	Optra2000	1/4/2003	$2,000.00
Printer	HP	Deskjet 900XJ2	1/4/2002	$500.00
Printer	HP	Deskjet 900XJ2	1/4/2001	$500.00
Printer	HP	Deskjet 900XJ2	1/4/2002	$500.00
Server	Dell	PowerEdgell	6/30/2003	$4,300.00
Server	Dell	PowerEdgell	6/30/2003	$4,300.00

Record: 1 of 7

Figure 11-14

Manufacturer	SumOfInitialValue	CountOfInitialValue
Compaq	$28,200.00	16
Dell	$49,600.00	17
HP	$1,500.00	3
Lexmark	$4,000.00	2
Micron	$27,150.00	15

Record: 1 of 5

Skill List

1. Create and modify reports
2. Add subreport controls to Access reports
3. Sort and group data in reports

In Skill Set 12, you will create and modify reports in Report Design View. You will build a new report and customize an existing report by adding, moving, and formatting controls. You'll also work with the subreport control, which allows you to preview or print multiple reports from one report object. In addition, you'll use sorting and grouping options to determine the order in which records are printed and how records are subtotaled and summarized on a report.

Skill Set 12
Producing Reports

Create and Modify Reports
Create a Report in Report Design View

Instead of using a report creation tool, such as AutoReport or the Report Wizard, you can use Report Design View to create a new report. When you create a report in Report Design View, you need to specify a table or query for the report's Record Source property. After you set the Record Source property, you specify where you want fields from the record source to appear on the report by dragging fields from the field list to the report.

Activity Steps

Step 6
It's generally more difficult to distinguish between text box and label controls in Report Design View (as compared to Form Design View) because the controls are formatted similarly. To determine what type of control is currently selected, click the Properties button. The title bar of the property sheet identifies the type of control that is selected.

file > **Baseball01.mdb**

1. Click the **Reports button**  on the Objects bar (if it's not already selected), double-click **Create report in Design view**, then maximize Report Design View

2. Click the **Properties button** on the Report Design toolbar to open the Report property sheet, click the **Data tab**, click the **Record Source list arrow**, then click **TeamStandings**
   As soon as you choose a table or query for the Record Source property, the field list opens showing the fields in the table or query.

3. Close the property sheet

4. Double-click **TeamStandings** on the title bar of the field list to select all of the fields, then drag them to the middle of the Detail section of the form
   Controls in the Detail section will print once for every record.

5. Click the **Label button** Aα on the Toolbox toolbar, click the left side of the Page Header section, then type **Team Standings Report**
   Controls in the Page Header section will print at the top of each page.

6. Click the **Text Box button** abl on the Toolbox toolbar, click the middle of the Page Footer section, click **Unbound** in the text box, type **=[Page]**, click the label to select it, then press **[Delete]**
   See Figure 12-1. Controls in the Page Footer section will print at the bottom of each page. The =[Page] expression adds the page number.

7. Click the **View button** on the Report Design toolbar, then click the report twice to zoom out and in to view the page header and page footer sections
   See Figure 12-2. This report shows the four fields of the TeamStandings query.

8. Close the report without saving it

Figure 12-1: Creating a report in Report Design View

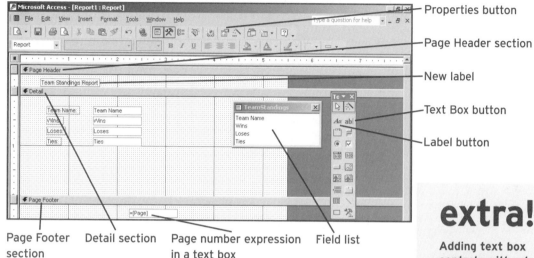

Properties button

Page Header section

New label

Text Box button

Label button

Page Footer section   Detail section   Page number expression in a text box   Field list

Figure 12-2: Previewing a report created in Report Design View

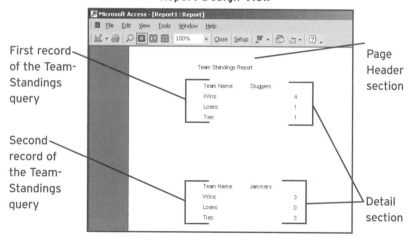

First record of the Team-Standings query

Second record of the Team-Standings query

Page Header section

Detail section

extra!

Adding text box controls without accompanying labels
When you add a text box control to a report, an accompanying label control is also created. The label appears to the left of the text box and describes its contents. If you do not want to automatically create a label control every time you add a text box to a report, you need to change the default properties for the text box control. To change the default properties for a text box, click the **Text Box button** on the Toolbox toolbar, click the **Properties button** on the Report Design toolbar, click the **Format tab** in the property sheet, click the **Auto Label list arrow**, click **No**, and then close the Default Text Box property sheet.

Skill Set 12
Producing Reports

Create and Modify Reports
Modify Report Sections Using Report Design View

You can modify report sections in many ways. For example, you can use the Report Header section to add a descriptive title to the first page of the report. Or, you can use the Report Footer section to add a concluding comment or calculation to the last page of the report. Also, you can move, resize, or format report controls in any section to make a report easier to read or look more professional. You make all modifications to a report in Report Design View. For more information about report sections, see Table 12-1.

Activity Steps

 BaseballO1.mdb

1. Click the **Reports button** 🗎 Reports on the Objects bar (if it's not already selected), click **Player Listing**, click the **Design button** 🔍 Design on the Database window toolbar, then maximize the report (if it's not already maximized)

2. Click **View** on the menu bar, then click **Report Header/Footer** to open the Report Header and Report Footer sections of the report

3. Click the **Label button** *Aa* on the Toolbox toolbar, click the left side of the Report Header section, type **Player Listing**, and then press **[Enter]**
   Controls that you add to the Report Header section print once at the top of the first page of the report. Controls in the Page Header section print just below the Report Header section on the first page and at the top of the report's subsequent pages.

Step 4
To count the number of players in the report, you can use any field that contains a value for each player, such as FName, LName, or TeamName. Be sure to surround a field name in an expression with brackets.

4. Click the **Text Box button** abl on the Toolbox toolbar, click the middle of the Report Footer section, click **Unbound** in the text box, type **=Count([LName])**, click the label to select it, double-click the text in the label, then type **Total Players**
   See Figure 12-3. Controls that you add to the Report Footer section print once at the end of the report. The =Count([LName]) expression will count the number of values in the LName field for every record in the report.

5. Click the **View button** 🔍 on the Report Design toolbar, then click the **Last Page button** ▶❙ on the navigation toolbar
   See Figure 12-4. The last page of the report shows the Total Players label and the result of the =Count ([LName]) expression, because those controls are in the Report Footer section. There are 36 players in this report.

6. Save and close the Player Listing report

Figure 12-3: Modifying a report in Report Design View

Report Header section

New label

Report Footer section

New label

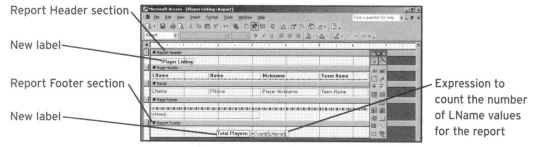

Expression to
count the number
of LName values
for the report

Figure 12-4: Previewing the Report Footer section of a report

Page Header section

Detail section

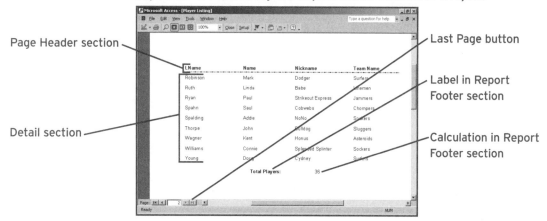

Last Page button

Label in Report
Footer section

Calculation in Report
Footer section

TABLE 12-1: Report sections

section	where does this section print?	what type of information does this section typically present?
Report Header	At the top of the first page of the report	Report title
Page Header	At the top of every page (but below the report header on page one)	Page number, current date, clip art
Group Header	Before every group of records	Value of the current group
Detail	Once for every record	Values for the rest of the fields in the report
Group Footer	After every group of records	Subtotal or count of the records in a group
Page Footer	At the bottom of every page	Page number or current date
Report Footer	At the end of the entire report	Grand total or count for all of the records in the entire report

Skill Set 12

Producing Reports

Add Subreport Controls to Access Reports

A **subreport** is a report within a report. You can use subreports to preview or print multiple reports as a single report object. The report that contains the subreport is called the **main report**. You add a subreport to a main report by adding a **subreport control** in Report Design View. You can add a subreport control by using the **SubReport Wizard.**

Activity Steps

 BaseballO1.mdb

1. Click the **Reports button** 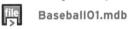 on the Objects bar (if it's not already selected), then double-click **Team Listing** to preview the report

2. Click the **View button** on the Print Preview toolbar to display the Team Listing report in Report Design View, then maximize the report (if it's not already maximized)

3. Using the resize pointer ‡, drag the bottom edge of the Report Footer section down about 1 inch so that you can add controls to it

4. Click the **Subform/Subreport button** on the Toolbox toolbar, then click the left side of the Report Footer section

5. Click the **Use an existing report or form option button**, click **Player Standings** in the list, then click **Next**

6. Click **None** in the list that determines which fields will be used for the link, click **Next**, click **Finish** to accept "Player Standings" as the name for the subreport, then maximize the Team Listing report (if it's not already maximized)
   See Figure 12-5. You can't see the entire Player Standings subreport in Report Design View; however, because you added it as a subreport to the Report Footer section of the Team Listing report, you can preview and print the subreport immediately after the Team Listing report.

7. Click the **View button** on the Report Design toolbar, then click the **Next Page button** on the navigation toolbar
   See Figure 12-6. The Player Standings report appears as the last page of the Team Listing report.

8. Save and close the Team Listing report

Step 4
If the SubReport Wizard doesn't appear, delete the existing subreport control, click the Control Wizards button on the Toolbox toolbar, then redo Step 4.

Figure 12-5: Adding a subreport to a main report

Report Footer section

Subreport control

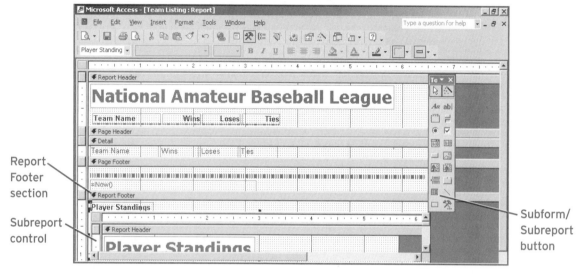

Subform/ Subreport button

Figure 12-6: Previewing a subreport added to the Report Footer section of a main report

Team Listing report

Next Page button

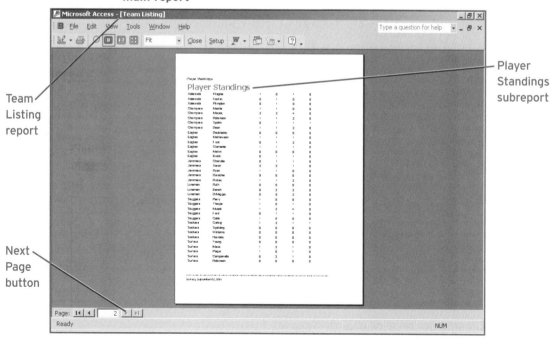

Player Standings subreport

Skill Set 12

Producing Reports

Sort and Group Data in Reports

Grouping means sorting records in ascending or descending order based on the value of a field. When you group records, you add either the **Group Header** section or the **Group Footer** section, or both. For example, if your database contains records for several international clients, you can group client records by a Country field so that a country name appears before each group of clients. You use the Sorting and Grouping window to specify grouping and sorting orders.

Activity Steps

 BaseballO1.mdb

1. Click the **Reports button** 🔲 Reports on the Objects bar (if it's not already selected), then double-click **Player Information**
   The records are sorted in ascending order based on the Team Name field.

2. Click the **View button** 🖳 on the Print Preview toolbar, maximize the report (if it's not already maximized), then click the **Sorting and Grouping button** 🗐 on the Report Design toolbar
   The Sorting and Grouping window shows that the records are currently sorted in ascending order based on the Team Name field.

3. Click the Group Header property box, click the **list arrow**, click **Yes**, click the Group Footer property box, click the **list arrow**, click **Yes**, click the **second Field/Expression cell**, click the **list arrow**, then click **LName**
   See Figure 12-7. The records will be grouped by the Team Name field and sorted within each Team Name group by the values in the LName field. The Team Name Header and Team Name Footer sections appeared when you changed the properties to Yes.

A grouping field is really just a sorting field with its Group Header and/or Group Footer properties set to Yes.

4. Close the Sorting and Grouping window, click the **Team Name text box** in the Detail section, then using the move pointer 🖑, drag the text box up into the Team Name Header section

5. Click the **Text Box button** 🔲 on the Toolbox toolbar, then click the Team Name Footer section below the Home Runs text box

6. Click **Unbound** in the text box control, type **=Sum([Home Runs])**, click the label to select it, double-click the text in the label, then type **Total**
   The calculated control will total the number of Home Runs for each team because it is placed in the Team Name Footer section.

7. Click the **View button** 🔲 on the Report Design toolbar and click the top of the report to zoom in on the first group
   See Figure 12-8.

8. Save and close the Player Information report

Figure 12-7: Setting grouping and sorting properties for a report

Grouping symbol

Team Name Header section

Team Name Footer section

Group Footer property

Sorting and Grouping button

Team Name field is used for grouping

LName field is used for sorting

Group Header property

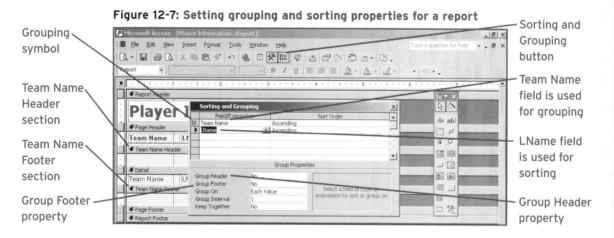

Figure 12-8: Previewing a report that uses a Group Header and Group Footer section

Team Name Header section displays team name before each group

Team Name Footer section displays a subtotal of home runs after each group

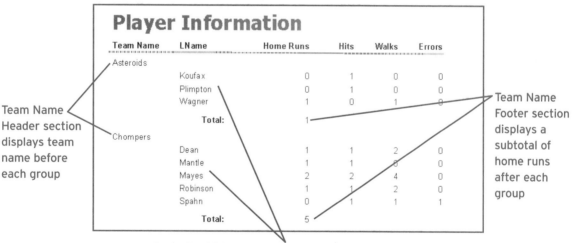

Records within each group are further sorted in ascending order by the LName field

Skill Set 12

Producing Reports

Target Your Skills

 Baseball01.mdb

1 Use the Schedule report to create the report shown in Print Preview in Figure 12-9. Set the Group Header and Group Footer properties for the Ballpark field to Yes, and sort the Game Date field in ascending order within the Ballpark groups. Move the Ballpark text box into the Ballpark Header section and add a text box control to the Ballpark Footer section to count the number of Team Name values for each group. Label the new text box control "Total."

 Baseball01.mdb

2 Add the Player Nicknames report as a subreport to the Current League Standings report as shown in Figure 12-10. Use the SubReport Wizard to make your selections, and select None when prompted to specify a field to create a link. Accept "Player Nicknames" as the name for the subreport.

Figure 12-9

Ballpark	Game Date	Home Team
Edwards Field		
	6/2/2003	Sluggers
	6/9/2003	Linemen
	6/16/2003	Sluggers
	6/23/2003	Linemen
	6/30/2003	Sluggers
	7/7/2003	Sluggers
	Total:	6
South Park		
	6/2/2003	Surfers
	6/9/2003	Chompers

Figure 12-10

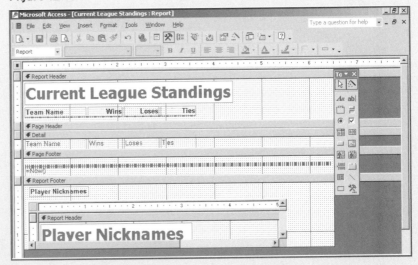

Skill List

1. Establish one-to-many relationships
2. Establish many-to-many relationships

In Skill Set 13, you will use the Relationships window to create relationships between database tables. Relationships allow tables to share information, which minimizes redundant data in your database. The process of determining how tables should be organized and related is called **database normalization**. A properly normalized database provides increased data entry productivity and accuracy, increased reporting flexibility, and decreased storage requirements. You'll also work with **referential integrity**, a set of rules that, when applied to a one-to-many relationship, helps maintain the integrity of the data in the database.

Skill Set 13

Defining Relationships

Establish One-To-Many Relationships

A one-to-many relationship links two tables in an Access database. For example, you can connect a Students table to an Enrollment table using a one-to-many relationship to relate one student to many classes. The fields that define the student (such as StudentID, FirstName, LastName, and Address) need to be entered only once in the Students table. As a student enrolls in additional classes, only one field that uniquely identifies the student, such as StudentID, needs to be entered in the Enrollment table. This field serves as the link between the two tables. It is called the foreign key field in the Enrollments table and the primary key field in the Students table. If you apply referential integrity to the one-to-many link, you ensure that no records are entered in the Enrollment table before the corresponding student is established in the Students table. You create one-to-many relationships and enforce referential integrity using the Relationships window.

Activity Steps

 EastCollege01.mdb

1. Click the **Relationships button** on the Database toolbar to open the Relationships window

2. Click the **Show Table button** 🔲 on the Relationship toolbar, click **Students**, click **Add**, click **Enrollment**, click **Add**, click **Courses**, click **Add**, then click **Close** in the Show Table dialog box

3. Drag the **StudentNo** field from the Students field list to the StudentNo field in the Enrollment field list
   See Figure 13-1.

4. Select the **Enforce Referential Integrity check box**, then click **Create**
   The bold field in a field list is the primary key field for that table. It is always the "one" side of a one-to-many relationship. The foreign key field is the "many" side (indicated by an infinity symbol) of a one-to-many relationship.

5. Drag the **CourseID** field from the Courses field list to the CourseID field in the Enrollment field list

6. Select the **Enforce Referential Integrity check box**, then click **Create**
   See Figure 13-2.

7. Save and close the Relationships window

Step 2

If you accidentally add a field list to the Relationships window twice, click the title bar of one of the duplicate field lists, then press [Delete].

Figure 13-1: Edit Relationships dialog box

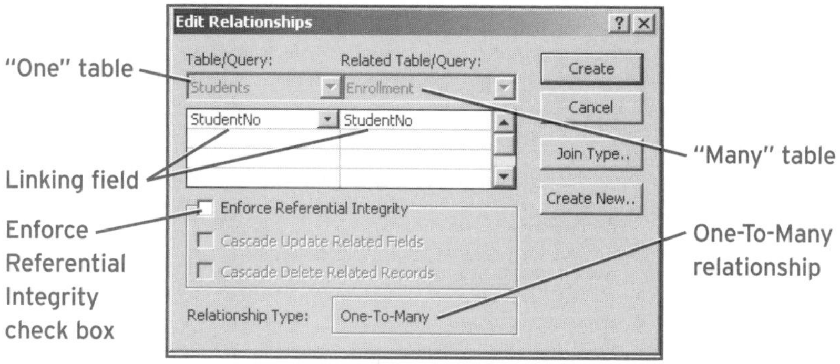

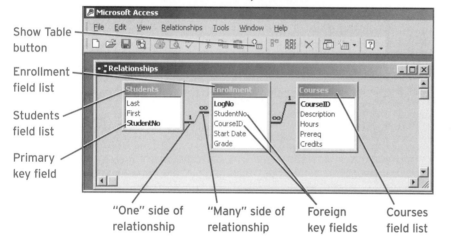

"One" table — Table/Query:

Linking field

Enforce Referential Integrity check box

"Many" table

One-To-Many relationship

extra!

Understanding enforce referential integrity options

When you select the Enforce Referential Integrity check box, the Cascade Update Related Fields and Cascade Delete Related Records check boxes become available. These options should be used with caution because they both make automatic changes to the "many" table when you are working in the "one" table. If you select the **Cascade Update Related Fields** check box and change the linking field in the "one" table, all matching entries in the linking field in the "many" table will be automatically updated. (For example, if the CustomerNumber field is the linking field between the Customers and Sales tables, and you change the CustomerNumber entry in the Customers table, all matching records in the Sales table will be automatically updated.) Similarly, if you select the **Cascade Delete Related Records** check box and you delete a record in the "one" table, all related records in the "many" table will also be automatically deleted.

Figure 13-2: Final Relationships window

Show Table button

Enrollment field list

Students field list

Primary key field

"One" side of relationship

"Many" side of relationship

Foreign key fields

Courses field list

Skill Set 13

Defining Relationships

Establish Many-To-Many Relationships

A **many-to-many** relationship exists between two tables when one record in the first table relates to many records in the second table, and one record in the second table relates to many records in the first table. For example, in a school database, one class relates to many students and one student can take many classes. To make a many-to-many relationship possible, you must create a third table, called a **junction table**. Each original table has a one-to-many relationship with the junction table, which produces the many-to-many relationship between the two original tables. In the school database example, you could use an Enrollments table to serve as the junction table between the Students and Classes tables. One student would relate to many enrollments and one class would relate to many enrollments. Table 13-1 has more information on table relationships.

Activity Steps

 WestCollege01.mdb

1. Click the **Relationships button** ⬚ on the Database toolbar to view the Relationships window
   In this database, one course relates to many students and one student can take many courses. A junction table will join the tables.

2. Close the Relationships window, then double-click **Create table in Design view**

Step 3
Access does not require you to have a primary key field in each table, but since primary key fields uniquely identify each record, it's good database practice to add a primary key field to each table.

3. Type **EnrollmentID**, press [↓], type **StudentID**, press [↓], type **CourseID**, click **EnrollmentID**, then click the **Primary Key** button 🔑 on the Table Design toolbar
   See Figure 13-3. In this junction table, the EnrollmentID field will serve as the primary key field, the StudentID field as the foreign key field to connect this table to the Students table, and the CourseID field as the foreign key field to connect this table to the Courses table.

4. Click the **Save button** 💾 on the Table Design toolbar, type **Enrollment** in the Table Name box, click **OK**, then close Table Design View

5. Click the **Relationships button** ⬚ on the Database toolbar

6. Drag the **StudentID** field from the Students field list to the StudentID field in the Enrollment field list, select the **Enforce Referential Integrity check box**, then click **Create**

7. Drag the **CourseID field** from the Courses field list to the CourseID field in the Enrollment field list, select the **Enforce Referential Integrity check box**, then click **Create**
   See Figure 13-4.

8. Save and close the Relationships window

Figure 13-3: Creating a junction table

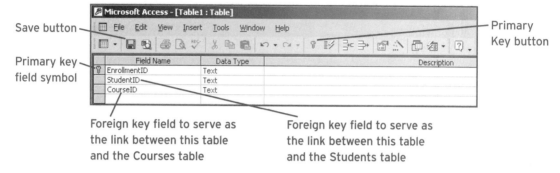

Save button

Primary key field symbol

Primary Key button

Foreign key field to serve as the link between this table and the Courses table

Foreign key field to serve as the link between this table and the Students table

Figure 13-4: Final Relationships window with junction table

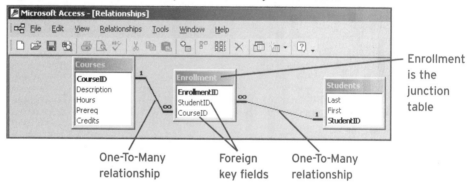

Enrollment is the junction table

One-To-Many relationship

Foreign key fields

One-To-Many relationship

TABLE 13-1: Relationship types

relationship	description	example	notes
One-to-One	A record in Table X is related to only one record in Table Y	The Students table has only one matching record in the Graduation table (which tracks the student's graduation date and final major)	This relationship is not common, because all fields related this way could be stored in one table
One-to-Many	A record in Table X is related to many records in Table Y	One product in the Products table is related to many records in the Sales table	The one-to-many relationship is the most common relationship
Many-to-Many	A record in Table X is related to many records in Table Y, and a record in Table Y is related to many records in Table X	One record in the Teachers table is related to several records in the Courses table, and one course in the Courses table is related to several records in the Teachers table	To create a many-to-many relationship in Access, you must establish a junction table between two original tables

Skill Set 13

Defining Relationships

Target Your Skills

 Metro01.mdb

1 In this database, one doctor can practice at many clinics, and one clinic can support many doctors. Therefore, a many-to-many relationship exists between the Clinics and Doctors tables. Create a junction table named Assignments with the fields and relationships shown in Figure 13-5. Enforce referential integrity on the relationships.

 City01.mdb

2 In this database, one doctor accepts many insurance companies, and one insurance company is used by many doctors. Therefore, a many-to-many relationship exists between the Insurance Companies and Doctors tables. Create a junction table named Authorizations with the fields and relationships shown in Figure 13-6. Enforce referential integrity on the relationships.

Figure 13-5

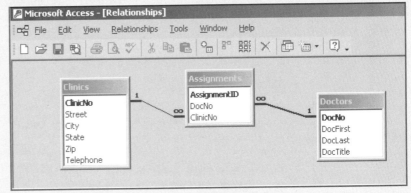

Figure 13-6

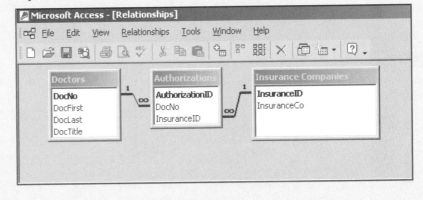

Skill List

1. Create and modify a data access page
2. Save PivotTable and PivotChart views to data access pages

In Skill Set 14, you will build **data access pages**, dynamic Web pages that are created using the page object. A **dynamic** Web page reflects current data when it is opened or refreshed because it retains a connection to the database. You can use data access pages for data entry and reporting. You will also add PivotTables and PivotCharts to data access pages. A **PivotTable** allows you to sort, filter, and analyze data. A **PivotChart** is a graphical representation of data, and like the PivotTable, allows you to analyze data by sorting, filtering, and using other data analysis features.

Skill Set 14

Operating Access on the Web

Create and Modify a Data Access Page

You can use Page Design View to create a new data access page or to modify an existing one. When you create a data access page in Page Design View, you determine what data will be displayed by using the fields from the **Field List**, a window that shows fields from the tables and queries in the database. In Page Design View, you can also modify the size and position of the fields, formatting characteristics (such as fonts, colors, and themes), and the title of the data access page.

Activity Steps

 Cars01.mdb

1. Click the **Pages button** on the Objects bar (if it's not already selected), double-click **Create data access page in Design view**, click **OK** if an alert box appears informing you about Access 2000, then maximize Page Design View

2. Click the **Field List button** 🔳 on the Page Design toolbar to toggle on the Field List, then click the **plus sign** to the left of Inventory in the Field List to view all the fields of the Inventory table
   Expanding a table or query in the Field List shows the object's fields.

3. Drag each field from the Inventory table in the Field List to the "Drag fields from the Field List and drop them on the page" section as shown in Figure 14-1
   When you are adding a field to the data access page, a blue rectangle indicates the border of the section.

4. Click in the **Click here and type title text** placeholder, then type **Car Inventory**

5. Click **Format** on the menu bar, click **Theme**, click **Capsules** in the Choose a Theme list, then click **OK**

6. Click the **View button** 🔳 on the Page Design toolbar to display the data access page in Page View
   See Figure 14-2. Page View shows you how the Web page would appear if saved and opened in Internet Explorer.

7. Close the data access page without saving it

Step 3

If your data access page doesn't look like Figure 14-1, you can move controls in the body by dragging them to a new location, just as if you were working in Form Design View or Report Design View.

Figure 14-1: Adding fields to a data access page in Page Design View

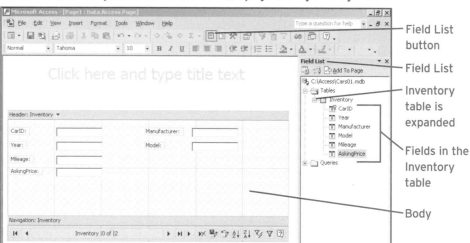

Figure 14-2: The final data access page in Page View

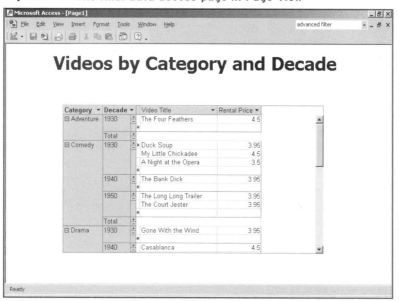

Save PivotTable and PivotChart Views to Data Access Pages

Create a PivotTable on a Data Access Page

You can add a **PivotTable List control** to a data access page to arrange data in a PivotTable. A **PivotTable** summarizes data by columns and rows to make it easy to analyze. A typical PivotTable uses one field as a column heading, another as a row heading, and a third to summarize data (usually subtotal, average, or count) within the body of the PivotTable. To add a PivotTable List control to a data access page, you must work in Page Design View. If you drag an entire table or query object to a data access page, the **Layout Wizard** will appear to help you determine the layout for the fields.

Activity Steps

 Cars01.mdb

1. Click the **Pages button** [Pages] on the Objects bar (if it's not already selected), double-click **Create data access page in Design view**, click **OK** if an alert box appears, then maximize Page Design View

2. Click the **Field List button** on the Page Design toolbar to toggle on the Field List, click the **plus sign** to the left of the Queries folder in the Field List, then drag the **Inventory Value** query to the "Drag fields from the Field List and drop them on the page" section

3. Click the **PivotTable option button** in the Layout Wizard dialog box, then click **OK**

4. Click the **PivotTable List control** to display a hashed border
See Figure 14-3. You will determine the total inventory value (based on the AskingPrice field) for all cars based on manufacturer and year.

5. Close the Field List, right-click the **Manufacturer field**, click **Move To Column Area** on the shortcut menu, right-click the **ModelYear field**, click **Move To Row Area** on the shortcut menu, right-click the **AskingPrice field**, point to **AutoCalc** on the shortcut menu, click **Sum**, then drag the **sizing handles** on the PivotTable List control to expand it

6. Click the **View button** on the Page Design toolbar, click the **Manufacturer list arrow**, deselect the **(All) check box**, select the **Ford check box**, select the **Toyota check box**, then click **OK**

7. Click the **collapse button** in the Ford column, then click the **collapse button** in the Toyota column
See Figure 14-4.

8. Close the page without saving it

Step 4
You cannot move the fields in a PivotTable List control unless the PivotTable displays a hashed border, which indicates that you're editing the control. Click a PivotTable List once to select it. Click a selected PivotTable to edit it.

Figure 14-3: Creating a PivotTable in Page Design View

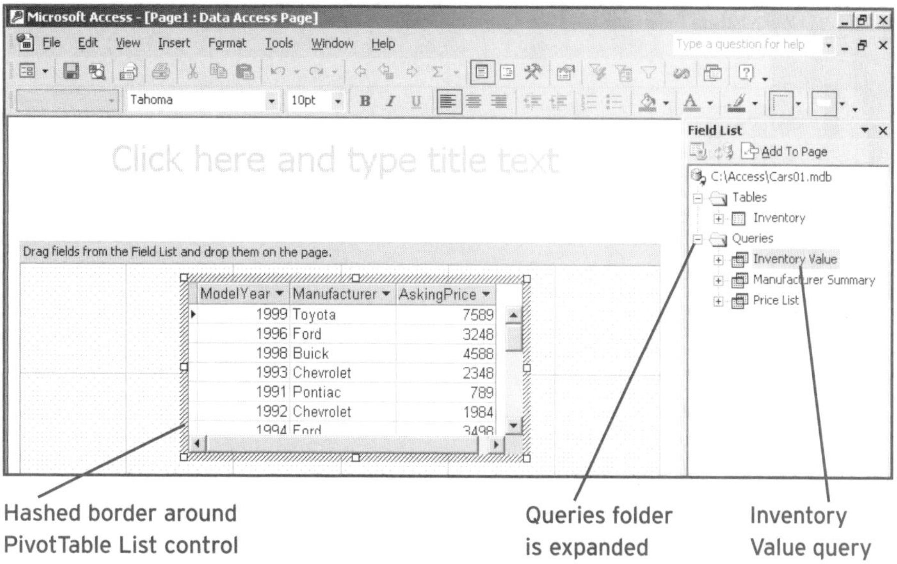

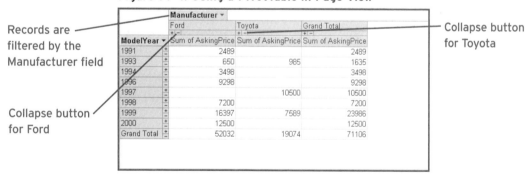

Hashed border around
PivotTable List control

Queries folder
is expanded

Inventory
Value query

Figure 14-4: Using a PivotTable in Page View

Records are
filtered by the
Manufacturer field

Collapse button
for Ford

Collapse button
for Toyota

ModelYear ▼	Sum of AskingPrice (Ford)	Sum of AskingPrice (Toyota)	Sum of AskingPrice (Grand Total)
1991	2489		2489
1993	650	985	1635
1994	3498		3498
1996	9298		9298
1997		10500	10500
1998	7200		7200
1999	16397	7589	23986
2000	12500		12500
Grand Total	52032	19074	71106

Skill Set 14

Operating Access on the Web

Save PivotTable and PivotChart Views to Data Access Pages
Create a PivotChart on a Data Access Page

You can add a **PivotChart control** to a data access page to arrange data in a PivotChart. A **PivotChart** graphically summarizes data. A typical PivotChart uses one field as an x-axis label (the **Category field**), another field for the legend area (the **Series field**), and a third to summarize data (usually subtotal, average, or count) within the body of the PivotChart. For example, you could use a PivotChart to graph the total value of your products summarized by two fields, such as Supplier and Product. To add a PivotChart control to a data access page, you must work in Page Design View. Dragging an entire table or query object to a data access page displays the Layout Wizard, which you use to determine the layout for the fields.

Activity Steps

 Cars01.mdb

1. Click the **Pages button** [Pages] on the Objects bar (if it's not already selected), double-click **Create data access page in Design view**, click **OK** if an alert box appears informing you about Access 2000, then maximize Page Design View

2. Click the **Field List button** on the Page Design toolbar to toggle on the Field List, click the **plus sign** to the left of the Queries folder in the Field List, then drag the **Inventory Value** query to the "Drag fields from the Field List and drop them on the page" section

3. Click the **PivotChart option button** in the Layout Wizard dialog box, click **OK**, then drag the **sizing handles** on the PivotChart control to expand it within the borders of the "Drag fields from the Field List and drop them on the page" section
See Figure 14-5.

4. Click the **plus sign** to the left of Inventory Value in the Field List to display the fields within that query

5. Drag the **ModelYear** field to the "Drop Category Fields Here" section, drag the **Manufacturer** field to the "Drop Series Fields Here" section, then drag the **AskingPrice** field to the "Drop Data Fields Here" section

6. Click the **View button** on the Page Design toolbar, click the **Manufacturer list arrow**, deselect the **(All) check box**, select the **Chevrolet check box**, then click **OK**
See Figure 14-6. You can filter the data in a PivotChart.

7. Close the data access page without saving it

The PivotChart and PivotTable List controls that you add to a data access page work similarly to the PivotChart and PivotTable views you can display for tables, queries, and forms.

Figure 14-5: Creating a PivotChart in Page Design View

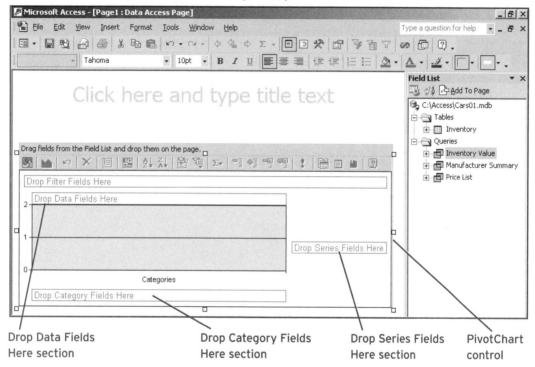

Drop Data Fields
Here section

Drop Category Fields
Here section

Drop Series Fields
Here section

PivotChart
control

Figure 14-6: Using a PivotChart in Page View

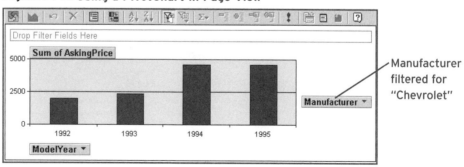

Manufacturer
filtered for
"Chevrolet"

Skill Set 14

Operating Access on the Web

Target Your Skills

 Government01.mdb

1 Use Page Design View to create the PivotTable shown in Figure 14-7. Base the PivotTable on the State Analysis query. Move the State field to the Row Area and the Party field to the Column Area of the PivotTable. Resize the PivotTable to fill the screen, and add the title "PivotTable of State Representatives."

Figure 14-7

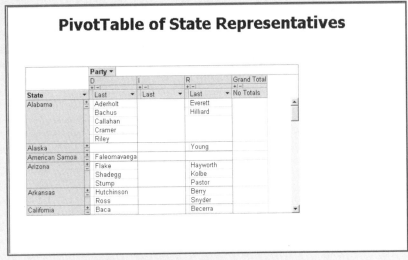

 Government01.mdb

2 Use Page Design View to create the PivotChart shown in Figure 14-8. Base the PivotTable on the State Analysis query. Resize the PivotChart to fill the screen. Add the Last field to the Drop Data Fields Here section, the Party field to the Drop Series Fields Here section, and the State field to the Drop Category Fields Here section. Use the State field to filter the data so that only the data for Alabama and Colorado appears.

Figure 14-8

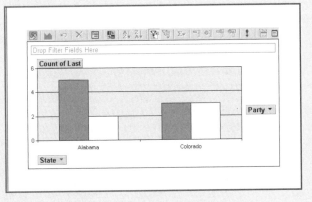

Skill Set 15

Skill List

1. Import XML documents into Access
2. Export Access data to XML documents
3. Encrypt and decrypt databases
4. Compact and repair databases
5. Assign database security
6. Replicate a database

In Skill Set 15, you'll work with Access tools to secure and protect a database. Using encryption, you'll convert database objects and data into a format that is indecipherable to other programs. Using compact and repair tools, you'll organize and compress a database to help it run as efficiently as possible. You'll use passwords to protect a database from unauthorized use, and you'll learn about replication tools that allow you to give remote or traveling users the ability to use and update a database, even when they do not have a physical connection to the database. You'll also import and export XML files into and out of a database.

Import XML Documents into Access

Using **XML** (**Extensible Markup Language**) you can deliver data from one application to another over an intranet or the World Wide Web. The XML file format allows you to share data with many other software applications. An **XML document** is a text file that contains data and Extensible Markup Language tags that identify field names and field values. You can import an XML file as a new table of data into Access. An **XSD** (**Extensible Schema Document**) file accompanies the XML file to further define the structure of the data.

Activity Steps

 Service01.mdb
zips.xml
zips.xsd

Step 2
Access can import many types of files, as listed in the Files of type list in the Import dialog box.

1. Click **File** on the menu bar, point to **Get External Data**, then click **Import**

2. Click the **Look in list arrow**, navigate to the drive and folder where your Project Files are stored, click the **Files of type list arrow**, click **XML Documents**, click **zips.xml**, then click **Import**

3. Click **OK** in the **Import XML** dialog box, then click **OK** when the import process is finished

4. Double-click the **Zips** table to open it in Table Datasheet View
   See Figure 15-1. Twenty-one records with three fields, Zip, City, and State, are imported into the database.

5. Close the Zips table

Figure 15-1: The imported Zips table

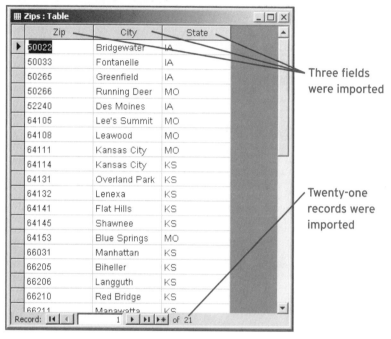

Three fields were imported

Twenty-one records were imported

extra!

Defining the World Wide Web Consortium The **World Wide Web Consortium**, also known as **W3C**, is an international league of companies and associations that supports initiatives to sustain the growth and health of the World Wide Web. W3C recommended XML as a standard way to describe and organize data so that it can be used by multiple programs consistently.

Skill Set 15

Using Access Tools

Export Access Data to XML Documents

The **recordset** consists of the fields and records that are displayed when you open an object. Access can export the recordset of a table to many different file formats, including an XML document. Once your data is in an XML file format, it can be transferred to and used by other software applications that are written to read XML data. When you export Access data to an XML document, you also have the option to export an XSD (Extensible Schema Document) file, which contains structural information about the fields (such as field properties), and an **XSL (Extensible Style Language)** file, which contains formatting information about the data (such as font size and color).

Activity Steps

 Service01.mdb

1. Click the **Tables button** [▦ Tables] on the Objects bar (if it's not already selected), then click **Names**

2. Click **File** on the menu bar, then click **Export**

3. Click the **Save in list arrow**, navigate to the drive and folder where your Project Files are stored, click the **Save as type list arrow**, click **XML Documents**, then click **Export**
   The Export XML dialog box appears, prompting you for information about what you want to export. *See Figure 15-2.*

4. Click **OK** in the Export XML dialog box to export both the data as an XML document and the schema as an XSD document
   A **schema** contains structural information about the data in an XSD file.

5. Start Internet Explorer, click **File** on the menu bar, click **Open**, then click **Browse**

6. In the Microsoft Internet Explorer dialog box, click the **Look in list arrow**, navigate to the drive and folder where your Project Files are stored, click the **Files of type list arrow**, click **All Files**, click **Names.xml** in the files list, click **Open**, then click **OK**
   See Figure 15-3. The XML document opens in the browser window and shows you both the data and tags in an XML document.

7. Close Internet Explorer

Step 6
Another way to view an XML document is to locate it within Windows Explorer and then double-click the filename to automatically open it in Internet Explorer.

Figure 15-2: Export XML dialog box

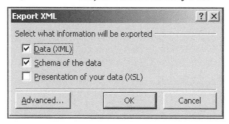

Figure 15-3: Names.xml file displayed in Internet Explorer

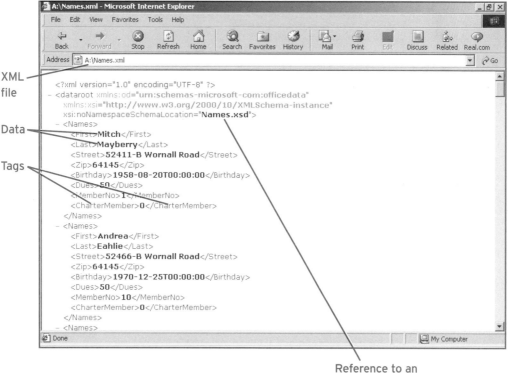

Skill Set 15

Using Access Tools

Encrypt and Decrypt Databases

Encrypting means making database objects and data indecipherable to other programs (such as a word processor or a utility program used to read data). **Decrypting** reverses encryption. Because you can open an encrypted database within Access itself, encryption is usually used in conjunction with other security measures, such as setting user IDs, passwords, and user permissions. Using both encryption and another form of security protects your database from anyone who might attempt to open it within Access and from anyone who might attempt to read the data using other types of programs. Additional threats to your database are described in Table 15-1.

Step 1
If you are using a floppy disk to complete this activity, please copy Service01.mdb to a new floppy disk before doing these steps so that you have plenty of space to complete the encryption and decryption processes.

Activity Steps

 Service01.mdb

1. Close any open databases, but leave Access running
   To encrypt a database, Access must be running, but the database that you want to encrypt must be closed.

2. Click **Tools** on the menu bar, point to **Security**, then click **Encrypt/Decrypt Database**

3. In the Encrypt/Decrypt Database dialog box, click the **Look in list arrow**, navigate to the drive and folder where your Project Files are stored, click **Service01**, then click **OK**

4. Type **Service01E** (for "encrypted") in the File name box, then click **Save**

5. To decrypt a database, click **Tools** on the menu bar, point to **Security**, then click **Encrypt/Decrypt Database**

6. Click **Service01E** in the Encrypt/Decrypt Database dialog box
   See Figure 15-4.

7. Click **OK**, type **Service01D** (for "decrypted") in the File name box, then click **Save**
   You can also encrypt and decrypt a database without renaming it. The encrypted or decrypted database will replace the existing database. However, it's always a good idea to have a backup of any file that you are overwriting, should anything go wrong during the encryption or decryption process.

Figure 15-4: Encrypt/Decrypt Database dialog box

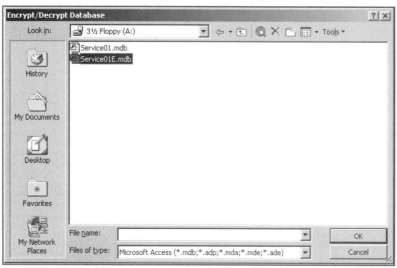

TABLE 15-1: Database security threats

incident	what can happen	appropriate actions
Virus	Viruses can cause many kinds of damage, ranging from profane messages to destruction of files	Purchase the leading virus-checking software for each computer, and keep it updated
Power outage	Power problems such as **brown-outs** (dips in power often causing lights to dim) and **spikes** (surges in power) can cause damage to the hardware, which can render the computer useless	Purchase a **UPS** (Uninterruptible Power Supply) to maintain constant power to the file server (if networked) and **surge protectors** (power strip with surge protection) for each user
Theft or intentional damage	Theft or intentional damage of computer equipment or data destroys valuable assets	Place the file server in a room that can be locked after hours, use network drives for user data files that are backed up on a daily basis, use off-site storage for backups, set database passwords and encryption so that files that are stolen cannot be used, and use computer locks for equipment that is at risk, especially laptops

Skill Set 15

Using Access Tools

Compact and Repair Databases

When you delete data or objects in an Access database, the disk space formerly occupied by the deleted information remains unused. This means that as you work with a database over time, it becomes fragmented, using more disk space and running slower. **Compacting** a database rearranges the database on your disk, and reuses the space formerly occupied by the deleted objects. A compacted database minimizes disk storage requirements and improves performance. The compacting process also automatically repairs damaged databases, which can help you find and correct structural problems before they become bigger issues.

Changes that you make in the Options dialog box affect every database. So if you are using a shared computer, it is best to use the default options rather than customizing the Access environment for all databases.

Activity Steps

file > ServiceO1.mdb

1. Click **Tools** on the menu bar, point to **Database Utilities**, then click **Compact and Repair Database**

2. To automatically compact and repair a database each time it is closed, click **Tools** on the menu bar, click **Options**, then click the **General tab** in the Options dialog box (if it is not already selected)
   See Figure 15-5.

3. If the ServiceO1 database is stored on your hard drive, select the **Compact on Close check box**, then click **OK**

4. If the ServiceO1 database is stored on a floppy disk, click **Cancel**
   The Compact on Close option can corrupt your database if it is stored on a floppy disk that doesn't have sufficient room to complete the process. For more information on the Compact on Close option, see the Extra! on page 17 of the Getting Started Skill Set.

Figure 15-5: Options dialog box

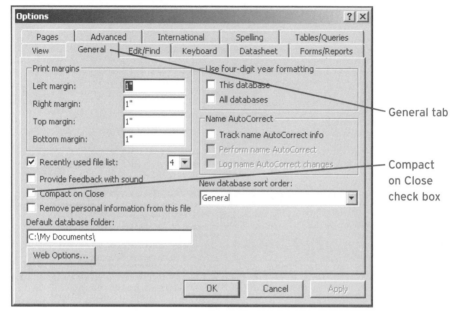

General tab

Compact
on Close
check box

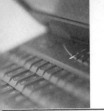

Skill Set 15

Using Access Tools

Assign Database Security
Set a Database Password

You can secure an Access database in many ways, as described in Table 15-2. Setting passwords is a common method to secure information. You can set three types of passwords for an Access database: database, security account, and Visual Basic for Applications (VBA) passwords. If you set a **database password**, all users must enter a password before they can open the database file. Once they open it, users have full access to the database. **Security account passwords** act at the user level rather than at the file level. Setting this type of password enables you to limit what a user can do to the database, such as read, delete, or edit data. **VBA passwords** prevent unauthorized users from modifying VBA code.

Activity Steps

 Service02.mdb

1. Close any open databases, but leave Access running, click the **Open button** on the Database toolbar, navigate to the drive and folder where your Project Files are stored, click **Service02** in the Open dialog box, click the **Open button list arrow**, then click **Open Exclusive**
   To set or change a database password, the database must be opened in **Exclusive Mode**, an environment that doesn't allow users to work in the database simultaneously.

2. Click **Tools** on the menu bar, point to **Security**, then click **Set Database Password**

3. Type **ames4321** in the Password box, press **[Tab]**, then type **ames4321** in the Verify box
   See Figure 15-6.

4. Click **OK**, then close the database

5. To test the password, open the **Service02** database

6. Type **ames4321** in the Password Required dialog box, then click **OK**

7. To unset the database password, close the database, click the **Open button** on the Database toolbar, click **Service02** in the Open dialog box, click the **Open button list arrow**, click **Open Exclusive**, type **ames4321** in the Password Required dialog box, then click **OK**

8. Click **Tools** on the menu bar, point to **Security**, click **Unset Database Password**, type **ames4321** in the Unset Database Password dialog box, then click **OK**

Step 4
Passwords are case sensitive and harder to guess if they contain both characters and numbers.

Figure 15-6: Set Database Password dialog box

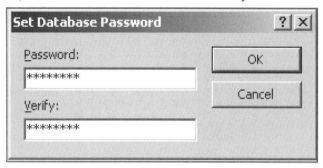

TABLE 15-2: Methods to help secure an Access database

method	description
passwords	Protects the database from unauthorized use, and can be implemented at the database, workgroup, or VBA level
encryption	Compacts the database and makes the data indecipherable to other programs
startup options	Hides or disables certain functions when the database is opened
show/hide objects	Shows or hides objects in the Database window, which can prevent users from unintentionally deleting objects
split a database	Separates the data (table objects) from the rest of the objects (such as forms and reports) into two databases that work together; splitting a database allows you to give each user access to only those specific database objects that they need, instead of all the objects in the database

Skill Set 15

Using Access Tools

Assign Database Security
Create Workgroups and Permissions

You can set permissions to restrict user activities in a database and add a level of security. **Permissions** specify the activities that users are allowed to complete, such as modifying or entering new data. You assign permissions to a user by assigning permissions to a **workgroup**, a list of database users who have the same needs. See Table 15-3 for a list of permissions. To set up workgroups, you create a workgroup information file or add users to an existing one. A **workgroup information file** defines users, passwords, and user permissions. Only the workgroup's administrator (Admin), the user who has all permissions, can set permissions. If you create a new workgroup information file, you must join the workgroup as the administrator. If your database has never been secured, you are automatically the administrator of a default workgroup information file, so you can bypass the steps to join a workgroup as an administrator and then set up users, workgroups, and permissions.

Activity Steps

 Service03.mdb

1. Click **Tools** on the menu bar, point to **Security**, then click **User and Group Accounts**

2. Click **New** in the User and Group Accounts dialog box, type **Joe** in the Name box, type **swim50** in the Personal ID box, then click **OK**
   You can add users and workgroups (group accounts) because you are the administrator of the default workgroup information file.

3. Click the **Groups tab**, click **New**, type **Accounting** in the Name box, type **money121** in the Personal ID box, then click **OK**

4. Click the **Users tab**, click **Accounting** in the Available Groups list, click the **Name list arrow**, click **Joe**, then click **Add**
   See Figure 15-7.

5. Click **OK** in the User and Group Accounts dialog box
   Now you can set permissions within a database file.

6. Click **Tools** on the menu bar, point to **Security**, then click **User and Group Permissions**

7. Click the **Groups option button**, click **Accounting** in the User/Group Name list, click the **Object Type list arrow**, click **Query**, click the **Member Activity** query in the Object Name list, select the **Read Data check box** as shown in Figure 15-8, then click **OK**

8. To delete the new group and user, click **Tools** on the menu bar, point to **Security**, click **User and Group Accounts**, click the **Users** tab, click **Joe** in the Name list, click **Delete**, click the **Groups** tab, click **Accounting** in the Name list, click **Delete**, then click **OK**

Step 1
As the administrator, you can set up a new workgroup information file for a database. Click Tools on the menu bar, point to Security, click Workgroup Administrator, then click Create to create a new workgroup information file for a database.

Figure 15-7: User and Group
Accounts dialog box

New
Accounting
group

Default
groups

Add

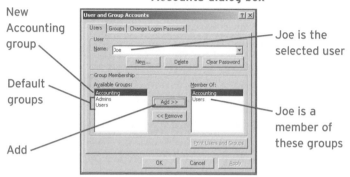

Joe is the
selected user

Joe is a
member of
these groups

Figure 15-8: User and Group
Permissions dialog box

Accounting
group is
selected

Groups
option
button

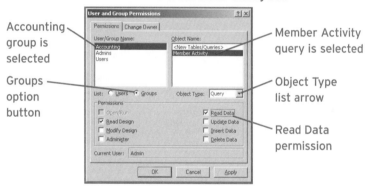

Member Activity
query is selected

Object Type
list arrow

Read Data
permission

TABLE 15-3: Workgroup permissions

permission	description
Open/Run	Open the specified database, form, or report, or run the specified macro
Open Exclusive	Open a database in Exclusive Mode
Read Design	View objects (tables, queries, forms, reports, or macros) in Design View
Modify Design	View, modify, and delete objects (tables, queries, forms reports, or macros)
Administer	For a database, set a database password, replicate a database, or change start properties; For objects (tables, queries, forms, reports, macros), have full access including the ability to assign permissions
Read Data	View data in tables and queries
Update Data	View and modify, but not insert or delete, records in tables and queries
Insert Data	View and insert, but not modify or delete, data in tables and queries
Delete Data	View and delete, but not modify or insert, data in tables and queries

Skill Set 15

Using Access Tools

Replicate a Database

If you want to copy a database to another computer, such as a home computer or a laptop that you use when traveling, you can create a replica of the database. A **replica** is a special copy that keeps track of changes made in both the original database (called the **Design Master**) and the copy so that the files can be reconciled and updated at a later date. The Design Master and all replicas created from the Design Master are called the **replica set**. The process of making the copy is called **replication**, and the process of reconciling and updating changes between the replica and the master is called **synchronization**.

Activity Steps

 Service04.mdb

1. Click **Tools** on the menu bar, point to **Replication**, click **Create Replica**, then click **Yes** in the alert box informing you that the database will be closed and converted into the Design Master

2. Click **No** when prompted to make a backup, navigate to the drive and folder where you want to store your replica, click **OK** to create a replica of the database with the filename "Replica of Service04," then click **OK** in the alert box that appears

3. Double-click the **Names** table, then change Daniels in the Last field of the first record to **Zamboni**
See Figure 15-9. Replica icons appear to the left of the tables within a replicated database, and "Design Master" appears on the title bar. Data entered or edited in the Design Master can be resynchronized with replica databases (or vice versa).

4. Close the Names table, close the Service04 database, click the **Open button** 📂 on the Database toolbar, double-click **Replica of Service04** to open the replica database, double-click the **Names** table to observe that the first record still shows "Daniels," then close the Names table

5. Click **Tools** on the menu bar, point to **Replication**, click **Synchronize Now**, click **OK**, click **Yes** to temporarily close the database, then click **OK** when informed that the synchronization was successful

6. Double-click the **Names** table
See Figure 15-10. Note that the edit to the first record, originally entered in the Design Master, was synchronized with the replica.

7. Close the Names table

Replication works well when the Design Master is located on a file server and replicas are located in a Briefcase folder on a laptop.

Figure 15-9: Changing an entry in the Design Master

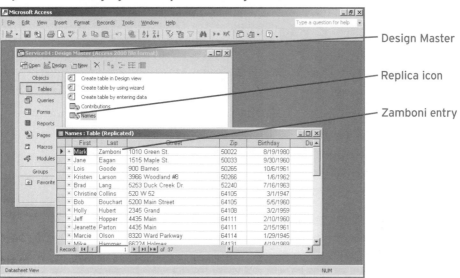

Design Master

Replica icon

Zamboni entry

Figure 15-10: Viewing the change in the replica after synchronization

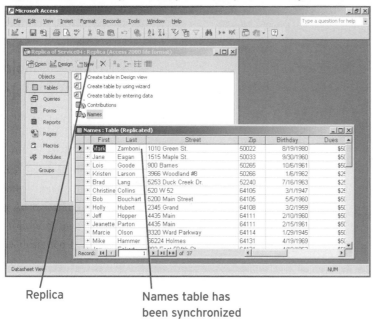

Replica

Names table has been synchronized

Skill Set 15

Using Access Tools

Target Your Skills

 Travel01.mdb

1 Import the countries.xml file into the Travel01 database, then open the Countries table in Table Datasheet View as shown in Figure 15-11. Compact and repair the Travel01 database.

Figure 15-11

 Travel01.mdb

2 Export the Cities table in the Travel01 database to an XML file named Cities. Export both the XML data as well as the schema of the data. View the Cities.xml file in Internet Explorer as shown in Figure 15-12.

Figure 15-12

Skill Set 16

Creating Database Applications

Skill List

1. Create Access modules
2. Use the Database Splitter
3. Create an MDE file

In Skill Set 16, you will work with tools that help you transform an Access database into a full application. In this context, **application** refers to an Access database that has been customized to meet the needs of a specific audience. For example, you could add command buttons that perform specific actions to make a form and a database easier to use. You could also split a database into multiple parts to improve its overall performance and to add a level of security. Or, you could create an **MDE** database, a special copy of a database that is used both to improve database performance and to restrict users from making changes in Design View of most objects.

Skill Set 16

Creating Database Applications

Create Access Modules
Create a Class Module in a Form Using the Command Button Wizard

Modules store **Visual Basic for Applications (VBA)** programming code. **VBA** is a programming language packaged within each program of the Microsoft Office suite. VBA enables you to customize a program. For example, you might use VBA to help users navigate through various forms, making the database easier to use. Access has two types of modules: **global modules**, which contain VBA code used throughout an entire database, and **class modules**, which contain VBA code used only in the specific form or report object in which the code is stored. For example, when you use the **Command Button Wizard** to create a custom command button, you create VBA code, which is stored in a class module in the form.

Activity Steps

 Inventory01.mdb

1. Click the **Forms button** on the Objects bar (if it's not already selected), verify that **Equipment Entry Form** is selected, click the **Design button** on the Database window toolbar, then maximize Form Design View

Step 5
Even if you delete a command button in Form Design View, the associated VBA code remains. To delete the VBA code, open the Code window, then delete every line from the Sub statement to the End Sub statement for that button.

2. Click the **Toolbox button** on the Form Design toolbar to toggle on the Toolbox toolbar (if it's not already displayed), click the **Command Button button** on the Toolbox toolbar, then click about 1 inch to the right of the Processor text box on the form
The Command Button Wizard includes six different categories of command buttons. Each category contains several common actions that you can assign to a command button.

3. Click **Record Operations** in the Categories list, then click **Print Record** in the Actions list
See Figure 16-1.

4. Click **Next**, click **Next** to accept the image, type **PrintRecord** as a meaningful button name, then click **Finish**
See Figure 16-2.

5. Click the **Code button** on the Form Design toolbar to view the class module that you created by using the wizard
See Figure 16-3. You can enter and edit VBA statements in this window. The **Sub statement** marks the beginning of the VBA code, and the **End Sub statement** marks the end.

6. Close the Microsoft Visual Basic window, then click the **View button** on the Form Design toolbar

7. Click the **PrintRecord button** to test it, then save and close the Equipment Entry Form

Figure 16-1: Command Button Wizard dialog box

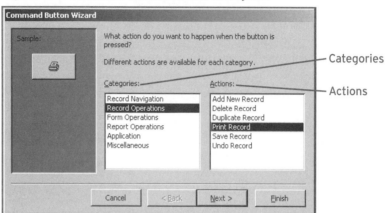

Figure 16-2: A new command button in Form Design View

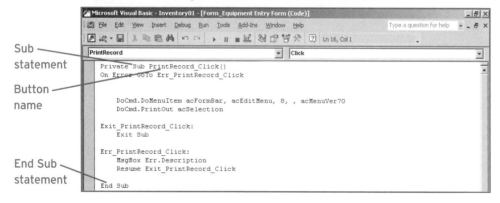

Figure 16-3: Viewing the VBA code in a class module

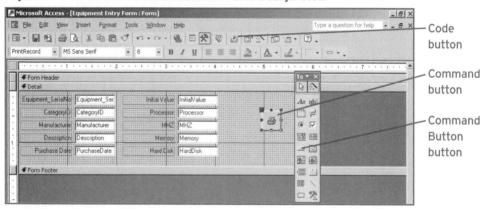

Skill Set 16

Creating Database Applications

Create Access Modules
Create a Global Module to Store a Custom Function

When you click the Modules button on the Objects bar, global modules are displayed in the Database window. It's common to use global modules to store custom functions, VBA code that performs calculations in queries, forms, and reports. Although Access provides many built-in functions such as Sum, Count, and Avg (average), you might want to create a new function that simplifies a custom calculation. For example, you might use VBA to create a custom function called YearsOfService that calculates the number of years an employee has worked for a company.

Activity Steps

 Personnel01.mdb

1. Click the **Modules button** [Modules] on the Objects bar, then click the **New button** [New] on the Database window toolbar

2. Create the VBA function named **YearsOfService** by entering the VBA code as shown in Figure 16-4
   The Option Compare Database statement is provided automatically in new modules. It sets rules for how text is sorted in a Text field.

3. Click the **Save button** [save] on the Standard toolbar, type **Custom Functions** in the Module Name box, then click **OK**
   You defined the YearsOfService function using two existing Access functions, Int and Now. The value of the DateOfHire argument is subtracted from Now(). (Now() represents the current date.) This subtraction results in the number of days that the employee has worked. The number is then divided by 365 to calculate the number of years. The Int function determines the integer portion of the answer.

4. Close the Microsoft Visual Basic window, click **Queries** [Queries] on the Objects bar, then double-click **Create query in Design view**

5. Click **Add** in the Show Table dialog box to add the Employees field list to Query Design View, then click **Close**

6. Scroll down, double-click the DateHired field to add it to the first column of the query design grid, click the **Field cell** in the second column, then type Service:YearsOfService([DateHired])
   See Figure 16-5. You created a new calculated field named Service that uses the YearsOfService custom function you previously created in a global module.

7. Click the **View button** [view] on the Query Design toolbar
   See Figure 16-6. The Service field calculates the years of service.

8. Save the query using the name Years of Service, then close it

Step 2
VBA is not case sensitive, but using uppercase and lowercase characters in the function name helps clarify the code.

Figure 16-4: Defining a custom function in the Microsoft Visual Basic window

Enter this
VBA code

Automatically
entered

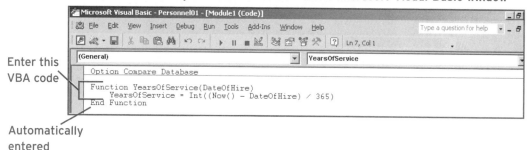

Figure 16-5: Creating a calculated field using the custom
function in Query Design View

Calculated
field name

Expression
using the new
YearsOfService
function

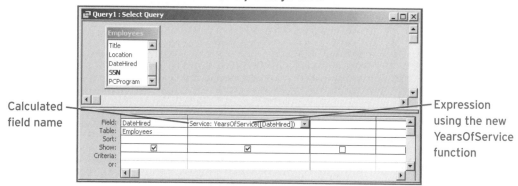

Figure 16-6: Query Datasheet View of
calculated field

New calculated
field named
Service

Answer is
calculated
using the new
YearsOfService
function

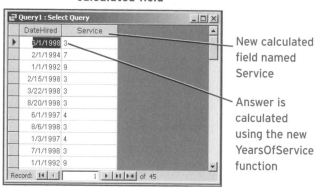

Skill Set 16

Creating Database Applications

Use the Database Splitter

The **Database Splitter** feature splits a database into two files: the **back-end database**, which contains tables (all the data) typically stored on a shared file server, and the **front-end database**, which contains other database objects, such as queries, forms, and reports, stored on user computers. You can copy and customize the front-end database for as many users as needed. Each front-end database contains linked tables that connect it to the data stored in the back-end database. Front-end database users share a single copy of data stored in the back-end database and have fast access to all other objects stored on their own computer. A split database adds a level of customization, because a database administrator can customize each front-end database to contain only the queries, forms, and reports that each user needs. A split database also adds a level of security, because users can't modify a table's design from a front-end database.

Activity Steps

 Derby01.mdb

1. Click **Tools** on the menu bar, point to **Database Utilities**, then click **Database Splitter**

2. Click **Split Database** in the Database Splitter dialog box

3. Click the **Save in list arrow**, navigate to the drive and folder where your Project Files are stored, then click **Split** to save the back-end database with the name Derby01_be

4. Click **OK** when informed that the split was successful, then click the **Tables button** 🔲 Tables on the Objects bar (if it's not already selected)
   See Figure 16-7. The original Derby01 database is now a front-end database and contains no data. Instead, it contains a link to the Stats table, which is stored in the Derby01_be back-end database. Therefore, front-end database users can view, edit, and enter data in tables, but they cannot modify table objects in Table Design View.

5. Click the **Forms button** 🔲 Forms on the Objects bar
   A front-end database retains the original query, form, and report objects that it had before it was split.

6. Right-click the **Start button** on the taskbar, click **Explore**, navigate to the folder that contains your Project Files, then double-click **Derby01_be**
   The back-end database contains the Stats table. Normally, the back-end database would be on a server, so everyone using a front-end database could access the data stored in the back-end database.

7. Click the **Forms button** 🔲 Forms on the Objects bar
   The back-end database contains no other objects.

Step 3
You can give a back-end database any valid filename, but "be" in the default filename can remind you that it is the "back-end" database.

Figure 16-7: Front-end database

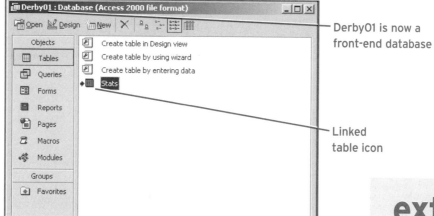

DerbyO1 is now a
front-end database

Linked
table icon

extra!

Understanding client/server computing

Splitting a database into a front-end and back-end database is an excellent example of client/server computing. **Client/server computing** can be defined as two or more information systems cooperatively processing to solve a problem. In most implementations, the **client** is defined as the user's PC and the **server** is defined as the shared file server, mini-, or mainframe computer. The server usually handles corporate-wide computing activities, such as data storage and management, security, and connectivity to other networks.

Skill Set 16

Creating Database Applications

Create an MDE File

An Access **MDE file** is a special copy of a database that prevents others from opening or editing form, report, or module objects in Design View. Users can still enter data in the MDE file just like they can in the original database, but they can't view or copy the development work of the form, report, and module objects. An MDE file is much smaller than an **MDB file** (a regular database file), making it easier to distribute and run faster than the original MDB file. To create an MDE file using Access 2002, your database must be in an Access 2002 file format.

Activity Steps

 Technology01.mdb

1. Click **Tools** on the menu bar, point to **Database Utilities**, point to **Convert Database**, then click **To Access 2002 File Format**

2. Type **Technology2002** in the File name box, click the **Save in list arrow**, navigate to the drive and folder where your Project Files are stored, click **Save**, then click **OK** when informed about Access 2000

3. Close the database, but leave Access running

4. Click **Tools** on the menu bar, point to **Database Utilities**, then click **Make MDE File**

5. Click **Technology2002**, then click **Make MDE**

6. Type **TechnologyMDE** in the File name box, click **Save**, then close Access

7. Right-click the **Start button** on the taskbar, click **Explore**, navigate to the folder that contains your Project Files, then double-click **TechnologyMDE**

8. Click the **Forms button** 🔲 Forms on the Objects bar
   See Figure 16-8.

9. Click each object button on the Objects bar
   The Design button is not available for any database object in an MDE file except for tables and queries.

Step 1
By default, databases created in Access 2002 are Access 2000 version databases so that they can be opened in Access 2000 without going through any conversion process. Access file format version information appears on the Database window title bar.

Figure 16-8: Using an MDE file

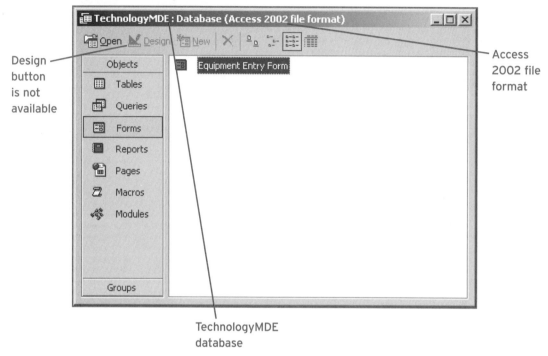

Design button is not available

Access 2002 file format

TechnologyMDE database

Skill Set 16

Creating Database Applications

Target Your Skills

 Physicals01.mdb

1 In Form Design View of the Patient Entry Form, use the Command Button Wizard to add three command buttons to the form as shown in Figure 16-9. Use the Go To First Record action, the Go To Last Record action, and the Close Form action for the command buttons. Use the default pictures for each button, and use the meaningful button names of GoToFirst, GoToLast, and CloseForm. Test the buttons in Form View.

 WellVisits01.mdb

2 Create an MDE file from the WellVisits01 version Access 2000 database by converting it to an Access 2002 version database with the name WellVisits2002, and then making an MDE file named WellVisitsMDE from the WellVisits2002 database. The final WellVisitsMDE file is shown in Figure 16-10.

Figure 16-9

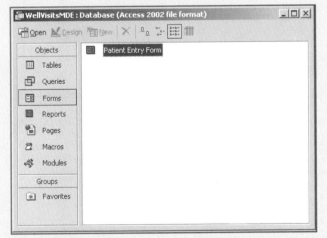

Figure 16-10

Access 2002 Core Projects Appendix

Projects List

Project 1 – Contact Database for Step One Consulting

Project 2 – Event Database for Great Prairie Jazz Festival

Project 3 – Winners Database for Classic Car Races

Project 4 – Photography Database for French Archeology Project

Project 5 – Conference Database for E-Commerce Forum

Project 6 – Properties Database for Powder Trails Realty

Project 7 – Sales Database for Precious Pets

Project 8 – Great Hiking Trails Database

The Access Core skill sets cover the skills you need to create and work with simple Access databases. You learn how to create, format, and modify the principal database objects: tables, forms, reports, and data access pages. You also learn how to import data into Access and how to export data from Access tables into other Office applications. In the following projects, you'll practice your skills by opening and working with databases designed for a variety of purposes.

Project for Skill Set 1

Creating and Using Databases

Contact Database for Step One Consulting

You've just been hired by Step One Consulting, a small firm based in Minneapolis that offers corporate clients seminars in written and oral communications. You've been asked to expand the database the company uses to manage its contacts. To get an idea of the kinds of tables included in a contact database, you'll use the Database wizard to create a Contact Management database. Then you'll open another version of the database, navigate through some of the tables and forms, view and navigate a subdatasheet, and format one of the datasheets.

Step 5
Click the list arrow next to Gerrie Wilcox, then select Susan Ing.

Activity Steps

1. Start Access, click **General Templates**, and then select the **Contact Management** template from the Databases tab

2. Save the database as **Contacts.mdb**

3. Step through the Database wizard, accepting the default for Step 2, selecting the **Sumi Painting** style for screen displays and the **Soft Gray** style for printed reports, and then entering **Step One Consulting Contacts** as the database title

4. From the database window, view the **Calls table**, view the **Contacts form**, explore some of the other tables and forms, then close the database

5. Open **AC_Project1.mdb**, open the **Calls table**, navigate to **Record 26**, then change the name to **Susan Ing**

6. Open the **Contacts form**, navigate to **Record 4**, change **Tom** to **Thomas** in the FirstName field, then close the form

7. Open the **Contacts table**, expand the subdatasheet for Munesh Nanji, compare your screen to Figure AP 1-1, then collapse the subdatasheet

8. Open the Datasheet Formatting dialog box, apply the **Aqua** background color and the **Blue** gridline color, close the dialog box, then compare the formatted datasheet to Figure AP 1-2

 close AC_Project1.mdb

Figure AP 1-1: Subdatasheet for Contacts table

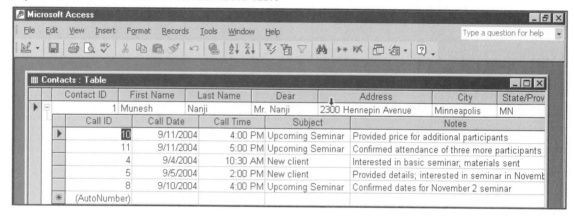

Figure AP 1-2: Formatted datasheet for Contacts table

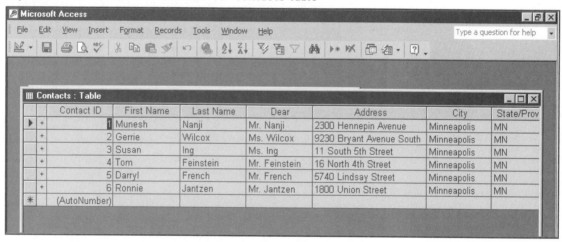

Project for Skill Set 2

Creating and Modifying Tables

Event Database for Great Prairies Jazz Festival

For the past two years, the Great Prairie Jazz Festival in the Red River Valley has welcomed jazz artists from around the world for a three-day festival of the best in avant-garde and mainstream jazz. This year, the festival administration has decided to use Access to organize data about the performers invited to play at 15 venues during the festival. You will help by creating a new database containing two tables. The Performers table will contain contact information about each performer or group, and the Venues table will list the time and place where the performances take place. You will use the Table Wizard to create the Performers table, and then you will work in Table Design view to create the Venues table.

Step 2
Remember to click the Rename Field button to change the name of a field.

Step 8
In the Lookup Wizard, select the I will type in the values I want option, and type the three entries into the cells of one column.

Activity Steps

1. Create a database called **Festival.mdb**

2. Use the Table Wizard to create a table from the **Mailing List** sample that includes the following fields: **FirstName**, **LastName**, OrganizationName changed to **GroupName**, **Address**, **City**, State changed to **State/Province**, **PostalCode**, and **Country/Region**

3. Complete the Wizard by naming the table **Performers** and setting a primary key

4. Enter the data for the first two records shown in the table in Figure AP 2-1, then close the table

5. Create a new table in Design view using the following fields: **Date**, **Time**, **Venue**, **Performer**, and **Phone**

6. Select the **Date/Time** data type for the Date field

7. Save the table as **Venues** and click **Yes** to create a primary key

8. Use the Lookup Wizard to create a lookup field for the Venue field that contains the following three choices: **Main Stage**, **Amphitheater**, and **Lakeside**

9. Add the **Phone Number** input mask to the Phone field, select the option to show symbols, then enter data for the three venues as shown in Figure AP 2-2

 close Festival.mdb

Figure AP 2-1: Records for the Performers table

Record 1		Record 2	
FirstName	Cara	FirstName	Paul
LastName	Hammond	LastName	Robbins
GroupName	Cara Hammond Quartet	GroupName	Paul Robbins Trio
Address	1500 West 9th Street	Address	340 Bathurst Street
City	Vancouver	City	Toronto
State/Province	BC	State/Province	ON
PostalCode	V7H 1E7	PostalCode	M5W 1R7
Country/Region	Canada	Country/Region	Canada

Figure AP 2-2: Records for the Venues table

▦ Venues : Table						_ □ ×
ID	Date	Time	Venue	Performer	Phone	
1	8/3/2004	2 to 4 p.m.	Amphitheater	Paul Robbins Trio	(415) 444-7888	
2	8/3/2004	2 to 4 p.m.	Lakeside	The Three Saxes	(604) 555-2344	
3	8/3/2004	8 to 10 p.m.	Main Stage	Cara Hammond Quartet	(604) 555-3322	
▶ (AutoNumber)						

Project for Skill Set 3

Creating and Modifying Queries

Winners Database for Classic Car Races

Classic sports-racing car drivers compete in races throughout North America from April to October each year. As an avid fan of these races, you've created a database containing a table that lists the winners of the top 25 races in the United States and Canada. In this project, you'll create three queries. The first query will list only winners who drove Ferraris, and the second query will list only winners who drove Aston Martins and competed in the United States. The third query will list all the drivers who won races in Canada and will include a calculated field that calculates the U.S. dollar value of the prize money awarded to the drivers.

Activity Steps

 open AC_Project3.mdb

1. View the contents of the **2004 Winners table** and the **2004 Prize Money table**
   The 2004 Winners table includes the name of the winning driver, the make, model, and year of the winning car, the location of the race, and the Race ID. The 2004 Prize Money table includes the Race ID, the location of the race, and the prize money awarded.

Step 5
The required expression that appears in the blank field to the right of PrizeMoney is USFunds: [PrizeMoney]/1.5 because one U.S. dollar is equivalent to 1.5 Canadian dollars (approximately).

2. Use the Simple Query Wizard to create a detailed query that includes the **FirstName**, **LastName**, **Car**, **Model**, **Year**, and **Country fields** from the 2004 Winners table and the **Race ID**, **Raceway**, and **PrizeMoney fields** from the 2004 Prize Money table; accept the default name for the query

3. Modify the query grid so the query lists each winner who drove a **Ferrari**, then save a copy of the query as **Ferraris**
   The completed query appears as shown in Figure AP 3-1.

4. Revise the 2004 Winners Query to list only those winners who drove an **Aston Martin** and who competed at raceways in the USA, then save a copy of the query as **Aston Martins**

5. Open the 2004 Winners Query, remove the current criteria, then create a calculated field named **USFunds** that divides the **PrizeMoney** field by **1.5**

6. Enter **Canada** in the Criteria cell for Country, view the query results, then return to Design view and format the calculated field to display the Currency symbol
   The completed query appears as shown in Figure AP 3-2.

 close AC_Project3.mdb

Figure AP 3-1: Ferrari query results

	FirstName	LastName	Car	Model	Year	Country	RaceID	Raceway	PrizeMoney
	Marty	Graham	Ferrari	Testa Rosa 250	1959	USA	1	Adirondack	$3,000.00
	Scott	Archie	Ferrari	Dino 250	1960	USA	4	Silver Field	$2,100.00
	Haden	Jack	Ferrari	V6 3 liter	1959	USA	1	Adirondack	$3,000.00
▶	Gilbert	Ronnie	Ferrari	Berlinetta	1960	USA	1	Adirondack	$3,000.00
*							Number)		

Ferraris : Select Query

Figure AP 3-2: Canadian Winners query results

	FirstName	LastName	Car	Model	Year	Country	RaceID	Raceway	PrizeMoney	USFunds
▶	Lundy	Jack	Cooper	Climax 1,100 c.c.	1959	Canada	3	Brantford	$2,400.00	$1,600.00
	Jones	Frank	Jaguar	D-Type	1960	Canada	3	Brantford	$2,400.00	$1,600.00
	Wilkes	Paul	Lotus	Eleven	1959	Canada	6	Westwood	$2,500.00	$1,666.67
	Petersen	Buzz	Corvette	Stingray	1961	Canada	3	Brantford	$2,400.00	$1,600.00
	Phillips	Wally	Porsche	1500 RS	1958	Canada	6	Westwood	$2,500.00	$1,666.67
	Jeffries	Roger	Elva	Mark 2	1960	Canada	6	Westwood	$2,500.00	$1,666.67
	Collins	Alan	Alfa Romeo	Sprint Veloce	1958	Canada	6	Westwood	$2,500.00	$1,666.67
*						Number)				

2004 Winners Query : Select Query

Project for Skill Set 4

Creating and Modifying Forms

Photography Database for French Archeology Project

As a student of archeology at the University of Victoria, you have created a database that contains data for a history project on archeological sites in France. The database contains three tables: the Sites table lists information about each site you are cataloging, the Photos table lists information about photographs taken at the sites, and the Site Categories table lists the four site categories (Neolithic, Magdalenian, Bronze Age, and Roman). After entering several records in Datasheet view for the Sites and Photos tables, you decide to create forms for entering the data.

Activity Steps

 open AC_Project4.mdb

1. Use the Form Wizard to create a form for the **Sites table** that includes all the fields except the CategoryID field and uses the **Columnar** format and the **SandStone** style, then name the form **Sites**

2. In Design view, select and then fill all the text boxes with **light green**, then apply the **Raised** special effect (middle selection in the top row of Special Effect selections)

3. Select all the labels and text boxes, then increase the font size to **11-point**

4. Enter a new record in the form, as shown in Figure AP 4-1

5. Use the AutoForm tool to create a form for the **Photos table**

6. Save the form as **Site Photos**

7. Reduce width of the ID and CategoryID textboxes to approximately ¾"

8. Enter a new record in the form, as shown in Figure AP 4-2

 close AC_Project4.mdb

Figure AP 4-1: Data for Record 16 of the Sites form

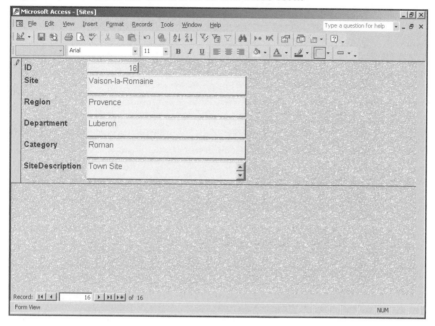

Figure AP 4-2: Data for Record 9 of the Site Photos form

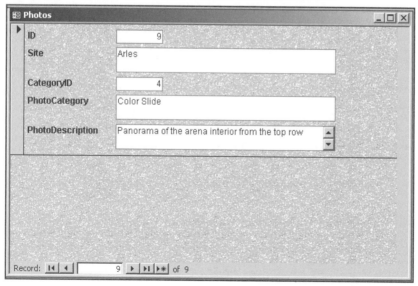

Project for Skill Set 5

Viewing and Organizing Information

Conference Database for E-Commerce Forum

You work for an organization in Mexico City that is sponsoring a two-day forum on e-commerce issues for entrepreneurs from all over North and South America. At present the conference database contains two tables: the Delegates table lists the names and addresses of the people who have signed up for the conference, and the Workshops table lists the various workshops offered at the conference. In this project, you will add two new records to the database as well as edit and delete some other records. You will also create a crosstab query to count the number of delegates from Brazil and Mexico City, and then use the two different filter features to show only records conforming to certain criteria.

Activity Steps

 open AC_Project5.mdb

1. Enter the record for Kevin Sylvano in the **Delegates table**, as shown in Figure AP 5-1

2. Delete the record for **Jorge Ramirez**, edit the record for **Juanita Sanchez** by changing her street address to **av. Angelico 622**, then close and save the Delegates table

3. Open the **Workshops form**, change the text in the **Day 1 Afternoon field** for **Record 2** to **E-Commerce Storefront Services**, enter the data shown in Figure AP 5-2 for **Record 3**, then close the form

4. Use the Crosstab Query Wizard to create a query from the **Brazil and Mexico Delegates query** that designates **Country** as the row heading, **City** as the column heading, and uses the **Count** function
   Figure AP 5-3 shows the results of the crosstab query.

5. Close the query, open the **Delegates table** in Datasheet view, then sort the records in alphabetical order by **Track**

6. Open the **Workshops query** in Design view, sort the records in **Ascending** order by **Country**, then view the query results

7. In the **Delegates table**, use the Filter by Selection button to show only participants who live in **Colombia**

8. Remove the filter, then use the Filter by Form feature to filter the records to show only participants who live in **Mexico City** and are signed up for **Track A**

9. Close the **Delegates table** without saving it

 close AC_Project5.mdb

Figure AP 5-1: New record for the Delegates table

ID	FirstName	LastName	Address	City	Code	Country	Trac
1	Pedra	Juarez	Al Maracatins, 1325	Sao Paulo	03088-013	Brazil	A
2	Philippe	Siqueros	Paseo de la Reforma No. 1978	Mexico City	11400	Mexico	B
3	William	Slade	1750 Trade Center Way	Naples, FL	33196	USA	B
4	Astrud	Fernandes	Tr Batuira 18	Guarulhos	7041140	Brazil	C
5	Ramona	Estêves	Sierra Tarahumara No. 345	Mexico City	10500	Mexico	A
6	Alessandro	Almacenes	Av. 10 de Agosto 1545	Quito		Ecuador	C
7	Conchita	Alvarez	Calle 92 no. 14-88	Bogota	90343	Colombia	B
8	Oscar	Tornearia	136 Vila Prudente	Sao Paulo	03638-111	Brazil	B
9	Jorge	Ramirez	Av 6 De Diciembre 125	Quito		Ecuador	A
10	Dawn	Grenville	648 Fifth Ave.	New York, NY	10149	USA	A
11	Maria	Gironella	Calle Shiller 407, Polanco	Mexico City	11580	Mexico	B
12	Carlos	Rivera	Carlos Pellegrini, 1139	Buenos Aires	1028	Argentina	C
13	Pablo	Mendez	Edificio Concasa Carrera 43	Barranquila	4	Colombia	C
14	Manuel	Figuentes	Rio Lerma 41	Mexico City	6580	Mexico	A
15	Juanita	Sanchez	av. Angelica 645	Sao Paulo	2115990	Brazil	B
16	Kevin	Sylvano	1601 42nd Street	New York, NY	10144	USA	C
(A							

Record: 17 of 17

Figure AP 5-2: Text added to Record 3 in the Workshops form

Workshops

Session ID	3
Track	C
Day 1 Morning	E-Marketing Made Easy
Day 1 Afternoon	Domain Name Issues
Day 2 Morning	Don't Eat the Cookies
Day 2 Afternoon	E-Mail Marketing Tips

Record: 3 of 3

Figure AP 5-3: Crosstab query results

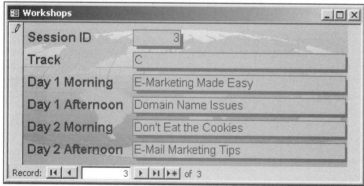

Brazil and Mexico Delegates_Crosstab : Crosstab Query

Country	Total Of FirstNa	Guarulhos	Mexico City	Sao Paulo
Brazil	4	1		3
Mexico	4		4	

Project for Skill Set 6

Defining Relationships

Properties Database for Powder Trails Realty

You work for Powder Trails Realty, a small real estate agency in Whistler, British Columbia that employs five agents. To keep track of which agents are responsible for which properties, you've created a database containing two tables. The Properties table lists the various homes for sale, and the Agents table lists the five agents. You want to create a relationship between these two tables that allows you to quickly determine which agent is responsible for which properties.

Activity Steps

 open AC_Project6.mdb

1. Open the Relationships window, then add the **Properties** and **Agents tables**

2. Create a **one-to-many relationship** from the Agents table to the Properties table using the **AgentID** field
   Compare the Relationships window to Figure AP 6-1.

3. Edit the relationship to select the **Enforce referential integrity** option button in the Edit Relationships dialog box

4. Close the Relationships window, save changes when prompted, then use the Query Wizard to find out which properties are handled by **Mary Gregson** and **Tony Esperanzo**; include all the fields from the Agents table and all the fields *except* the AgentID field from the Properties table and name the query **Mary and Tony Properties**
   The completed query appears as shown in Figure AP 6-2. Mary and Tony are responsible for two properties each.

 close AC_Project6.mdb

Figure AP 6-1: Relationship established

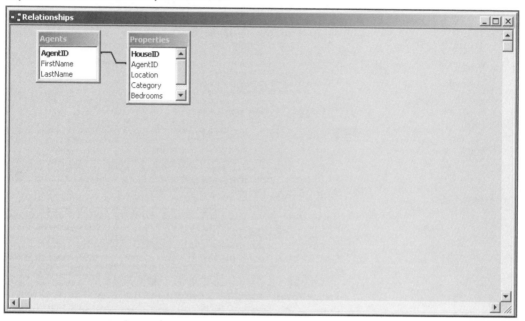

Figure AP 6-2: Completed query

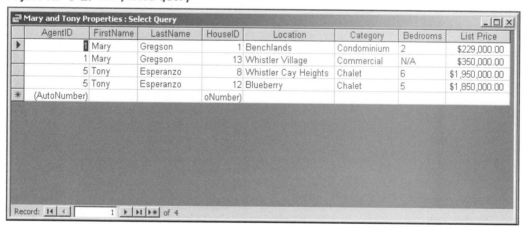

Project for Skill Set 7

Producing Reports

Sales Database for Precious Pets

Precious Pets is a small pet store that caters to pet lovers in Carmel, California. The store sells pets in five categories: cats, dogs, rodents, reptiles, and birds. The owner of Precious Pets has asked you to create reports from two tables in the Precious Pets database. The first report lists all the reptiles and rodents sold from April 1 to 5, 2004, and the second report lists all the pet sales from April 1 to 5, 2004 sorted and totaled according to category.

Activity Steps

 open AC_Project7.mdb

1. Use the Report Wizard to create a report from the **Reptiles and Rodents query** that includes the following fields: **Sale Date**, **Animal**, and **Price**

2. Make **Sale Date** the grouping level and change the interval for the grouping option for Sale Date to **Day**, sort the records in Ascending order by **Animal**, select the **Outline 1** layout, select the **Soft Grey** format, and name the report **Reptile and Rodent Sales**

3. In Design view, delete the two **Sale Date** labels, then move the two **Animal** labels to the right until the left edge of the labels is even with **3** on the ruler bar and the completed report appears in Print Preview as shown in Figure AP 7-1

4. Preview and print a copy of the report, then save and close it

5. Open the **April 1 to 5 Sales report** in Design view, add subtotals to the Price field, change the label to **Subtotal:**, then format the calculated control with the Currency style

6. Add a date calculated control to the right side of the report header and enter **Current Date:** as the label text

7. Format the Animal categories (e.g., Bird and Cat) with 16 pt and Bold

8. Print preview the report
   The completed report appears in Print Preview as shown in Figure AP 7-2.

 close AC_Project7.mdb

Figure AP 7-1: Reptile and Rodent Sales report

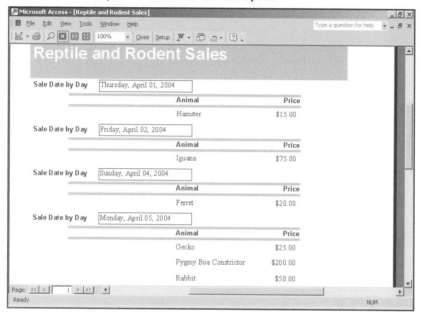

Figure AP 7-2: April 1 to 5 Sales report

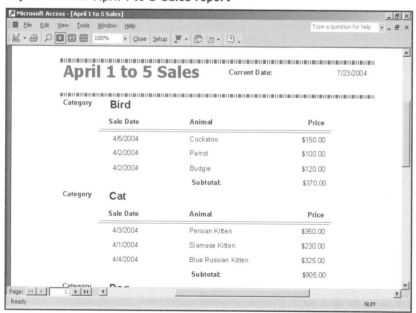

Project for Skill Set 8

Integrating with Other Applications

Great Hiking Trails Database

As an avid hiker in the many natural parks throughout North America, you have decided to create a database containing information about your hikes. At present, the data you want to include in your hiking database is saved in two places—an Excel workbook and another Access database. In this project, you will create a new database and then import a file from Excel and a report and table from Access. Then you will import one of the tables into a new Excel workbook and save the report as a Web page. Finally, you will create two versions of a data access page—one that you can enter information into and one that reports up-to-date database activity.

Activity Steps

1. Start a new database and name it **Trails.mdb**

2. Import the Excel file **AC_Project8A.xls** into Access; specify that the first row of the Excel worksheet contains column headings, then accept the remaining defaults and name the table **Day Hikes**

3. Import both the table and the report called **Overnight Hikes** from the Access database **AC_Project8B.mdb** into the **Trails.mdb** database

4. Export the **Overnight Hikes table** to an Excel workbook

5. Export the **Overnight Hikes report** to a Web page called **Overnight.html**, then view the table in your Web browser

6. Use the Data Access Page wizard to create a data access page from the **Day Hikes table** that includes all the fields, has no grouping level, is *not* sorted on any of the fields, and has the title **Day Hikes**

7. Apply the **Watermark** theme to the data access page, enter **Great Day Hiking Trails** as the page title, save the data access page as **Day.htm** and accept the warning, view the page in Page view, then compare it to figure AP8-1

8. Use the Data Access Page wizard to create a data access page for data reporting from the Overnight Hikes table that includes all the fields, designates **State/Province** as the grouping level, is *not* sorted on any of the fields, and has the title **Overnight Hikes**

9. Apply the Nature theme, enter **Great Overnight Hiking Trails** as the page title, then view the first record for British Columbia
The data access page appears as shown in Figure AP 8-2.

10. Save the data access page as Night.htm

 close Trails.mdb Overnight Hikes.xls, Overnight.html Night.htm

Step 4
Click the Save formatted checkbox in the Export dialog box.

Step 9
If the Nature theme is not available, select another theme from the list.

Figure AP 8-1: Great Day Hiking Trails data access page

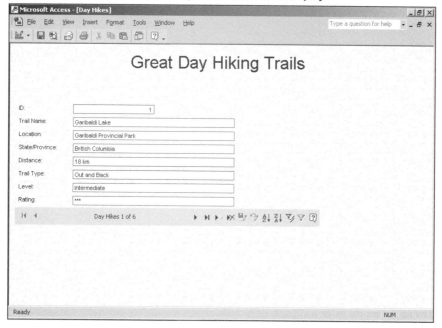

Figure AP 8-2: Great Overnight Hiking Trails data access page

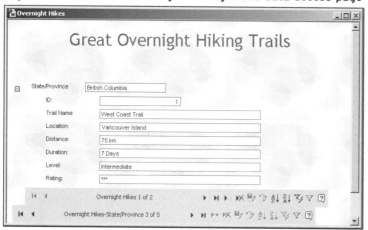

Access 2002 Expert Projects Appendix

Projects List

The Access Expert skill sets cover many of the techniques and advanced tools used to create custom versions of database objects. In addition, the skill sets include methods for defining relationships, operating Access on the World Wide Web, using Access tools to perform such activities as encrypting and replicating databases, and using Access to create database applications. In the following projects, you will practice these skills by developing and using databases to maintain information for various business applications.

Project for Skill Set 9

Creating and Modifying Tables

Database for Italia Vacations, Inc.

Italia Vacations Inc., manages a Web site that lists holiday villas for rent in various regions of Italy. The company maintains two databases: one database contains the Villas table, which lists the holiday villas available for rental, and the other database contains the Customers table, which lists the customers who have rented villas. In this project you will first use data validation to ensure that all users enter information consistently in the Villas table, and then you will create a link between the two databases so that information entered in the Customers table is accessible to both databases.

Step 3

Click the I will type the values that I want option button in the first Lookup Wizard dialog box.

Step 5

This input mask will require that phone numbers be entered as (011) followed by a space, followed by a 0 in brackets, followed by three digits, followed by a hyphen, followed by four digits.

Activity Steps

 open AE_Project9A.mdb

1. In the **Villas table**, create a Validation Rule for the Source field to specify that only **C or W** be entered, then create Validation text that states **Enter C for Catalog or W for Web**

2. Switch to Datasheet view and save when prompted, click **No** when prompted to test existing records, enter **D** in the Source column of the last record, then correct the error by entering **W** when prompted

3. In the **Villas table**, use the Lookup Wizard to create a Lookup field for the Region field that includes the regions shown in Figure AP 9-1

4. In Datasheet view, enter **Tuscany** as the region for the last record in the Villas table

5. Create a custom input mask called **International Phone Number** for the Phone Number field that specifies the settings for a phone number shown in Figure AP 9-2

6. Save when prompted, enter the phone number **(011) (0)343-5569** in the last record, then close the table

7. Use the Link Tables command to link to the **Customers table** in the **AE_Project9B.mdb** database

8. Open the **Customers table** in **AE_Project9A.mdb**, then add a new record for a customer called **Gerry Hansen** who lives at **140 Aspen Way, Boulder, CO, USA 81423**, and will stay for **2 weeks** at **Villa 14** starting **August 21, 2004**

9. Close the Customers table, close the AE_Project9A.mdb database, then open **AE_Project9B.mdb** and verify that the new record has been added to the Customers table in this database

 close AE_Project9B.mdb

Figure AP 9-1: Values for Lookup field

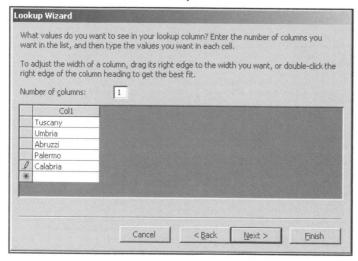

Figure AP 9-2: Custom input mask

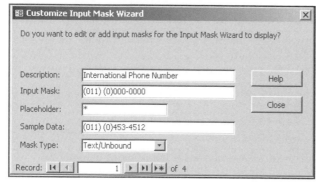

Project for Skill Set 10

Creating and Modifying Forms

Sales Database for Pioneer Antiques

Pioneer Antiques sells items from America's past, particularly those items related to the Old West. The company sells its wares from a retail store located in Tuscon, AZ and from its company Web site, www.pioneerantiques.com. The Sales database contains the Sales table, which lists each item sold, and the Customer table, which lists each customer. In this project, you will create a form for entering data in the Sales table and then modify the form by creating a subform that lists the customers. You will then create a switchboard and modify startup options so that a salesperson can quickly access the Sales form to enter new data.

Activity Steps

 open AE_Project10.mdb

1. Using the **Sales table** as the Record Source property, create a form in Design view that appears as shown in Figure AP 10-1

2. Use the form to add a record with the data: **Georgian Candlesticks, Silver, 1792, Gilliam McKim**, buyer ID **20**, then save the form as **Sales**

3. Open the **Customer form**, then add a subform called **Sales subform** under the Zip Code label that contains all the fields from the **Sales table**; accept the default settings in the Subform wizard

4. Navigate to the record for **Gretchen Kingsley**, compare your screen to Figure AP 10-2, adjust column widths in Design view, if necessary, then close and save the form

Step 3
If necessary, increase the width of the Sales subform to approximately 6".

5. Use the Switchboard Manager to create a new switchboard called **Antiques Switchboard** that includes two items: **Open Sales Form** that opens the **Sales form** in edit mode and **Open Customer Form** that opens the **Customers form** in edit mode

6. Close the Edit Switchboard Page dialog box and the Switchboard Manager dialog box, then use the new switchboard to open the **Sales form**

7. Close the **Sales form** and the switchboard, modify the switchboard by moving the Open Customer Form command above the Open Sales Form command, then view the modified switchboard

8. Close the Switchboard, set startup options to display the switchboard on startup, then close the database

9. Open the database, use the command button on the switchboard to go directly to the **Sales form**, then add the following new record: **Punched Tin Lantern, Metalware, 1810, Gail Jenkins**, buyer ID **15**

 close AE_Project10.mdb

Figure AP 10-1: Sales form created in Form Design view

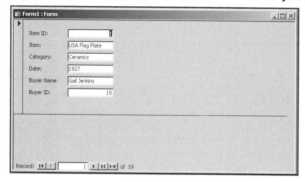

Figure AP 10-2: Customer form with Sales subform

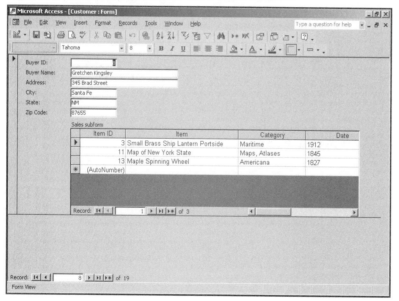

Project for Skill Set 11

Refining Queries

Product Database for Viva Arts

Viva Arts is a wholesale supplier of art materials to artists throughout the United States and Canada. In this project you will modify the Inventory table in the store's database so that the store manager can quickly create queries to obtain specific information about the inventory.

Activity Steps

 open AE_Project11.mdb

1. In Design view, create a query that includes all the fields from the **Inventory table** and finds only the supplies that are in the Paint category AND that cost more than $8.00, then save the query as **Premium Paints**
   The query results list 10 items.

2. In Design view, create a query that includes all the fields from the **Inventory table** and lists all products in the **Canvas** OR **Paper** OR **Canvas Board** categories, then save the query as **Surfaces**
   The query results list 15 items.

3. From the **Inventory table**, create an Advanced filter to select only the **Aquaflo** brand of **paints** in the **6 oz. size** that cost less than $7.00
   The criteria for the filter should appear as shown in Figure AP 11-1.

Step 1
Enter >8 in the
Price criteria cell.

4. Apply the filter, then save it as a query object called **Aquaflo Acrylic Paints**
   Five items are listed after the filter is applied.

5. In the **Paints query**, create a parameter query that uses the text **[Enter Brand]**, view the query, type **Reiva** in the Enter Parameter Value dialog box, view the six records that appear, then close and save the query

6. Create a new query that includes all the records in the Inventory table, then save the query as **Inventory Query**

7. From the **Inventory Query**, create a Make Table action query that creates a table called **High Cost** containing only items from the Inventory table that cost more than $100.00, delete those items from the Inventory table, then view the new table, which contains six records

8. Using the **Categories query**, create a query that uses the **SUM aggregate function** to calculate the total worth of all the items in the query grouped by Category, save the query as **Total Items by Category**, then run the query, and compare it to Figure AP 11-2

 close AE_Project11.mdb

Figure AP 11-1: Advanced Filter query criteria

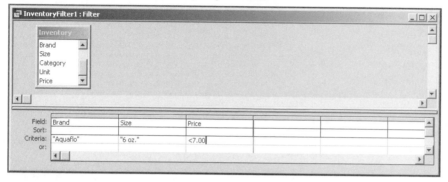

Figure AP 11-2: Total Items by Catetory query

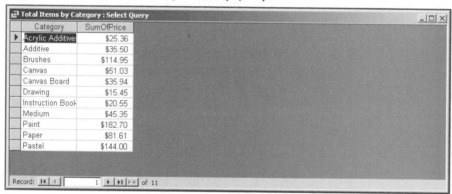

Project for Skill Set 12

Producing Reports

Customer Database for Custom Mouse Pads

Custom Mouse Pads supplies souvenir stores and corporate customers with mouse pads that feature photographic images, reproductions of art work, and logos. You've been asked to create a new report that shows all the mouse pads sold in the Art category and then to modify a report that lists all the mouse pads sold in the Photograph category.

Activity Steps

 open AE_Project12.mdb

1. Create a report in Design view that uses the **Art Mouse Pads query** as the record source

2. Move and size the labels, add **Purchases of Art Mouse Pads** as the Page Header, modify the header by increasing its font size to 18-point and adjusting its size and position, add a text box to the footer that contains **=[Page]**, then remove the label
   Your screen should match Figure AP 12-1.

3. Save the report as **Art Mouse Pads**, then close it

4. Open the **Photograph Mouse Pads report**, add a Report Footer, then add a control in the Report Footer that uses the Sum function to total the quantity of images purchased and includes the label **Total Images**
   The required control is =Sum([Quantity]).

5. View the report in Print Preview, move to the last page of the report, then verify that 25,400 mouse pads have been purchased

6. In Design view, sort the **Photograph Mouse Pads report** in Ascending order by **Country** and show the **Group Header**

7. Move the **Country text box** in the Detail section up into the Country Header section, then move the **CompanyID text box** to close the gap in the Details section

8. Increase the height of the Details section by approximately 3", add a subreport control that shows the **Companies report** for each record (accept all defaults in the SubReport Wizard), then view the report in Print Preview
   The first record appears in Print Preview as shown in Figure AP 12-2.

 close AE_Project12.mdb

Step 2
You separate a label and text box combination by clicking and dragging the large square handle. To increase the size of a label or text box, drag the right middle sizing handle.

Figure AP 12-1: Art Mouse Pads report

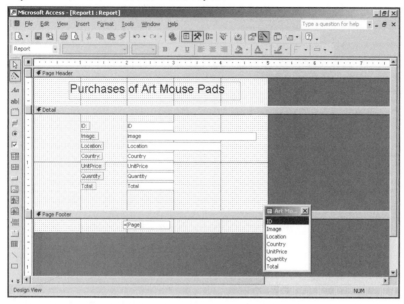

Figure AP 12-2: Photograph Mouse Pads and Companies Report in Print Preview

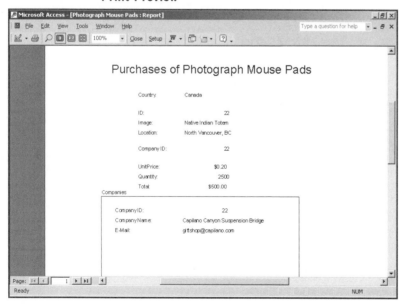

Project for Skill Set 13

Defining Relationships

Client Database for Fit 'n Fun Health Club

The Fit 'n Fun Health Club maintains a database of the various fitness classes offered at the club. This database includes three tables: a list of Members, a list of Classes and Instructors, and a Registration table that identifies the members registered in each class. You first need to create a one-to-many relationship between the Members table and the Registration table. Then you will create a many-to-many relationship between the Members table and the Classes table that uses the Registration table as the junction table.

Activity Steps

 open AE_Project13.mdb

1. Using the **MemberID field**, create a one-to-many relationship with referential integrity enforced from the **Members table** to the **Registration table** to show that one client can take many classes

2. View the **Members table**, then determine how many classes **Ron Dawson** is taking
   Ron takes two classes, as shown in Figure AP 13-1.

3. Using the **Registration table** as the junction table and the **ClassID field**, create a many-to-many relationship with referential integrity enforced between the **Members table** and the **Classes table**
   The relationships should appear in the Relationships window as shown in Figure AP 13-2.

4. In the **Classes table**, determine how many members are taking the Aerobics class taught be Michelle Leung on Wednesdays
   As shown in Figure AP 13-3, two members have registered for Michelle's class.

 close AE_Project13.mdb

Figure AP 13-1: Classes taken by Ron Dawson

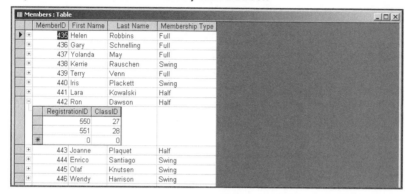

Figure AP 13-2: Relationships established

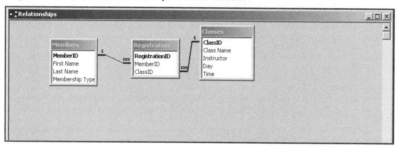

Figure AP 13-3: Members registered in the Wednesday Aerobics class

Project for Skill Set 14

Operating Access on the Web

Rentals Database for Classics Plus Video Club

The Classic Plus Video Club rents classic videos to students at various universities and colleges in the Chicago area. The club's database contains two tables: the Inventory table, which contains the list of videos available, and the Rentals table, which contains the list of students who have rented videos. First, you'll create a data access page from the Rentals table so that club personnel can enter video rental data online. Then, you'll create a data acesss page with a PivotTable and a data access table with a PivotChart.

Activity Steps

 open AE_Project14.mdb

1. Create a Data Access Page in Design view that includes all the fields from the Rentals table

2. As shown in Figure AP 14-1, size and position the fields, enter **Video Rentals** as the page title, then apply the **Poetic** theme (or select another theme if Poetic is not available)

3. Save the page as **Rentals.htm**

4. Create a Data Access Page in Design view that includes a PivotTable from the Inventory table as follows:

   a. Remove the **Video ID**, **Artist or Director**, and **Rentals in 2004** fields

   b. Move the **Category** and **Decade** fields to the Row area

   c. Enter **Videos by Category and Decade** as the title for the data access page

5. Modify the size and position of the PivotTable so that it appears as shown in Figure AP 14-2 in Page view, then save the page as **Categories.htm**

6. Create a Data Access Page in Design view that includes a PivotChart from the Inventory table by doing the following: move the **Category field** into Category, the **Decade field** into Series, and the **Rentals in 2004** field into Data

7. Show only data for the **Comedy** and **Drama** categories

8. Resize the chart and add a title as show in Figure AP 14-3, then save the page as **RentalData.htm**

 close AE_Project14.mdb

Step 2
To move both the text box and label, click and drag the text box. To move just the label, click and drag the label.

Step 4
If Drop Areas are not visible, right-click the PivotTable area, then click Drop Areas.

Figure AP 14-1: Data Access Page from the Rentals table

Figure AP 14-2: Data Access Page with PivotTable

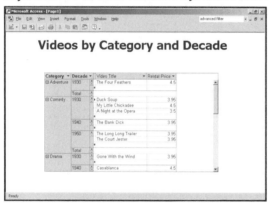

Figure AP 14-3: Data Access Page with PivotChart

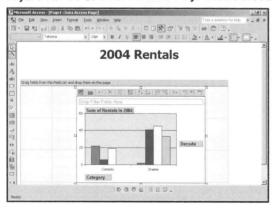

Project for Skill Set 15

Using Access Tools

Database of Golden Golf Tours

Golden Golf Tours offers a wide range of tours to golfers interested in combining travel with golf. In this project, you will work with the company's database to import data currently saved in XML format, export one the of the tables to XML format for transfer over the World Wide Web, and then use Access tools to encrypt the database, compact and reopen it, assign security, and replicate it.

Activity Steps

 open AE_Project15.mdb

1. Import the **Flights.xml** document into the database
   The XML document contains information about flight arrivals and departures for each of the golf tours.

2. Export the **Courses table** to an XML file, click **OK** in the Export XML dialog box to export both the data as an XML document and the schema as an XSD document, then view the XML file in the browser
   The XML file appears in the browser as shown in Figure AP 15-1.

3. Close the browser and return to Access, close the database, open it in Exclusive mode, assign the password **gogolf** to the database, close the database, then open it using the password

4. Create a workgroup called **Golf** with **tours** as the Personal ID that contains two people: **Mark Green** (Personal ID is **soccer**), and **Cheryl Wong** (Personal ID is **snow**)
   Figure AP 15-2 shows Mark Green being added to the Golf workgroup in the User and Group Accounts dialog box

5. Assign the users of the Golf workbook the permission to open and run the AE_Project15.mdb database

6. Close the database, encrypt it using the filename **AE_Project15_Encrypt.mdb**, open the encrypted database, compact and repair it, then close it

7. Remove the **gogolf** password from the **AE_Project15.mdb file**, remove the Golf workgroup and the two users, then replicate the AE_Project15.mdb file to a file called **Replica of AE_Project15.mdb**, without creating a backup copy of the Design Master

8. Open **AE_Project15.mdb**, open the **Tours table**, change **Riviera** to **Lavender** in Record 6, then close the database and exit Access

9. Open **Replica of AE_Project15.mdb**, apply the Synchronize function, then verify that the change was made to Record 6 in the replicated database

 close AE_Project15.mdb

Figure AP 15-1: Courses.xml file shown in browser

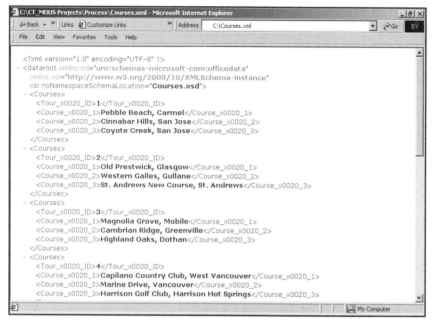

Figure AP 15-2: User and Group Accounts dialog box

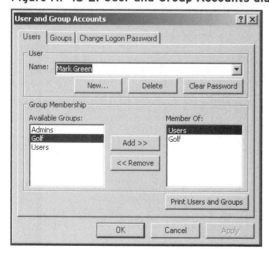

Project for Skill Set 16

Creating Database Applications

Product Database for Snaps Photo Supplies

Snaps Photo Supplies sells cameras, film, and other photographic supplies to photography enthusiasts in Atlanta. You've been asked to create database applications to help automate the form completion process, so that users can quickly enter required information. You'll create two command buttons using the Command Button Wizard, and then you'll create a new Global module that will convert entries in Celsius temperatures to Fahrenheit. This module will be used to calculate the ferotyping temperatures of photographic paper listed in the Papers table.

Activity Steps

 open AE_Project16.mdb

1. Open the **Supplies form** in Design view, then use the **Command Button Wizard** to create a command button called **Add New Record** that uses the pencil image, and a command button called **Delete Record** that uses the trash can 1 image

2. Position the command buttons in the lower right corner of the form as shown in Figure AP 16-1

3. Use the Add New Record button to add a new record with the data shown in Figure AP 16-2, then use the Delete Record button to delete record 15

4. Create a new Global module that consists of the VBA function named **CelsiusToFahr** by entering the VBA code shown in Figure AP 16-3

5. Save the module with the name **Temperature Function**

6. In Query Design view, add the Papers table, add the TempC field to the query grid, click in the **Field cell** in the second column, type **TempF: CelsiusToFahr([TempC])**, run the query, verify that the first temperature is converted to 212, then save the query as **Conversions**

7. Use the Database Splitter to create a back-end database called **AP_Project16_be.mdb**

8. Convert the database to the Access 2002 file format, save the database as **Snaps.mdb**, then close it

9. Make an MDE file for the Snaps.mdb file, then save the file as **SnapsMDE**

 close SnapsMDE.mdb

Figure AP 16-1: Form with command buttons

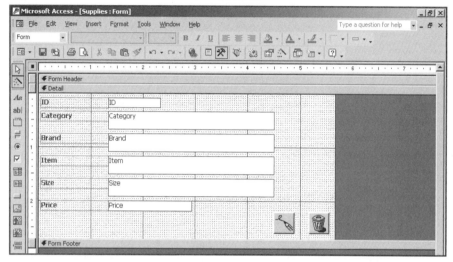

Figure AP 16-2: New record added

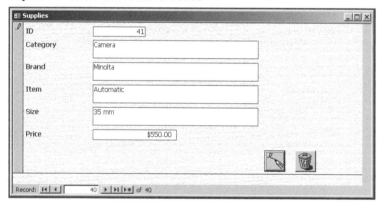

Figure AP 16-3: VBA code for Global module

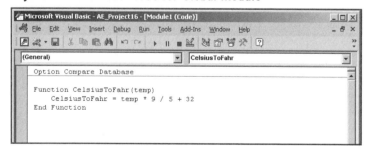

Glossary

action query one of four queries (make-table, append, delete, or update), all of which change data when you run them

administrator the user who has all permissions to all database activities, including modifying the workgroup information file

aggregate functions functions such as SUM, COUNT, or MAX, that allow you to create statistics on groups of records

Analyze It with Microsoft Excel a tool used to export a set of records to Microsoft Excel

AND conditions two or more criteria entered in the same row of Query Design View, each of which must be true for a given record to display in Query Datasheet View

append query an action query that adds the fields and records selected in the query to the designated table

application an Access database that has been customized to meet the needs of a particular audience

AutoForm a tool used to quickly create a new form based on the selected table or query

AutoFormat a collection of formatting characteristics and design elements that you apply to a given form or report

AutoNumber a data type that Access controls and sequentially increments by one integer for each new record

Avg an aggregate function that averages the values in the given field

back-end database in a split database situation, the database that stores all the table objects

blank database template a template that creates a database with no objects

Briefcase a special type of folder designed to help keep files that are used on two computers synchronized

brown-out a dip in power that sometimes causes computer damage

browser software used to find, download, and display Web pages

calculated control a text box control that contains an expression that calculates a value

calculated field a field created in Query Design View (using an expression) whose contents depend on the values in other fields

Cascade Delete Related Records an option that you can impose on a one-to-many relationship; if a record in the "one" side of the relationship is deleted, all matching records from the "many" table will also be deleted

Cascade Update Related Fields an option that you can impose on a one-to-many relationship; if the value of the linking field in the "one" side of the relationship is updated, all matching fields in the "many" table will also be updated

Category field a field used in the x-axis area on a chart

class modules modules containing VBA code that can be used within a given form or report

client in most client/server computing environments, the user's PC

client/server computing two or more information systems cooperatively processing to solve a problem

combo box a data entry control that provides the features of both the list box control and the text box control

Command Button Wizard a wizard used to create a command button for a form

Compact on Close a feature that automatically compacts and repairs your database every time you close it

Compacting rearranging the database on your hard disk to reuse space formerly occupied by deleted objects

comparison operators characters such as > (greater than) or < (less than) that you can use to further define criteria in a filter or query

constant a value that never changes

control any item on a form or report such as a label, text box, or command button

Count an aggregate function that counts the number of values in the given field

criteria limiting conditions that determine which records are displayed in a particular view

crosstab query a query that creates a summarized presentation of records by grouping data by one or more fields

Crosstab Query Wizard a wizard that helps you create a crosstab query

Currency a data type that allows a field to store only monetary values

custom functions new user-created functions created within a module using VBA code

DAP *see data access page*

data access page a special type of Web page that maintains a connection with the database

data type determines what type of data (text, numbers, dates, pictures) can be stored by a field

data validation a process that compares a field entry with criteria that define a set or range of acceptable entries for a field

database developer one who creates new database objects such as queries, forms, and reports

database normalization the process of determining how tables should be organized and related

database password a password that must be entered to open the database file

Database Splitter a feature that splits a database into two files: the back-end database that stores all the data, and the front-end database that stores all the other database objects

database user anyone who enters, edits, views, or uses database information, but doesn't design or create new database objects

Database window displays the name of the current database in its title bar and has icons that represent the existing database objects

Database window toolbar a toolbar at the top of the Database window that helps you create, modify, or view objects

Database Wizard a wizard that provides sample databases and database options from which you can choose to quickly create a new database

datasheet a spreadsheet-like grid that stores data

Datasheet View a view of a table or query used to enter and edit data in a spreadsheet-like format

date calculated control a text box control that uses an Access function to calculate and display today's date on a report

Date function an Access function that displays today's date in the m/d/yyyy format

Date/Time a data type that allows a field to store only valid dates and times

decrypt to reverse the encryption process

default switchboard the switchboard that opens first when using more than one switchboard in a database

delete query an action query that deletes the fields and records selected in the query

delimited text file a file of unformatted data where each field value is separated by a common character, such as a comma or a tab; used to convert data from proprietary software into a format that other programs can import

Design Master the original database from which replicas are made

Design View a view used to modify the structure of an object

Detail a section that prints once for every record

development database a test database used by a database developer to create and test new objects

dynamic the ability of a Web page linked to a database to reconnect to the database to display up-to-date data every time the Web page is opened or refreshed

encrypt to make database objects indecipherable to other programs

export to convert data from an Access database to an external file, such as a Word document

expression any combination of field names, constants, and operators used to create a value

Extensible Markup Language a standard file format that is used to deliver data from one application to another over an intranet or the World Wide Web; an XML file

Extensible Schema Document a file that accompanies an XML file to further define the structure of the data stored in the XML file; an XSD file

Extensible Style Language a file that accompanies an XML file to further define formatting information about the data; an XSL file

field one category of information such as a person's title, city, or country

field list in Form Design View or Report Design View, a list of fields from the selected record source

file extension one to three characters attached to the end of a filename, which tells the computer what type of information is stored in a file; Access uses the mdb file extension

filter a tool used to temporarily isolate a subset of records in a Datasheet View or in Form View

Filter by Form a filter tool that allows you to specify more than one limiting condition for filter criteria

Filter by Selection a filter tool that allows you to quickly isolate a subset of records that match the value that is currently selected

First an aggregate function that returns the value from the first record in the record source

foreign key field the field on the "many" side of a one-to-many relationship used to tie the "many" table to the "one" table

form an Access object that provides an easy-to-use data entry screen

Form Design View a view used to define the layout and formatting characteristics of a form

Form View a view of a form that is used to enter and edit data

Form Wizard a wizard that helps you quickly create a new form

formatting changes the way something appears, but not its actual value

front-end database in a split database, it stores all the database objects except for the table objects (the front-end database contains linked table objects that link it to data stored in the back-end database)

function a built-in formula that helps you quickly build an expression

global modules appear in the Database window when you click the Modules button on the Objects bar; they contain VBA code that can be used throughout the database

Group Footer a section that prints after every group of records

Group Header a section that prints before every group of records

Grouping sorting records in ascending or descending order based on the value of a field and providing a header and/or footer section before or after the records that contain the same value for that field

Help system a collection of definitions, examples, and linked documents that provide extensive information about Access

HTML *see Hypertext Markup Language*

HTML template a file that contains formatting characteristics, such as font sizes and colors, that you can apply to Web pages in order to give them a consistent appearance

Hyperlink a data type that stores Web page addresses

Hypertext Markup Language the language used to create Web pages

import to convert data from an external data source, such as an Excel workbook into an Access database

Import Spreadsheet Wizard a wizard used to import data from an Excel workbook into an Access database

Input Mask a field property that specifies the number and types of characters that can be entered into a field, and also defines a visual guide as data is entered into a field

Input Mask Wizard a wizard that helps you determine an input mask

junction table a table that establishes separate one-to-many relationships with two tables that have a many-to-many relationship

Last an aggregate function that returns the value from the last record in the record source

Limit to List a field lookup property that limits the values for the selected field to those in the list

linked table a link to data stored in a "real" table in another database

Linked Table Manager a tool used to change the path between the original table and linked table

linking field the field that is common to two tables and used to tie them together in a one-to-many relationship

lookup field a field that contains a drop-down list of values that are provided by Lookup properties

Lookup properties properties which provide a drop-down list of values for a field

Lookup Wizard a wizard that helps you identify the list of values for a lookup field

macro a database object that stores a set of actions that can be automatically replayed by running the macro

Macro Design View a view used to define macro actions

main form a form that contains a subform control

main report a report that contains a subreport control

make-table query an action query that creates a new table of data based on the fields and records selected in the query

many-to-many relationship the relationship between two tables when one record in one table is related to many records in the other table, and vice versa

Max an aggregate function that finds the maximum value in the given field

MDE file a special copy of a database that prevents others from opening or editing a form, report, or module in Design View

Memo a data type that allows a field to store lengthy text beyond 255 characters

Merge It with Microsoft Word a tool used to export Access data to a Microsoft Word document to create a mail merge

Microsoft Visual Basic window a window used to write Visual Basic for Applications (VBA) programming code

Min an aggregate function that finds the minimum value in the given field

module a database object that stores Visual Basic for Applications (VBA) programming code

multi-user a database's ability to support many people entering and updating data at the same time

navigation buttons buttons on the navigation toolbar that help you move through the displayed records

navigation toolbar a toolbar in the lower-left corner of Datasheet View and Form View that contains navigation buttons

Now function an Access function that displays both today's date as well as the current time

Number a data type that allows the field to store only valid numeric entries

objects the major parts of a database; the object types include tables, queries, forms, reports, pages, macros, and modules

Objects bar a bar that is positioned on the left side of the Database window, which gives you access to the seven types of objects used to store and manage data in a database

Office Assistant an animated character that provides tips and interactive prompts that offer assistance while you are working

OfficeLinks a set of tools used to export Access data to Microsoft Excel and Microsoft Word

OLE Object a data type that stands for Object Linking and Embedding; it allows a field to link or embed an external file such as an Excel workbook, a photo, or a sound clip

one-to-many relationship the relationship between two tables when one record in the "one" table is linked to many records in the "many" table

one-to-one relationship the relationship between two tables when one record in one table is related to one record in another table, and vice versa

operators a symbol representative of a particular action, such as + (add), - (subtract), * (multiply), / (divide), and ^ (exponentiation)

OR conditions two or more criteria entered in two or more rows of Query Design View, only one of which must be true for a given record to display in Query Datasheet View

orphan records a record in the "many" table of a one-to-many relationship that doesn't have a matching record in the "one" table

page a database object that creates dynamic Web pages

Page Design View a view used to create and modify data access pages

Page Footer a section that prints at the bottom of every page

Page Header a section that prints at the top of every page (but below the report header on page one)

Page View a view that displays the final data access page just as it will appear in Internet Explorer

Page Wizard a wizard that quickly creates new data access pages

parameter criteria a query criterion that prompts you for the actual criteria entry each time you run the query

parameter query a query that contains parameter criteria

permissions activities that users are allowed to complete with various objects, as defined by the workgroup information file

PivotChart a graphical presentation of data in a PivotTable that you can use to sort, filter, and analyze data interactively

PivotChart control a control used to add a PivotChart to a DAP (dynamic access page)

PivotTable a presentation of data that calculates statistics about groups of records, and with which you can interactively sort, filter, and analyze the data in new ways

PivotTable List control a control used to create a PiviotTable

Preview a view of an object that shows how it will look when it is printed

primary key field contains unique data for each record

production database a database that's used on a regular basis by database users

properties individual characteristics of an item such as a field, control, or object

Properties button a button on many different toolbars that opens the property sheet for the selected object, control, or section

property sheet a window that displays all the properties for a selected item

Publish It with Microsoft Word a tool used to export data to Microsoft Word

query a database object that selects fields and records from one or more tables and displays them in a datasheet

Query Datasheet View a view used to view, enter, edit, and delete data in a spreadsheet-like arrangement of data compiled by a query

query design grid the lower pane of Query Design View that determines which fields and records (and their order) will be displayed by Query Datasheet View

Query Design View a view used to define the fields and records to be displayed in Query Datasheet View

record all the fields for one item in a table, such as all the fields that describe an employee

record source a table or query that a form, report, or page object is based on

Record Source property a form or report property that determines which record source will be displayed in a form or report

recordset the fields and records that are displayed when you open an object as determined by the object's Record Source property

referential integrity a set of rules that, when applied to a one-to-many relationship, helps you keep inappropriate data from being entered into the database, and helps you from creating orphan records in a database

relational database a database that contains multiple tables linked together in one-to-many relationships

replica a special copy of a database that keeps track of changes so that you can resynchronize the copy with another copy of the database

replica set the Design Master and all replicas created from the Design Master

replication the process of creating copies, called replicas, of a database

report a database object whose main purpose is to create a professional printout

Report Design View a view used to define the layout and formatting characteristics of a report

Report Footer a section that prints at the end of the entire report

Report Header a section that prints at the top of the first page of the report

Report Wizard a wizard that helps you quickly create a new report

ScreenTip descriptive information that automatically appears in a small box when you point to a toolbar button

sections areas of a report that determine where and how often the controls placed within those areas print on the report

security account passwords passwords defined by the workgroup information file that give different users different permissions to various objects

select query a type of query that selects fields and records from one or more tables and displays them in a datasheet

Series field a field used in the legend area on a chart

server in most client/server computing environments, a shared file server, mini-, or mainframe computer

Simple Query Wizard a wizard that helps you build a select query

sorting to arrange records in either ascending or descending order based on the contents of a field

spike a surge in power that sometimes causes computer damage

startup options commands that are automatically applied to your database when you open it

StDev an aggregate function that calculates the standard deviation of the values in the given field

subdatasheet a datasheet within a datasheet

subform a control within a form that displays another form

SubForm Wizard a wizard that assists you in creating a subform control

subreport a control within a report that displays another report

SubReport Wizard a wizard that assists you in creating a subreport control

Sum an aggregate function that totals the values in the given field

surge protector equipment that protects a computer from a power spike

switchboard a special form that helps users navigate through the database

Switchboard Manager a tool used to create and modify switchboard forms

synchronization the process of reconciling the changes between the replicas and the Design Master so that all databases contain the latest updates

table a database object that stores all the data in the database

Table Datasheet View a view used to view, enter, edit, and delete data in a spreadsheet-like arrangement

Table Design View a view used to enter, modify, and delete fields in a table

Table Wizard a wizard that provides sample tables and fields from which you can choose to create a new table

template a sample database for a subject area such as inventory, event, contact, or expense management, which you can use to quickly create your own database

Text a data type that allows a field to store any combination of text or numbers up to 255 characters

Text Box button a button on the Toolbox toolbar that allows you to add a new text box control to a form, page, or report

txt a file extension for a text file

Uninterruptible Power Supply equipment that maintains constant power to computer equipment during power brown-outs, spikes, and total loss of power; UPS

update query an action query that updates field values as defined in the query for the records selected in the query

UPS *see Uninterruptible Power Supply*

Validation Rule a field property used to set criteria for data validation

Validation Text a field property used to display a message if a user attempts to enter an unacceptable value into the field (as determined by the criteria in the Validation Rule property)

value the data that you enter into a field, such as Mark in the FirstName field

Var an aggregate function that calculates the variance of the values in the given field

VBA *see Visual Basic for Applications*

VBA password a password that prevents unauthorized users from modifying VBA code

view a presentation of an object that supports different database activities

Visual Basic for Applications a programming language packaged within each program of the Microsoft Office suite that can be used to extend the features of the software; VBA

W3C *see World Wide Web Consortium*

workgroup a list of database users who have the same needs

workgroup information file a file that contains user IDs, passwords, and permissions; used to create a secure database

World Wide Web Consortium an international league of companies and associations that support initiatives and standards that sustain the growth and health of the World Wide Web; also known as the W3C

XML *see Extensible Markup Language*

XML document a text file that contains data and XML tags to identify field names and field values

XSD *see Extensible Schema Document*

XSL *see Extensible Style Language*

Yes/No a data type that stores only one of two values: Yes or No

Index

A

Access. *See also* database
  exiting, 16–17
    Compact on Close, 17
  starting, 2–3
action query. *See also* query
  creating and running, 144–145
    append query, 144
    delete query, 144
    make-table query, 144
    update query, 144
aggregate function, use in queries, 146–147
Analyze It With Microsoft Excel, 102. *See also* Excel
AND condition, 136–137
append query, 144. *See also* query
application, 189
AutoFormat. *See also* formatting
  modifying form properties, 58–59
AutoForms, form creation, 54–55

B

Briefcase folder, 187
browser, data access page requirements, 109

C

calculated control. *See also* control
  adding to report
    date calculated control, 92–93
    subtotals for record groups, 90–91
calculated field, 43. *See also* field
  adding to select query
    format values in calculated field, 50–51
    with Query Design View, 48–49
Cascade Delete, 161
Cascade Update, 161
Category field, 170
client, 195
client/server computing, 195
column, key column, 38
combo box, 116
Command Button Wizard, module creation, 190–191

Compact on Close, database, 17
Conference database. *See also* database
  creating, 120–121
constant, 48
Contact Management database. *See also* database
  creating, 112–113
control. *See also* calculated control
  modifying on form, 60–61
  on report, 88
criteria, 46
crosstab query, 68. *See also* query
Crosstab Query Wizard, 68

D

DAP. *See* data access page
data
  entering and editing, keystrokes for, 65
  exporting
    to Excel workbook, 102–103
    to Web page, 104–105
  importing
    from another Access database, 100–101
    from Excel workbook, 98–99
data access page (DAP), 97, 165. *See also* Web page
  browser requirements, 109
  creating
    for data entry, 106–107
    for data reporting, 108–109
    with Page Design View, 106, 166–167
    with Page View, 106
    with Page Wizard, 106
  PivotChart creation on, 170–171
  PivotTable creation on, 168–169
data reporting, with data access page, 108–109
data type, field, 34
data validation, 112
  Validation Rule property, 112
  Validation Text property, 112

243

security, passwords, 182–183
security threats, 179
select query, 43. *See also* query
    adding calculated field to
        format values in calculated field,
          50–51
        with Query Design View, 48–49
    creating and modifying
        with Query Design View, 46–47
        with Simple Query Wizard, 44–45
Series field, 170
server, 195
Simple Query Wizard, using, 44–45
sizing handle, 60, 88
sorting
    records
        in Datasheet View, 70–71
        in Query Design View, 72–73
subdatasheet. *See also* database
    navigating, 26–27
subform. *See also* form
    adding controls to, 132–133
subreport. *See also* report
    adding to report, 154–155
subreport control, 154
SubReport Wizard, 154
switchboard, 123
    creating, 126–127
        startup options, 130
    default switchboard, 126
    modifying, 128–129
Switchboard Manager, 126

T

table, 6
    creating and modifying, 32–33
        with Design View, 34–35
        with Table Wizard, 32–33
    junction table, 162
    linked tables, 114
Table Design View, table creation, 34–35
Table Wizard, using, 32–33
task pane, 2

template
    database, 20
        database wizards, 20
Text Box, adding controls without labels, 151
Text Box button, 151
text file. *See* delimited text file
toolbar
    docked, 20
    managing, 12–13
    navigation toolbar, 24
        buttons, 67
.txt file extension, 99

U

update query, 144

V

Validation Rule property, 112
Validation Text property, 112
value, 6
    format values in calculated field, 50–51
VBA. *See* Visual Basic for Applications
view, 12, 22. *See also* Design View
    Datasheet View, 22
    Design View, 22
    Form View, 22
    Preview, 22
Visual Basic for Applications (VBA), 190

W

W3C. *See* World Wide Web Consortium
Web page. *See also* data access page
    dynamic Web page, 106, 165
    exporting data to, 104–105
Winners database. *See also* database
    creating, 116–117
workbook. *See* Excel workbook
workgroup, creating, 184–185
workgroup information file, 184
World Wide Web Consortium (W3C), 175

X

XML. *See* Extensible Markup Language
XSD. *See* Extensible Schema Document
XSL. *See* Extensible Style Language